VIRILIO LIVE:

Selected Interviews

Theory, Culture & Society

Theory, Culture & Society caters for the resurgence of interest in culture within contemporary social science and the humanities. Building on the heritage of classical social theory, the book series examines ways in which this tradition has been reshaped by a new generation of theorists. It also publishes theoretically informed analyses of everyday life, popular culture, and new intellectual movements.

EDITOR: Mike Featherstone, *Nottingham Trent University*

SERIES EDITORIAL BOARD
Roy Boyne, *University of Durham*
Mike Hepworth, *University of Aberdeen*
Scott Lash, *Goldsmiths College, University of London*
Roland Robertson, *University of Pittsburgh*
Bryan S. Turner, *University of Cambridge*

THE TCS CENTRE
The Theory, Culture & Society book series, the journals *Theory, Culture & Society* and *Body & Society*, and related conference, seminar and postgraduate programmes operate from the TCS Centre at Nottingham Trent University. For further details of the TCS Centre's activities please contact:

Centre Administrator
The TCS Centre, Room 175
Faculty of Humanities
Nottingham Trent University
Clifton Lane, Nottingham, NG11 8NS, UK
e-mail: tcs@ntu.ac.uk
web: http://tcs.ntu.ac.uk

Recent volumes include:

Simulation and Social Theory
Sean Cubitt

The Contradictions of Culture
Cities, Culture, Women
Elizabeth Wilson

The Tarantinian Ethics
Fred Botting and Scott Wilson

Society and Culture
Principles of Scarcity and Solidity
Bryan S. Turner and Chris Rojek

Modernity and Exclusion
Joel S. Kahn

VIRILIO LIVE:
Selected Interviews

edited by John Armitage

SAGE Publications
London • Thousand Oaks • New Delhi

First published 2001

SAGE Publications Ltd
6 Bonhill Street
London EC2A 4PU

SAGE Publications Inc
2455 Teller Road
Thousand Oaks, California 91320

SAGE Publications India Pvt Ltd
32, M-Block Market
Greater Kailash – I
New Delhi 110 048

British Library Cataloguing in Publication data

A catalogue record for this book is
available from the British Library

ISBN 0 7619 6859 8
ISBN 0 7619 6860 1 (pbk)

Library of Congress control number 2001131844

Typeset by Line Arts, Pondicherry.
Printed and bound in Great Britain by Athenaeum Press,
Gateshead

CONTENTS

This book is dedicated to Julie Lawrence, my sister

ACKNOWLEDGEMENTS

An editorial task of this extent is inevitably a cooperative endeavour. I want to offer my deepest thanks to Paul Virilio, who not only gave me his permission to publish his words in this book but who also took time out from a frenzied writing schedule to produce the Preface for it. Mike Gane and Nicholas Zurbrugg commented on an earlier draft of the Introduction. To Mike and Nicholas my sincere thanks. Thanks are also due to Douglas Kellner for refereeing Virilio interviews in German. Additionally, I owe a debt of gratitude to Mike Featherstone, the editor of *Theory, Culture and Society*, and to Chris Rojek, senior commissioning editor at Sage, for encouraging my work on Virilio from the beginning.

To the Virilio interviewers, translators and publishers, dispersed across the world, and who gave their work and permissions, a genuine thank you. However, I was not able to locate all the interviewers, translators and publishers of the interviews published in this volume. On behalf of Sage Publications, I would like to say that every effort has been made to trace all the copyright holders of the material reprinted herein, but if any have been inadvertently overlooked the publishers will be pleased to make the necessary arrangements at the first opportunity. For their willingness to allow either the publication of an interview originally published in a language other than English or an interview that has not been published previously, I would especially like to thank Andreas Ruby, Niels Brügger and Nicholas Zurbrugg.

I am particularly grateful to Patrice Riemens, the Scarlet Pimpernel of cyberspace, who translated Virilio's Preface, various Virilio interviews, and who offered sometimes-dizzying dromological companionship in Amsterdam and Paris. My colleagues in the Division of Government and Politics at the University of Northumbria, UK and, in particular, John Fenwick and Ken Harrop provided much-appreciated intellectual, financial and administrative support. I am also grateful to Arthur Affleck. His research assistance was invaluable in the final stages of the preparation of this book. Lastly, I want to extend my heartfelt thanks to my partner in love, life and the odd academic crime, Joanne Roberts. On numerous occasions, Joanne generously put her own research aside to comment on many of the draft sections of this book.

John Armitage

PREFACE

Paul Virilio

I do not agree with Montesquieu, when he wrote 'the more one talks, the less one thinks'. All that matters is the nature of the exchange. To talk does not necessarily mean to chatter, and to have a dialogue with another person does not necessarily mean to sermonize but to respond to that person in a proper fashion, inclusive of thoughtful arguments.

For thirty years now I have held a professorship of architecture, and I know from experience that talk can provoke. The spoken word is a mental voyage, a voyage in thought and action. The interview is at once the *exhalation* of thought and the *inspiration* for theory. Otherwise, how can we explain, for instance, Flaubert's 'Shouting Alley' in that remote corner of the Croisset Estate, near Rouen, where he used to scream out his writings?

The fact is that writing takes a long time, whereas the spoken word is an exploration of speed, not only in terms of its *delivery*, but also in terms of its *conceptualization*.

The spoken word shifts thought into overdrive. This acceleration also speeds up the revelatory possibilities of thought and intuition. However, the spoken word is primarily involved with re-conceptualizing thought through the reverberations inherent in dialogue itself. Dialogue is the canonical form *par excellence*, and it was a form cherished by the ancient philosophers; philosophers who were not concerned with the mere blurting out of messages, as so many seem to be in these loud-mouthed times.

When two people are in a dialogue, the VERB TAKES ON HUMAN FORM. Without the echo of the human voice, without the interplay of the exchange, the *force behind the meaning of the words deteriorates*. Moreover, dialogue sometimes results in a theoretical breakthrough.

For me, the *silent procedure* of writing corresponds to the 'sound barrier'. However, the sound barrier is a barrier that the spoken word can sometimes break through!

Of course, the spoken word in the form of, say, a radio interview, has a number of drawbacks. It can often result in misunderstandings, inaccuracies and repetitiveness. But one should also stress that an interview is but a draft, a blueprint for a text, and that reading and writing are an essential follow up after the verbal expression, after the breath of the shared word.

Moreover, let us be totally honest. Very few interviews are totally satisfactory to a writer, and nothing can substitute for *the retinal persistence of the written text*.

But a dialogue is a movement from one person to the Other. It is, as they say, the practice of alterity. It is therefore necessary to say that I seldom encounter an interviewer who is convinced beforehand of the validity of my words or of the relevance of my work. This results in the interview often turning into *an effort of clarification*, which might be useful, but which is also tiring, and sometimes very trying.

Another aspect of the interview form, but this time a more positive one, is the element of surprise, the element of amazement, or, in other words, a recognition of the fact that ACCIDENTS OCCUR ALONG THE WAY as the discourse unfolds.

It is indeed very often in the exchange, in the clash of opinions with one's interviewer, that the unforeseen happens, and the unexpected truth of the union materializes. And in fact, my penchant for spontaneity often makes me disinclined to amend afterwards particular figures of speech, or particular images and metaphors that might, in print, appear too harsh. Then you have to take into account the man himself. I am half Latin and half Breton. A Latin person is a born public speaker with just a hint of the demagogue, whereas a native of Brittany normally takes to silence and to contemplation.

Therefore, if writing is a contemplative act, then speech is an action since it never returns before it has achieved its task.

But let us conclude with a short passage from Jacques le Majeur's 'Epître de Saint Jacques', and taken from his *Contre l'intempérance du language*:

> When we put a bit in a horse's mouth in order to let ourselves be obeyed, we in fact direct his whole body. Or take ships: large as they may be, and even if propelled forward by strong winds, they are still steered by a small rudder, at the helmsman's will and pleasure. In the same fashion, the tongue is a small organ, and yet it can boast of great achievements!

Translated by Patrice Riemens.

INTRODUCTION

John Armitage

Paul Virilio is perhaps the most provocative French cultural theorist on the contemporary intellectual scene. Renowned for his fascination with the military–industrial complex and for his concept of 'dromology', or the logic of speed, Virilio's theoretical and philosophical writings are enthusiastically received by other contemporary cultural theorists with related concerns, such as Jean Baudrillard. However, Virilio's increasingly influential and consistently challenging theories introduced in texts like *Bunker Archeology* (1994) and *Strategy of Deception* (2000), remain a source of continual controversy and intellectual debate.[1] By presenting Virilio's cultural theory in interview form, *Virilio Live: Selected Interviews* offers the reader a new method of approaching his work and the controversies it generates. In this Introduction, the first section delineates Virilio's biographical history, the significance and theoretical development of his complex and routinely misinterpreted cultural theory. The second section describes the core cultural themes and Virilio's important theoretical contributions embodied in the twelve interviews selected for this book. The third section provides a theoretical interpretation of these interviews and clarifies their important relationship to the contemporary debate over postmodernism. The penultimate section briefly evaluates the significance of Virilio's interviews.

Meet Paul Virilio

As Virilio indicates in the Preface, he was born in Paris in 1932 to a Breton mother and an Italian father. Virilio was evacuated in 1939 to the port of Nantes, where he was traumatized by the spectacle of the *Blitzkrieg* during the Second World War. After training at the École des Métiers d'Art in Paris, Virilio became an artist in stained glass, working with such eminent modernists as Matisse. However, in 1950, Virilio converted to Christianity, and, following military service in the colonial army during the Algerian war of independence (1954–62), he studied phenomenology with Merleau-Ponty at the Sorbonne. Captivated by military space and the organization of territory, Virilio's early writings appeared while he was acting as a self-styled 'urbanist' in *Architecture Principe*, an architectural group and review he established with the architect Claude Parent in 1963. Virilio produced his first major work, a photographic and phenomenological study of the architecture of war, *Bunker Archeology*, in 1975.

After participating in the *événements* of May 1968 in Paris, Virilio was nominated Professor by the students at the École Spéciale d'Architecture. An untrained architect, Virilio has never felt compelled to restrict his concerns to the spatial arts and is the inventor of an array of arresting concepts. These range from the 'oblique function' and the 'trajectory' to 'speed-space', 'chronopolitics', the 'information bomb', the 'integral accident' and the 'strategies of deception'. Virilio's phenomenological works, such as his untranslated *L'Insécurité du territoire* (1976), draw on the writings of Husserl and, above all, Merleau-Ponty. Nevertheless, one reason why Virilio's demanding cultural perspective and philosophical conceptions have only recently begun to influence current postmodern and other cultural debates in the English-speaking world is that he rarely leaves Paris and seldom appears in public outside France. Virilio retired in 1998 and currently devotes himself to writing and working with private organizations concerned with housing the homeless in Paris.

The significance of Virilio's cultural theory stems from his claim that, in a culture overshadowed by war, the military–industrial complex is of fundamental importance in debates over the creation of the city and the spatial organization of cultural life. In *Speed and Politics: An Essay on Dromology* (1986), for example, Virilio offers a credible 'war model' of the growth of the modern city and the evolution of human culture. Indeed, according to Virilio, the fortified city of the feudal period was a motionless and generally unassailable 'war machine' coupled to an attempt to modulate the circulation and momentum of the movements of the urban masses. Hence, the fortified city was a political space of habitable inertia, the political configuration and the physical underpinning of the feudal era. Nonetheless, for Virilio, the essential question is why did the fortified city disappear? Unlike Marx, Virilio postulates that the transition from feudalism to capitalism was not an economic transformation but a military revolution. Broadly, where Marx wrote of the materialist conception of history, Virilio writes of the military conception of history. To be sure, Virilio's somewhat unconventional answer to his own question is that the fortified city disappeared because of the advent of ever-increasingly transportable and accelerated weapons systems. In Virilio's terms, such innovations 'exposed' the fortified city and transformed siege warfare into a war of movement. Henceforth, the efforts of the authorities to govern the flow of the urban citizenry were undermined, heralding the arrival of what Virilio calls the 'habitable circulation' of the masses.

Virilio began his studies in 1958 on the 'Atlantic Wall' – the 15,000 Nazi bunkers built during the Second World War along the coastline of France to repel any Allied assault. Virilio's concepts of the oblique function and the trajectory were to be pre-eminent within the *Architecture Principe* group and review in rendering his contribution to architectural thought using the Gestalt or 'event' psychological theory of perceived mental forms. Such ideas culminated in the construction of a 'bunker church' in Nevers in 1966 and the Thomson–Houston aerospace research centre in Villacoubly in 1969. Subsequently, Virilio broadened his cultural and theoretical scope, arguing in the

1970s that the relentless militarization of the contemporary cityscape was prompting the arrival of speed or chronopolitics and the 'deterritorialization' of urban space. Reviewing the frightening 'dromological' fall-out from the communications technology revolution in information transmission, Virilio enquired into speed-space and started probing the connections between military technologies and the organization of cultural space in *Speed and Politics* and *Popular Defense and Ecological Struggles* (1990). Accordingly, in the 1980s, Virilio cultivated the next important stage of his theoretical work through aesthetic notions of 'disappearance'. Consequently, it is the 'fractalization' of the 'overexposed' city, war, cinema and the 'logistics of perception' that are Virilio's concerns in this period. These interests are the basis of Virilio's *The Aesthetics of Disappearance* (1991), *The Lost Dimension* (1991), *War and Cinema: The Logistics of Perception* (1989) and *The Vision Machine* (1994). Today, Virilio's cultural theory centres on the concepts of 'polar inertia', 'desert screen', the 'art of the motor', the information bomb, the integral accident and the strategies of deception.

Virilio's research seems most relevant to contemporary cultural theory in terms of its critical examination of the experience of the use of remote-controlled and cybernetic technologies such as the Internet. Significantly, other major contemporary cultural theorists such as Bauman (1999), Genosko (1999) and Lash (1999) are increasingly applying Virilio's challenging concepts. Even so, Virilio's most recent cultural theoretical works, such as *Polar Inertia* (1999), *Desert Screen* (2001), *The Art of the Motor* (1995), *Open Sky* (1997), *Strategy of Deception* and *The Information Bomb* (2000) often seem misinterpreted by postmodern cultural theorists such as Waite (1996) and by conservative critics like Sokal and Bricmont (1998). In fact, as we shall see in the sections that follow, Virilio's cultural theory has almost nothing to do with the kind of postmodern cultural theory that abandons all cultural values and, in Virilio's terms, naively celebrates technology. This explains why he characterizes himself as a 'critic of the art of technology'. It is also why I characterize Virilio as a 'hypermodernist', or a critic of postmodern technoculture who still defends the kinds of modernist values abandoned by many postmodern theorists but one who is also aware of modernism's contemporary 'excesses'.

Virilio live

In Part One, 'On Theory, Culture and Society', my interview with Virilio about modernism and 'hypermodernism' poses questions about the essential turning points of Virilio's life and his description of the background and development of his cultural theory. Here, Virilio explains how the core theme and central importance of his work is the cultural logic of contemporary militarism, and outlines his views of the artistic theory of modernism in the context of my conception of his 'hypermodern' agenda. Arguing that the modern military–industrial complex is developing ominous technological potentialities, Virilio's critique of hypermodern militarism attempts to signal the significance of the integral accident as well as the sudden changes and upheavals caused by the problem of generalized acceleration. Hence, Virilio conceives of the cultural logic of contemporary militarism as the product of technological speed, observing, 'it is clear that my work is a critical analysis of modernity, but through a perception of technology which is largely ... catastroph*ic* not catastroph*ist*'.

In Part Two, 'On Architecture', the first interview, by the cultural theorist Enrique Limon, turns on Virilio's concept of the oblique function. Here, Virilio explains that the idea of what he calls the oblique function is important because it highlights his philosophical commitment to phenomenology and Gestalt theory. Virilio's is also a commitment fixed on the possibility of a new 'third urban order' of 'topology', 'oriented surfaces' and the notion of putting 'the vertical city on trial'. The second interview, by the architectural critic Andreas Ruby, and published in English for the first time in this book, explains how Virilio's concept of the trajectory springs from the crucial and dromological 'relationship between the object and the subject'. As noted, Virilio's early architectural notions foreshadowed his critiques of speed-space, chronopolitics and computerized interactivity that surfaced in *Speed and Politics*, *War and Cinema* and *The Information Bomb*. It is these critiques that are discussed in Part Three, 'On Speed-Space and Chronopolitics', by Virilio and the three contemporary cultural theorists Chris Dercon, Niels Brügger and Friedrich Kittler.

As Virilio suggests to Dercon, his scepticism concerning the political economy of wealth is driven by his 'dromocratic' conception of power and by his resistance to the Fascist assumptions of Marinetti's Futurist manifestos. Similarly, in his interview with Brügger, translated into English here for the first time, Virilio argues that the political economy of the Greek city-state cannot be characterized under the political economy of wealth. For Virilio, a simple understanding of the management of the economy of the state will not suffice. On the contrary, the histories of socio-political institutions such as the military–industrial complex and artistic movements like Futurism demonstrate that war and the 'capacity for propulsion', rather than commerce and the urge for wealth, were the foundations of Greek culture. It is important to understand that Virilio is not suggesting that the political economy of wealth has been superseded by the political economy of speed. Rather, as he proposes to Brügger, in addition to the political economy of wealth, there is a dromocratic 'hierarchy', the political economy of speed. In his conversation with Kittler, Virilio develops his dromological enquiry to include considerations on the information bomb, 'the bomb that throws us into "real time"', and the catastrophic consequences if it explodes, a moment Virilio calls 'Information Chernobyl'. Here, Virilio describes the rationale of the information bomb as the logic of militarized technoscience in the era of computerized interactivity. For Virilio, then, the current era of interactivity is one in which humanity is gradually being transformed by a caste of 'technology monks' devoted to the construction of a 'new kind of civilization'. Technology monks are therefore the high priests of the new secular ideology Virilio calls 'technological fundamentalism', the religion of all those who believe in the absolute power of information and communications technologies. Thus, in the world according to Virilio, it is the 'monotheism' of cybernetic technologies, such as the Internet, which is responsible for integral accidents like the 1987 world stock market crash, brought about by accelerated automated program trading.

In the first interview in Part Four, 'On Art, Technoculture and the Integral Accident', with art critic Jérôme Sans, Virilio suggests that cultural theory must take account of interruptions in the rhythm of human consciousness or the 'mental persistence of the image'. Articulating his concept of 'picnolepsy' (frequent interruption) while alluding to Einstein's General Relativity Theory, Virilio argues that modern vision is the product of military power and time-based cinematic technologies of disappearance. Further, although there are political and cinematic aspects to our visual consciousness, what is indispensable to them is their ability to designate the technological disappearance of the grand aesthetic narratives and the advent of micro narratives. From Virilio's perspective, 'images have become a new form of light' that we cannot yet comprehend. In fact, for Virilio, people remain fascinated by the 'spectacularity' of the 'third window', the artificial light of TV and computer screens.

Significant here is Virilio's interview with the art critics Dominique Joubert and Christiane Carlut. Voicing his concerns about the aesthetics of disappearance, Virilio skilfully links the latter concept to the disappearance of poster art in the city and the crises of the physical dimension that he first raised in *The Lost Dimension*. As Virilio suggests, the 'logistics' of 'urban perception' are critically concerned with the disappearance of messages and signs into a militarized and cinematographic field of information transmission, stylization and the endless resequencing of film, video and TV images. In other words, the 'virtual screens' of advertising 'propaganda' have replaced the city walls.

In the following interviews with the art critics Catherine David and Pierre Sterckx, Virilio emphasizes his concept of 'delocalization' when discussing different kinds and works of contemporary art. Displaying a marked similarity to the poststructuralist Derrida's idea of 'deconstruction', Virilio's chief concern is with the links between art, spatial and temporal dislocation and the current 'event landscape' of absolute speed. According to Virilio, delocalization and the event landscape arise because, in the context of the ongoing 'virtualization of art', human actions no longer occur in 'real space' and, as a negative consequence, are 'devoid of references'. For Virilio, therefore, the art world – like the commercial world of advertising and consumerism – is presently 'disappearing' into the realm of computer images, a development he calls art's abandonment of its inscription on the terrain of the earth. Virilio thus conceptualizes a cybernetic delocalization where technological culture and technological creativity become detached from the 'here and now' and move into cyberspace or, as in the case of the Australian cybernetic performance artist Stelarc, invades and colonizes the corporeal space of the individual body. In the interviews with David and Sterckx, then, Virilio passionately questions the modification or the replacement of the human by the machine, arguing that contemporary art is witnessing the 'crucifixion' of the human body by the technologies of acceleration. Moreover, according to Virilio, technological dislocation not only results in the disappearance of the 'here and now' but also in the appearance of the 'virtual portal' or, 'the meeting of spectres' with the 'God of technology'. Delocalized art is thus distinct from traditional art, where the images produced are images of real space and time. Instead, it is an art where the difference between the images of real space and time are 'spectralized' or made 'telepresent' by the 'teletechnologies' of the mass media at 'the dark spot of art'. Analogous perhaps to the spirit of Lyotard's famous *Les Immateriaux* exhibition at the Beaubourg in Paris in 1985, Virilio's bold assertion in the interviews with David and Sterckx is that the plastic arts are dead. However, Virilio's perspective on the delocalization of art is consistent with his view that the only way to comprehend the development of contemporary art is to question its accelerating 'temporality' in the era of cybernetic globalization.

In the final, previously unpublished, interview in Part Four, with the cultural theorist Nicholas Zurbrugg, Virilio characterizes himself as a visionary, virtually painting with words, in order to clarify the hazards of polar inertia in the era of technoculture animated by alternating catastrophes and positive discoveries. Virilio begins with an examination of the disparity between 'new technological breakthroughs' such as 'a new kind of ship or plane' and the new kinds of integral accidents to which they give rise. He then goes on to explain the discrepancy between absolute speed and inertia in the development of technoculture in twentieth-century Western art. Outlining what he sees as the negative tradition of techno-evangelism stretching from Marinetti's Futurist enthusiasm to what he sees as the eugenicism implicit in Stelarc's modification of the human body, Virilio deplores the extent to which sustained intellectual and creative resistance to the nullifying impact of technology is almost non-existent. While celebrating the ways in which early twentieth century artists resisted the technologies of their time, Virilio argues that few artists and scientists seem to be resisting the seduction of contemporary technologies, concluding that it is all the more important for cultural critics to identify the 'accidents' of their time. For Virilio, the important thing to do now is to 'fight against' technology rather than 'sleep' before it. On the one hand, therefore, 'the most exciting thing' for Virilio is that 'every time a new technology appears, art diverges from it'. On the other, Virilio rather dramatically warns that in the 'positive' work of Marinetti, technoculture invariably becomes a kind of 'Fascist impulse'. For Virilio, most intellectuals and artists are virtually 'asleep' in front of the new technologies that they uncritically endorse. And cybernetic artists such as Stelarc are not so much to be welcomed as bearers of good tidings, but as feared prophets embodying the 'end' of both their own humanity and of 'a certain kind of art'. Virilio's interview with Zurbrugg therefore demonstrates his sense that apart from rare exceptions such as the work of video installation artists Bill Viola and Michael Snow, contemporary culture produces few important artistic works.

In the last part of the book, Part Five, 'On the Strategies of Deception', my second interview with Virilio elaborates on his most recent writings in *Strategy of Deception* and *The Information Bomb*. In this final interview, Virilio develops a critique of the informational and technological strategies employed in the Kosovo war by the European Union (EU) and the North Atlantic Treaty Organization (NATO) against the rule of Slobodan Miloševic in Serbia in 1998–9. Nevertheless, as Virilio observes in this specially commissioned interview, his is a critique of what he describes as 'strategically correct thinking'. Certainly, for Virilio, it is critical to reject the 'catastrophic modalities' of fusing military and humanitarian affairs through an analysis of the 'successful' strategy of the United States (US) and by resisting its domination of the EU and NATO. According to Virilio, then, 'cyberwar' is a form of US imperialism that is presently conducted through the development and deployment of the US's 'Revolution in Military Affairs' and what he now calls the 'military–scientific complex'. Moreover, by abandoning the political sensibility required in order to understand the emergence of the US's 'second deterrence' based on cyberwar, the EU and NATO have finally capitulated to 'the detonation of the information bomb'.

Virilio: live and direct

As becomes evident, Virilio's interviews offer compelling reading in terms of the ways in which they informally anticipate his subsequent more elaborate theoretical writings. Offering a major part of his ongoing analysis of contemporary culture, Virilio fascinatingly elucidates his general contributions to current debates addressing postmodernism and highlights how he can perhaps be best understood as what I would term a hypermodern critic of the art of technology.

Virilio's interviews are most significant, perhaps, because they move beyond the increasingly unproductive existing debate over the distinction between modernism and postmodernism. As my interview with Virilio in Part One indicates, for example, Virilio forcefully disassociates his ideas from what he sees as the uncritical superficiality of most postmodern cultural theory, arguing that he does 'not feel linked at all with postmodernity'.

Similarly, as Virilio's interviews with Limon and Ruby clearly indicate in Part Two, his architectural theory and practice are neither a reaction against modern architecture in general nor a reaction against the International Style in particular. Indeed, for Virilio, postmodern architecture is quite simply a catastrophe. Virilio's hostility to postmodern architecture is not hard to fathom since his own architectural work draws on the 'Brutalist' later architectural style of Le Corbusier, a project founded on exposed concrete and the dramatic collision of large oblique forms. Consequently, in his interviews with Limon and Ruby, Virilio not only acknowledges the modernist influence of Merleau-Ponty's phenomenology but also that of Gestalt theory and Einstein's writings on General Relativity Theory.

Furthermore, in the interviews in Part Three, Virilio argues that he perceives few links between his cultural theory and that of the works of post-structuralist cultural theorists such as Foucault's *Discipline and Punish* (1977). For instance, Virilio informs Brügger that, unlike Foucault's theories of incarceration, his theories are concerned with our 'imprisonment in speed'. In addition, and in contrast to Foucault, Virilio maintains that he is a humanist and a practising 'Anarcho-Christian'. Virilio's cultural theory thus runs counter to the perspective of anti-humanism and to the political and vehemently anti-Christian philosophy of Nietzsche, a thinker often cited approvingly by poststructuralists such as Foucault. Hence, there are only ambivalent, if occasionally convergent associations between Virilio's philosophical works and Foucault's poststructuralist texts. As Virilio suggests in his conversation with Kittler, in the era of information monotheism, he sees the 'greatest danger of all' as the prospect of a 'slide into a future without humanity'.

Moreover, as Virilio's interviews in Part Four significantly demonstrate, unlike many postmodern cultural theorists, he still defends modernist cultural values. In this way, Virilio characterizes his cultural theory as a critical examination of modernism's relationship to questions of technological perception, speed and the aesthetics of disappearance. Directing his gaze towards the literature, music and painting of high modernism, Virilio enthusiastically cites such leading modernist creators as Franz Kafka, Charlie Parker and Paul Klee. In turn, as Virilio stresses in his interview with David, his approach to postmodernism offers a critique from the viewpoint of past values, rather than a cynical celebration of the end of the world of human presence. It is in this sense of critiquing the most recent technological developments in postmodern culture in terms of modernism that Virilio is a visionary hypermodern thinker.

If Virilio defends certain postmodern practitioners, then it is because of the continuity between their work and the work of the earlier modern – and premodern – writers and thinkers that he admires. But at the same time, as Virilio indicates in his interview with Zurbrugg, he seems to find himself to be permanently at war with the 'Fascist impulse' that he perhaps rather mechanically equates with the Italian Futurist tradition.

Finally, as Virilio suggests in Part Five, his cultural theory of war also differs significantly from that of postmodern cultural theorists of war such as Baudrillard (1995). Unlike Baudrillard's cultural writings and interviews on war, for example, Virilio's war-strewn texts and conversations remain true to the idea of understanding human history, even as it crashes 'headlong into the wall of time'. Undeniably, nearly the whole of my discussion with Virilio on the strategies of deception is a sustained effort to comprehend the recent historical events that took place during the conflict in Kosovo. In this final interview, Virilio also questions the demise of the concept of a 'just war', contending that the idea of a just war must be rescued from its present deterioration into little more than 'secular holy war'. Far from sharing a Baudrillardian sense that perhaps 'the Kosovo War did not take place', Virilio argues that the very real significance of the Kosovo conflict is that it escalated warfare into the still more terrifying dimension of 'orbital space'.

In sum, as Virilio's interviews indicate, the complexity of his vision repeatedly advances *beyond* many of the more complacent assumptions of dominant postmodern cultural theory. By offering Virilio's cultural theory live and direct in interview format, *Virilio Live: Selected Interviews* allows the reader to share some of Virilio's most stimulating accounts of his ideas and the debates that they have initiated.

Questioning Virilio

Clearly, Virilio's cultural theory – and his interviews – court controversy. Virilio writes in the Preface, for example, that, for 'thirty years now I have held a professorship of architecture, and I know from experience that talk can provoke'. In other words, Virilio is well accustomed to high praise and to exasperated antagonism from architectural colleagues as well as to the hostility that occasionally arises from the twelve interviewers in this book to some of his more questionable assertions.

In Part One, for instance, I attempt to clarify the most affirmative dimensions of Virilio's cultural theory by defining them as aspects of a hypermodern perspective, rejecting many of the more negative conclusions of those who equate postmodernism with the collapse of all values. Virilio, I suggest, is most important as a defender of past values in the face of present crises.

In Part Two, Virilio's discussions of the trajectory, and of 'an architecture that understands the human body as a space-determining element', leads to Ruby's suggestion that Virilio's are the only writings that comprehend the human body and its environment in such a manner within contemporary architecture. Ruby is, of course, also referring here to the general disregard by other architects of Virilio's texts and, in particular, his remarkable existential meditation on the architecture of war in *Bunker Archeology*. Nevertheless, in the interview with Ruby, Virilio's reaction to modern architecture's neglect of his focus on the 'energized' human body is not one of despair. Rather, echoing his late philosopher friend, Deleuze, Virilio enthuses that the energized human body is a body 'with reflexes and anticipatory qualities, a body that is constantly in-becoming'. Yet, as Virilio indicates to Ruby, he senses that many modern architects 'have lost the dimension of the body that Vitruvius or Le Corbusier had but without gaining anything new in the process'. It is not necessary to labour the point that Virilio has a constructive approach both to sympathetic criticisms and to the denigration of his work through the provision of parallel examples taken from the rest of this book. What is necessary is to re-emphasize the fact that what *Virilio Live: Selected Interviews* confirms is the theoretical, cultural and social insight of this extraordinary critic of the art of technology. Virilio's achievement in these interviews is therefore that of successfully alerting the reader to the contemporary ascendancy of inauspicious visions of buildings turned into time-based

images, speed-space, chronopolitics, technological culture, the integral accident and the strategies of deception.

Nonetheless, it is also important to signal that, today, Virilio's cultural theory and interviews are also the subject of critical admonition from Waite and
others not for their similarities but for their dissimilarities from postmodern
cultural theory. For such authors, Virilio, the world's only critic of the art of
technology, remains an interesting but flawed critic of the art of *modernist*
conceptions of technology.

Conclusion

At their most original, Virilio's writings and interviews on contemporary
culture offer an indispensable beginning to our understanding of the consequences of dromology – or of cultural speed and acceleration – for contemporary society. As I have suggested, his work is most crucial in terms of the ways
in which it has instituted a speed-based philosophical examination of hypermodern cultural and social experience that is increasingly influential among
other cultural theorists of advanced societies. Virilio's frequently misunderstood and contentious phenomenological writings therefore stand apart from
postmodern cultural theory. Consequently, through the presentation of
Virilio's work in interview style, *Virilio Live: Selected Interviews* testifies to the
originality of his cultural theory. It also demonstrates the inadequacy of
postmodern cultural theorists' rejection of modernism and modernity when
analysing recent political events such as the war in Kosovo. In these respects,
this critic of the art of technology is associated with Merleau-Ponty's phenomenological critique of the positivistic view of perception, the body and subjectivity as well as with Deleuze's poststructuralist anarchist critique of Freudian
psychoanalysis and Marxist economic reductionism. Unlike these philosophers,
however, Virilio neglects to consider his cultural theoretical differences with
postmodernism. His writings are thus open to Waite's charge that they remain
embedded within the realm of modernism. For others, though, Virilio's cultural theory and interviews represent the beginning of a fascinatingly affirmative hypermodern analysis of the latest mutations in cybernetic society.

Note

1. In this Introduction I shall refer only to Virilio's most important writings and make use of
the English translations of such works. Virilio's main texts in French and English are detailed in
the Select Bibliography of the Works of Paul Virilio in this volume.

References

Baudrillard, Jean (1995) *The Gulf War Did Not Take Place*, trans. Paul Patton. Bloomington and
    Indianapolis: Indiana University Press.
Bauman, Zygmunt (1999) *In Search of Politics*. Cambridge: Polity Press.
Foucault, Michel (1977) *Discipline and Punish: The Birth of the Prison*, trans. Alan Sheridan.
    Harmondsworth: Penguin.
Genosko, Gary (1999) *McLuhan and Baudrillard: The Masters of Implosion*. London: Routledge.
Lash, Scott (1999) *Another Modernity, A Different Rationality*. Oxford: Blackwell.

Sokal, Alan and Bricmont, Jean (1998) *Intellectual Impostures: Postmodern Philosophers' Abuse of Science*. London: Profile Books.

Waite, Geoff (1996) *Nietzsche's Corps/e: Aesthetics, Politics, Prophecy, or the Spectacular Technoculture of Everyday Life*. Durham, NC and London: Duke University Press.

PART ONE

ON THEORY, CULTURE AND SOCIETY

1

FROM MODERNISM TO
HYPERMODERNISM AND BEYOND

Interview with John Armitage

Postmodernism and hypermodernism

JA: Professor Virilio, I would like to begin by charting your place within the contemporary intellectual landscape.[1] For instance, your work is closely associated with the cultural movement known as postmodernism. Certainly, your most recently translated study, *Open Sky* (1997 [1995]), is being received as such in the English-speaking world.[2] However, you have always been sceptical of the idea of postmodernism. Could you explain the basis of your critique of this concept?

PV: Postmodernism is a notion that makes sense in architecture, through the work of [Robert] Venturi (Venturi et al., 1977) and so on. Since I am teaching architecture, to me, postmodernism is a 'suitcase' word, a syncretism. In architecture, it is a clear-cut phenomenon: styles are mixed up, history is ignored, one goes for a 'melting pot' of approaches. But as far as thought is concerned, thought as developed in the years 1970–80, I simply cannot understand why people are talking about postmodernism. Poststructuralism? Yes, OK. Postmodernism? It doesn't make any sense to me. Hence, I do not feel linked at all with postmodernity. Moreover, as a teacher in a college of architecture, I believe postmodernism was a catastrophe in the history of modern architecture. Therefore there is no linkage between me and postmodernism. I know that many people tend to associate postmodernism with relativism, especially with cognitive relativism. Well, this is a new polemic that is cropping up, especially here in France, and which does not concern, let alone interest me in the slightest measure. Another thing is that I am a very marginal thinker, I do not relate to any established school of thought. Of course, I am a phenomenologist. When young, I was a pupil of [Maurice] Merleau-Ponty, I loved [Edmund] Husserl. You could call me a 'Gestaltist', I was enthusiastic about the psychology of form, Paul Guillaume, and the Berlin School: these are my intellectual origins.[3] I have been associated with the end phase of structuralism, with [Michel] Foucault, of course, and [Gilles] Deleuze. But I am essentially a marginal figure. The main influence in my work has been the Second World War, that is, strategy, spatial planning, and this body of thinking about total war of which I was victim in my youth.

JA: It seems to me that your work, which is primarily concerned with technological, urban and socio-cultural change, is the work of someone whose thinking addresses the problem of what might be called 'super-' or 'hypermodernism'?[4] I say this because your theoretical interventions appear to be aimed not only at intensifying but also at displacing traditional forms of thought about the modern world and the way it is represented. How do you respond to this interpretation?

PV: I totally agree. As a so-called 'war baby', I have been deeply marked by the accident, the catastrophe, and thus by sudden changes, and upheavals. I am a child of the *Blitzkrieg*, the 'lightning war', I am a child of history's acceleration, as Daniel Halévy put it in 1947.[5] Hence, it is clear that my work is a critical analysis of modernity, but through a perception of technology which is largely, I might say, catastrophic. I say catastro-*phic*, not catastro*phist*. This is because I have witnessed the drama of total war myself, I have lived through it, the millions of deaths, the cities razed to the ground, all that. As far as 'hyper-' or 'super-' modernism is concerned, I think we are not out of modernity yet, by far. I think that modernity will only come to a halt within the ambit of what I call the 'integral accident' (Virilio, 1989b [1986], 1997). I believe that technical modernity, modernity taken as the outcome of technical inventions over the past two centuries, can only be stopped by an integral ecological accident, which, in a certain way, I am forecasting. Each and every invention of a technical object has also been the innovation of a particular accident. From the sum total of the technosciences does arise, and will arise a 'generalized accident' (1997). And this will be modernism's end.

JA: Do you consider yourself a modernist author? Your writing style, for example, seems to many people to replace traditional narrative and structure with the 'stream of consciousness' technique ...

PV: Yes, I do. Well, let me put it this way: to be concerned with speed, like I am, means to be involved in music. For twenty years now I have been working on 'dromology', that is, on the importance of speed in history, and thus of acceleration (Virilio, 1986 [1977]). Now, if there is a realm where speed is really an important element, it is music, rhythm, tempo. And thus my writing is a dynamic, cinematic process. Moreover, and I state this as modestly as possible, it is my belief that philosophy is a mere subdivision of literature. To me, Shakespeare is really a great philosopher, perhaps above Kant and a few others.

Relativity

JA: *Open Sky* (1997 [1995]) brings to the fore one of the most under-appreciated themes of your writings, namely, your interest in Albert Einstein's theory of relativity. This scientific concept is also occasionally viewed as a facet of modernism. How does the theory of relativity relate to your current projects?

PV: Well, frankly, this is quite simple. There is no way one could study the phenomenon of acceleration in all these domains, whether that is in the realm of transportation, or in the realm of information, that is, in the transfer of information, without stepping full scale into the issue of relativity. It is unavoidable. Ours are cinematic societies. They are not only societies of movement, but of the acceleration of that very movement. And hence, of the shortening of distances in terms of time, but, I would also add, of the relation to reality. It is thus simply impossible to ignore the theory of relativity. We're all going through the gates of relativity. It is well known that the theory of relativity is very poorly popularized, it is not at all well understood by the general public. One cannot skip the theory of relativity for the mere reason that it is difficult to understand. Why so? Because we live it. We live it through mobile phones, through 'live' programmes on TV, through the telecommunications media, through Virtual Reality (VR), through cyberspace, through video-conferencing, through supersonic air travel, and so on. Thus, as we live it, we interpret it, in the musical sense of the word. Like one says, 'to interpret a musical score', we, all of us, interpret the theory of relativity through our own lived lives. We do that through our calendar, through our time planning, our relationships, our involvement in love affairs even. We do that through the telephone, for instance, we do that through education, and through 'tele-learning'. We have become deterritorialized. Our embedding in our native soil, that element of *hic et nunc*, (here and now), 'in situ', that embedding belongs, now, in a certain way, to the past. It has been overtaken by the acceleration of history – by the acceleration of reality itself – by 'real time', and by the 'live', all of which are in a stage beyond the *hic et nunc*, 'in situ' condition. Caught as we are between this territory-based embedding, which is of a geographic, geophysical nature, or even of a geostrategic nature in the case of the military, and total deterritorialization, what remains in order to interpret our world?

Nothing but relativity! Not the physicists' relativity, but our relativity, the relativity of our own lived lives, for which we are responsible, and of which we are the victims, at the same time. Relativity is no longer the exclusive domain of (natural) scientists, it has become the property of all those who live in the modern world.

Phenomenology and Marxism

JA: Before we move on to discuss your relationship to deconstruction (Derrida, 1973 [1967], 1976 [1967]) and poststructuralism, I would like to ask one or two questions about your own intellectual formation. For example, one of the leading philosophies in France and elsewhere in the immediate aftermath of the Second World War was structuralism ...

PV: Yes, indeed, absolutely so. And certainly not existentialism ...

JA: Even so, your own philosophical background developed through an engagement with Merleau-Ponty's *Phenomenology of Perception* (1962 [1945]). What would you say you learnt most from Merleau-Ponty's work and how has it influenced your own?

PV: First of all, I was a pupil of Merleau-Ponty, of Jean Wahl and of Vladimir Jankelevitch, to name three French philosophers who were teaching at the Sorbonne at that time. The one to whom I felt most attracted was quite naturally Maurice Merleau-Ponty, and his *Phenomenology of Perception*. Why? Because I am so totally involved with perception myself, through my childhood, through painting. Yes, I painted, I even worked with famous painters such as [Henri] Matisse and [Georges] Braque when I was young. I am a man of perception, a man of the gaze, I am a man of the visual school of thought. Therefore, Merleau-Ponty's *Phenomenology of Perception* appeared to me to form a crossroads with the psychology of form, with Gestalt and the whole Berlin School. And thus it is at this crossroads of the psychology of form, Gestalt theory and the *Phenomenology of Perception* that I position myself. And to that one of course has to add the reading of Einstein, of the big scientific names of the time, [Paul] Dirac, [Werner] Heisenberg and yes, of course, [Henri] Bergson.[6] So you have a crossroads there, and it's where I stand, at the intersection.

JA: Merleau-Ponty was, for a large part of his life, associated with the philosophy of humanist Marxism. One thing that has always surprised me about your writings, particularly within the intellectual context of post-war France, is the absence of any reference to Marx. What is your relationship, if any, to Marxism?

PV: I am no Marxist, nor have I ever been one. But my father was a communist. We'll come back to that later. You see, my mother was a Breton, and my father Italian. Like every young boy [*laughs*] I had to choose between my mother and my father. So, although I have a lot of respect for my father, I totally reject his political views. I absolutely cannot be a communist. I might well feel at home as a 'communard', as in the Paris Commune, or as an anarcho-syndicalist, these would suit me. But Marxism, no! Take it as a reaction against my father.

JA: Are you saying that your reasons for rejecting the Marxism of your intellectual contemporaries like Merleau-Ponty were autobiographical rather than theoretical?

PV: Yes, you're right, my intellectual contemporaries were communist to a man. I was not. But my reasons were theoretical also. This is because, when I was young, I converted to Christianity. I converted when I was 18, as an adult. The war had just ended then, and I had seen terrible things, and that was also one of the reasons for my conversion to Christianity. But then, you must know that I converted in the company of 'worker-priests'. Worker-priests are, in France, those priests who take an industrial job and go to live with the factory workers. They do not display their pastoral cross. I chose to convert with a worker-priest because I wanted something real, not some religious show with a guy in a costume. It is since that time that I have worked with Abbé Pierre.[7]

JA: Would it be correct, then, to suggest that you have no *theoretical* objections against socialism, against the left as a body of thought?

PV: No, of course not, I have nothing against socialism. I belong to the left, that is quite clear ...

JA: Nevertheless, in the immediate aftermath of the Second World War, many of your friends were not merely on the left but also committed Marxists ...

PV: True ...

JA: Can you recall why you felt it necessary to develop your own political perspective at that time? ...

PV: I feel that many of my contemporaries have totally blacked out the war from their minds. Many of them never experienced totalitarianism. I lived through that experience. With a communist father, who was Italian to boot, we had to make our escape from totalitarianism, from Nazism and so on. It was no joke to be both communist and Italian during the Second World War [in occupied France]. This meant that I never could get involved in something that appeared to me, right from the beginning, to be a totalitarian phenomenon. Yet I have always remained interested in the leftist dimension within Marxism.

'Anarcho-Christianity'

JA: You spoke earlier of your conversion to Christianity. What role does it play in your work? Do you see yourself, for example, as part of a French Catholic moral tradition that might include other Christian and existentialist critics of technology like Gabriel Marcel or Jacques Ellul?[8]

PV: Yes, I do see linkages, especially with Jacques Ellul, rather than with Gabriel Marcel, who is from an earlier generation. But I cannot really place myself within what you call a Catholic tradition. The reason is that I have always been utterly unable to write about my faith. I do not have the gift for that. I have always considered that my life as a follower of Christ was something happening through my everyday life, not through my theoretical writings. It is not that I refuse to do it, I would gladly write a book about it, but I simply do not have the gift for it. You see, I do not have much of a theological culture. My conversion was an affair of the heart, a love affair you may say, more than an intellectual one. Speaking of religion, I feel much more at ease with an ordinary, poor person. When I am writing, I am somewhere else.

JA: In the late 1950s and throughout most of the 1960s the philosophy of structuralism began to challenge Christian existentialism, phenomenology and humanist Marxism. Structuralism was, of course, profoundly *anti*-humanist. Could your own theoretical approach be described as anti-humanist?

PV: Oh, not at all. I am an anarcho-Christian. It sounds quite paradoxical, but to me the definition of man is subsumed, and I quote it often, in a saying by someone I have come to like very much, Hildegarde from Bingen. St Hildegarde wrote, composed music, played the harp, and was many other things at once. The saying is: '*Homo est clausura mirabilium dei*': 'Man is the closing point of the marvels of the universe' (i.e. God). Thus, for me, Man is not the centre of the universe, he is the end of the universe, the end of the world. This has nothing to do with ideas like 'transcendental ego' or 'egocentrism'. For me, there is nothing beyond man. Forget about technology, eugenism, robotics, prostheses. Forget also about [Friedrich Nietzsche's] '*Uebermensch*' [Superman]. I do not believe these ideas are at all humanist. I think they're far worse. This is a very important point for me, because I am absolutely against this new-fangled form of totalitarianism which I call technoscience and its cult. I see there a yet unheard-of eugenics programme, eugenics written very large, far beyond [Sir Francis] Galton's,[9] the idea behind this new brand of eugenicism being to perfect man, to make a better man. Well, there is no such thing as the possibility of 'improving' man, of tinkering man into something better. No way. Never.

JA: You would say that such a programme would not be a desirable aim?

PV: No indeed, I believe it is not. Yet it is exactly the programme of technoscience. Take, for instance, 'Dolly' [the recently cloned sheep], take neo-eugenicism, clones, take all new technologies. We see now a eugenic desire running amok.

From military space to cyberspace

JA: The initial significance of your theoretical work flows from your architectural and photographic enquiries, documented in *Bunker Archeology* (1994a [1975]), into the 'Atlantic Wall' – those 1,500 German bunkers constructed during the Second World War along the French coastline to prevent an Allied invasion ...

PV: There were in fact 15,000 of them, one zero more! And they stretched along the West European coast all the way up to Denmark. But about me: I spent my youth in the town of Nantes. Nantes lies at the mouth of the Loire, just before the Atlantic Ocean. Its true oceanic harbour is St Nazaire, where there was a German submarine base, and in fact an Allied landing took place there at some stage. Thus I spent the war time as a boy, with the sea just one hour away, yet without ever being able to go and see it: the seashore was a forbidden zone. So when liberation finally came, I rushed to the sea, to the beaches, like everybody else did. And there I encountered structures which were littering the beaches:

the bunkers of the Atlantic Wall. And thus at the same time as I saw the sea for the first time, I also discovered these mysterious, enigmatic architectural structures. To me, they were like the statues on Easter Island. And so, for ten years, I went on a quest after these structures. I sketched and photographed these bunkers in order to come to grips with the totalitarian dimension of the war. My first snapshots were taken in 1957, the last ones in 1965.

JA: What was the connection between this discovery and your thinking on military space?

PV: First, it was an emotional discovery, which you might compare with Victor Segalen's first encounter with Chinese sculpture. You can also call it an archaeological experience, and a shocking one. Another element, aside from this encounter with military space, and which led me to write *Bunker Archeology*, was that I wanted to get involved in the study of urban phenomena, in the city and its technique. I switched over to urbanism, to architecture and thus to the study of the technique's impact on the space of the city, and the way it alters the urban landscape. And at this point, you of course meet Gestalt theory, the psychology of forms. Military space is an organized form of perception. When I was a conscript – I served in the artillery – I was a gunner. Part of my military service was in Germany, in the French occupation zone. I was stationed in Freiburg, at the HQ of the First French Army. I ended up as a cartographic officer in the staff of Field Marshall Juin. In this function I made a good number of military surveys in the Black Forest region, to be used in manoeuvres taking place in the occupied zone. So everything is linked up. There is an aesthetic kind of involvement with bunkers, and an urbanistic one in the field of regional planning. Over thousands of kilometres, the coast was organized in such a way as to be controlled by sight. It is that logic that made me understand to what extent the war had been a total one. War had not only conditioned the people through manslaughter, Auschwitz and wholesale executions, it had also reorganized the territory, just like the Great Chinese Wall had done. One could say that military architecture was the first incarnation of Land Art. In fact, minimalist and Land artists like Robert Morris came to me later to reflect on my book, and said they had found it most interesting.[10]

JA: In *The Function of the Oblique* (Johnston, 1996) you, along with the architect Claude Parent, outline your efforts in the *Architecture Principe* group of the early 1960s to initiate an urban regime based on the theory of the 'oblique function', which, while founded on uneven planes and bodily disorientation, nevertheless resulted in the construction of several major works. Looking back, what do you think were the major achievements and disappointments of *Architecture Principe* and the theory of the oblique function?

PV: *Architecture Principe* was the name of a group. That period lasted five years in all (1963–8). You must know that this was at a time when many artists, philosophers and the like would come together to do things. For instance, we did quite a few things together with Archigram. You also had Paulo Soleri in the United States, and there was also the Metabolic Group in Japan.[11] And so, Claude Parent and myself decided to start a research group together, and the main thing I contributed to was a church. That was the St Bernadette church in Nevers, and that church is a so-called 'Bunker church'. Why? Because I wanted to 'Christianize' the bunker. Of course, at the time, the prevailing myth was that of the crypt – the atomic shelter. One was then living under the permanent threat of the atomic bomb, and hence the atomic shelter. And so, you get a cross-point between the theme of St Bernadette of Lourdes, and that of the bunker. In Lourdes, the Virgin Mary appeared to St Bernadette in a grotto. Now, both the grotto and the bunker are crypts, hidden places, as in the English word, cryptic. And thus there was an opportunity to make a cross-over happen between that monolithic branch of architecture and a religious building. There is another reason: I had frequently been to Germany, to look at bunkers, and there I had seen a lot of so-called '*Luftschutzraum*', air-shelters, and in Dusseldorf, I suddenly saw *Luftschutzraums* which had been converted into Protestant or Catholic churches. And a correspondence dawned on me as between these places of shelter from danger, and places of worship, which are also places of salvation. We had another big project, a factory, and we also designed a number of private homes with inclined planes. Now if you want me to explain the concept of the oblique function as succinctly as possible it is this: simply to have people inhabit places with inclined, not horizontal, planes …

JA: And the disappointments? …

PV: We published things. But, basically, this was a typical 'youth group'. And it broke up with the 'events' of May 1968. I was myself very much involved in those events, whereas Claude Parent was against the whole thing. So our ways parted, I went to the left, and he went to the right.[12]

JA: Much of your work in the late 1960s and early 1970s is overtly concerned with the idea of 'critical space'. Could you elaborate on this concept?

PV: Critical space is indeed a very important concept. You must see it as the direct outcome of me joining the École Spéciale d'Architecture, in 1968, at the formal request of the students there. And then, I immediately realized that the *prima materia* of the architect is not matter, bricks, stones and concrete, but space. And that it is necessary to construct space first before you can build up matter, with materials. Now, about the *critical* aspect of space: this means that space finds itself in a critical situation, just like one would speak of critical times, or of a critical situation. Space is under threat. Not only matter is threatened, space too is being destroyed. But it is being rebuilt at the same time. This is what I started to feel in the 1960s, and it was by then that I got the foreboding of cyberspace! I got the foreboding of virtual space, through Benoit Mandelbrot and the new geometry of fractals.[13] I came to see that the unity of space, which served as a basis for Le Corbusier, for the Archigram group, for all of us in sense, is in the process of being broken up. And the curious thing is that I published *The Lost Dimension* (1991b [1984]) in the same year as William Gibson published *Neuromancer* (1984). So here you have someone who writes on virtual space, on cyberspace, and someone who works on critical space. And both approaches will come to mesh into each other. To me, the reason why space is critical is because it is on the verge of becoming virtual space. Let me give you another example: whole dimensions no longer exist. For the modern architect, there exist the three dimensions, and time on top of them. This is what you might call 'ancient space'. It's modern space too, but it is conventional. From Mandelbrot onwards, dimensions are no longer whole, they are broken up. Space is fractured too. Nothing remains whole, as space, from approximately the 1970s onwards. And, to me, this is a great joy, since I am an anti-totalitarian. Newtonian absolute space disappears with the break-up brought about by fractals, and by Einsteinian relativity in the first place, of course. The entire unity of space, which was the basis of architecture, modern architecture included, is deconstructed, fractionalized. This is what I call an 'accident'. It is a far better situation than that of totalitarian space. Geometry has now encountered its accident in fractalization.

JA: In *The Lost Dimension* and elsewhere, you present critical analyses of the nature of electronic space and the spread of new information and communications technologies. Why is it necessary to criticize, say, the Internet and cyberspace?

PV: I do not criticize the Internet and cyberspace as such. What I criticize is the propaganda unleashed by Bill Gates and everything that goes with it. What I loathe are the monopolies of Microsoft, of Time Warner, etc. I cannot stand those! I am an Apple fan, I am for Apple's convivial approach. I am not fretting against technology *per se*, but against the logic behind it. But first and foremost I'd like to position myself as an art critic of technology. Everybody is familiar with the conventional art critic, the musicologist. But art criticism of technology is a taboo. 'Yes and Amen' is the only allowed position. Well, not for me, thanks!

Nietzsche, Derrida, power

JA: Although you were working on critical space in the late 1960s and early 1970s, it was also in that period when both structuralism and Marxism came under attack. Deconstructionists and poststructuralist philosophers like Jacques Derrida, for example, looked to Nietzsche rather than Marx for inspiration. Would it be correct to say that Nietzsche's philosophy is close to your own?

PV: It is true that I always have felt close to Deleuze and Derrida, who were very intimate friends, and Derrida still is, but I must confess that I have never been convinced by their 'Nietzscheanism'. I love 'Nietzschean music'. But, to me, Nietzsche is a man of the grand opera! His linkage with Wagner is not at all fortuitous. And I really admire the operatic part of Nietzsche. But his underlying philosophy? I'm sorry, I cannot stand it! It's physically repulsive! All that crap about the '*Uebermensch*', and 'The Will to Power'! I do, though, profoundly admire the dramatic, the literary dimension, in Nietzsche. But I cannot assign any philosophical value to that brand of thinking. Here we encounter Shakespeare again. It is clear that I prefer Shakespeare to Nietzsche, by far. When I link Nietzsche's writings to the opera, it is because, to me, philosophy is spread out over the arts. Take Marcel Duchamp: for me, he is a philosopher who happens to paint. Shakespeare is a philosopher who writes plays. Kant is a philosopher who writes philosophical treatises. But philosophy transcends all this. When reading Nietzsche, I admire the literary music, the 'heroization' of concepts. As half Italian, I admire! I clap my hands! I love theatre! To me, Nietzsche is like Verdi. I applaud. But at the same time, I cannot, simply cannot, accept his philosophy. You see, I remain an art critic.

JA: Do you see any points of contact between your work and that of Derrida? Derrida (1984, 1996 [1995]) has, for instance, not only written on Nietzsche but also on speed and technoscience ...

PV: No. The fact is that I do appreciate Derrida very much, but I do not encounter him. There are parallels in our work, but we do not share common ground. I cannot formulate it better. We are friends, but there are no points of contact in our writings.

JA: Earlier, you rejected the Nietzschean conception of power. How would you define power?

PV: This is a rather difficult type of question to respond to. The question of power is a long and vexed one. The ancient Chinese had an extraordinary phrase for it. When a representative of the Emperor would meet some local or regional power holder, his first words would be: 'Tremble and Obey!' To me, this is the best definition of power. Fear! That is, to instil fear, to frighten. The first thing power is about is fear, and from that compliance follows. Fear is of course also about emotions, about astonishment. And speed frightens. There is an awful lot more to say, naturally.

The political economy of speed

JA: Power and speed are central to perhaps what is your best known book, *Speed and Politics: An Essay on Dromology* (1986 [1977]). Could you explain the nature and significance of dromology?

PV: Dromology originates from the Greek word, *dromos*. Hence, dromology is the science of the ride, the journey, the drive, the way. To me, this means that speed and riches are totally linked concepts. And that the history of the world is not only about the political economy of riches, that is, wealth, money, capital, but also about the political economy of speed. If time is money, as they say, then speed is power. You see it with the velocity of the predators, of the cavalry, of railways, of ships and maritime power. But it is also possible to see it with the velocity of dispatching information. So all my work has been about attempting to trace the dromocratic dimension of societies from ancient Greek society right up to our present-day societies. This work is of course about unrelenting acceleration, but it is mostly about the fact that all societies are pyramidal in nature: the higher speeds belong to the upper reaches of society, the slower to the bottom. The wealth pyramid is the replica of the velocity pyramid. Examples are easy to find: it was true in ancient societies, through maritime power and cavalry, and through their ways of dispatching messages, and it holds true in our modern societies, through the transport revolution, and through the current revolution in data transport and information processing. Thus my work is all about stating that it is of paramount importance to analyse acceleration as a

major political phenomenon, a phenomenon without which no understanding of history, and especially history-that-is-in-the-making, since
the eighteenth century is possible.

JA: In *Speed and Politics* you also suggest that successive waves of acceleration imply both the 'disappearance' of physical geographical space and a
new politics of real time. What, for you, is the most important aspect of
the relationship between the physical dimension and the political space
of real time?

PV: Well, the old politics of acceleration were mainly about transport. That
is, the possibilities inherent in moving goods from one place to another,
or, perhaps equally importantly, moving *troops* from one point to
another. This means that acceleration bore next to no relationship to
information. You had pigeons, and other methods of despatching, but
through the ages there was hardly any acceleration of information transmission. But today, that is, since the beginning of the twentieth century,
acceleration is mainly about the increasing speed of information transmission. Sure, transportation has been constantly speeded up too, but,
today, the major development is the increasing speed of information
transmission, and the quest for the attainment of real time. Information
transmission is thus no longer concerned with the bringing about of a
relative gain in velocity, as was the case with railway transport compared
to horse power, or jet aircraft compared to trains, but about the absolute
velocity of electromagnetic waves.

Pure war and the politics of everyday life

JA: Your concerns about what might be called 'the dromocratic condition'
led, in the late 1970s, to the publication of your *Popular Defense and
Ecological Struggles* (1990 [1978]). This seems to me to be one of the few
books of yours which, while discussing the theoretical concept of 'pure
war', also makes a *practical* political case for 'revolutionary resistance'
against the tyranny of speed politics and, in particular, the military–
industrial complex. Could you elaborate upon these concepts? Are they
still relevant today?

PV: Here, one must state that the book might also have been titled *Pure War*
(Virilio and Lotringer, 1997 [1983]) since that is the heading of the
Introduction.[14] That was the time when we were living with the unadul-
terated balance of terror. What I mean is that one cannot understand
the concept of pure war outside of the atomic bomb, the weapon of the

apocalypse. At that time, and this has been somewhat forgotten, we were living with the potentiality of a pure war, which, nevertheless, failed to materialize. What is pure war? It is a war of a single utterance: Fear! Fear! Fear! Nuclear deterrence can be conceived of as pure war for the simple reason that nuclear war never took place. However, such deterrence did spawn a technoscientific explosion, inclusive of the Internet, and other satellite technologies. And so one saw that the history of warfare, of siege war, of the war of movement, of total war, of world war, all somehow merged into pure war. That is, into a blockade, into nuclear deterrence. What had been reached was the dimension of the integral accident, the moment of the total destruction of the world. And there it stopped. Thus, at that stage, the whole concept of resistance to war became a new phenomenon. It was no longer about resisting an invader, German or other, but about resisting the military–scientific and industrial complex. Take my generation: during the Second World War you had resistance, combat against the Germans who invaded France. During the 1960s and 1970s there was resistance, among others by me, not against an invader, but against the military–industrial complex, that is against the invention of ever crazier sorts of weapons, like the neutron bomb, and 'Doomsday machines', something that we saw, for instance, in Stanley Kubrick's film *Dr Strangelove*. Thus resistance to pure war is of another nature than resistance to an oppressor, to an invader. It is resistance against science: that is extraordinary, unheard of!

JA: At this point, I would like to ask a question on behalf of my students. For when I give a lecture on your work there is one question that comes up over and over again at the end of the session. It usually runs something like this: 'While I find Paul Virilio's analyses of pure war, and revolutionary resistance against the military–industrial complex extremely thought provoking, I'm not quite sure what he is suggesting I actually *do* about these issues at the political level, at the level of the everyday?' What, in your view, should one tell them?

PV: Well, tell them the following. I was a militant against the atomic bomb. I joined leftist movements during the events of May 1968. But I must say that I became very disappointed about political struggles, since they appear to me to lag very much behind developments both within the postindustrial revolution and technoscience. Thus I am, and many people with me, out of phase with real existing political movements. I feel henceforth marginalized, and the only action I can partake in takes place within the urban realm, with homeless people, with travellers, with people whose lives are being destroyed by the revolution brought about by the end of salaried work, by automation, by delocalization. You may call it street-corner work in a sense. For instance, together with Abbé Pierre, I was member of the High Committee for the Housing of Destitute People that was instituted by President [François] Mitterand and [Jacques] Chirac. I was on that Committee for three years. That work has stopped now, but, for the last fifteen years, I have been a member of private associations which work together with homeless people. These are Christian associations for the most part, and there lie my political activities these days. I am a disappointed man of the left. By the way, this is no fun because at the same time there is the rise of extremist political parties like [Jean-Marie] Le Pen's Front National, and so on.

Modernity and 'globalitarianism'

JA: If we can broadly define modernity as an attempt to understand the present period by contrasting it with the recent past, what key features, *other* than speed, would you point to in the contemporary era as being of most political significance?

PV: Globalitarianism! This is what transcends totalitarianism. Let's take an example, and excuse the neologism, but I cannot find another word. Totalitarianism covered my life, through the Second World War and through the period of nuclear deterrence, so you may say through Nazism first and then Stalinism. Totalitarianism was thus a central issue at that time. But now, through the single market, through globalization, through the convergence of time towards a single time, a world time, a time which comes to dominate local time, and the stuff of history, what emerges – through cyberspace, through the big telecommunications conglomerates, is a new totalitarianism, a totalitarianism of totalitarianism, and that is what I call globalitarianism. It is the totalitarianism of all totalities. Globalization, in this sense, is a truly important event. But, when people say to me, 'We'll become world citizens!', I reply, 'Forget it'. I was a world citizen long before globalization. After the war, I met Gary Davis, I went to meetings which took place in the Père Lachaise neighbourhood of Paris. I was 16–17–18 at that time. I was half Italian, I felt a world citizen. But when people say that Bill Gates, cyberspace and VR are the stuff of world citizenship, I say, no way! Globalitarianism is social cybernetics. And that's something infinitely dangerous, more dangerous even, perhaps, than the Nazi or communist brands of totalitarianism. It is difficult to explain globalitarianism but it is simple enough in itself. Totalitarianisms were singular and localized. Occupied Europe, for example, was one, the Soviet empire another, or China. That's clear. The rest of the world was not under totalitarianism. Now, with the advent of globalization, it is everywhere that one can be under control and surveillance. The world market is globalitarian. It is on purpose that I use the doublet total/totalitarian, and global/global-itarian. I consider this phenomenon a grave menace. It is manifest that Time Warner and the large conglomerates like Westinghouse, MCIWorldCom and all the other gigantic companies are not the exact equivalent of Hitler or Stalin. Yet, bad things are possible ...

JA: Undoubtedly, I believe that one of the leading microelectronics con-glomerates has even adopted 'One World, One Operating System' as its corporate logo ...

PV: Yes. I can't stand it. Let me remind you of a sentence by Saint-Just, one of the main protagonists of the French Revolution who got guillotined in the end, and who said once: 'There's this new idea in Europe: happi-ness.' Well, his other phrase, which I like very much is: 'If the people can be oppressed, even if they are not actually oppressed, then they are oppressed already.' It is a very interesting statement, because it says that the possibility is already the reality. Even if you are unaware of it, it has already happened. Hence the menace in the present period.

Lyotard

JA: Shortly after the publication of *Popular Defense and Ecological Struggles*, Jean-François Lyotard published his seminal book *The Postmodern Condition* (1984 [1979]). Does this book's renowned scepticism about the possibility of historical understanding, along with its rejection of the 'grand narratives' of progress, have any significance for you?

PV: Well, yes. We see here the fractalization of history, and Lyotard ex-pressed – at an early stage – the end of the grand ideological narratives. But then, there was a question put by a Jewish friend of mine, Gerard Rabinowich – it was just after the book's publication, and we had gath-ered among friends in St Germain des Prés. My friend asked: 'Well, Lyotard, what do *you* have to say about that grand narrative called jus-tice? Is that too a grand narrative belonging to the past?' A fine point indeed! Needless to say, Lyotard was at a loss for an answer. And indeed, to me, even if I accept the demise of the grand historical and ideological narratives in favour of the small narratives, the narrative of justice is beyond deconstruction. If that was the case, I would not be a Christian. You cannot deconstruct the absolute necessity of justice. Hence that issue remains intact. Justice cannot be divided up, be fractalized, on pain of descent into barbarism. We have reached a limit there.

Speed and inertia

JA: While some cultural theorists are sympathetic to your critique of speed, few of them appear to appreciate the stress you place on the relationship between absolute speed and its 'Other' – *inertia*? Indeed, you have written a book about speed and the environmental crisis entitled *Polar Inertia* (1999 [1990]). Why is speed inextricably bound up with inertia?

PV: That is quite simple. When what is being put to work are relative speeds, no inertia obtains, but acceleration or deceleration. We are then in the realm of mobility and emancipation. But when absolute speed, that is the speed of light, is put to work, then one hits a wall, a barrier, which is the barrier of light. Let me remind you that there exist three recognized barriers: the sound barrier, which was passed in 1947 by Chuck Jaeger, the barrier of heat, which was crossed in the 1960s with rockets, at what is called 'escape velocity' and, finally, the speed of light, which is the effectuation of the 'live' in almost all realms of human activity. That is, the possibility to transfer over distance sight, sound, smell and tactile feeling. Only gustation, taste, seems to be left out of it. From that moment onwards, it is no longer necessary to make any journey: one has already arrived. The consequence of staying at the same place is a sort of Foucauldian imprisonment, but this new type of imprisonment is the ultimate form because it means that the world has been reduced to nothing. The world is reduced, both in terms of surface and extension, to nothing and this results in a kind of incarceration, in a stasis, which means that it is no longer necessary to go towards the world, to journey, to stand up, to depart, to go to things. Everything is already there. This is, again, an effect of relativity. Why? Because the earth is so small. In the cosmos, absolute speed amounts to little, but at that scale, it is earth which amounts to nothing. This is the meaning of inertia. There is a definite relationship between inertia and absolute speed which is based on the stasis which results from absolute speed. Absolute stasis leads – potentially – to absolute stasis. The world, then, remains 'at home' [*in English*], already there, given. I repeat: this is a possibility, a potentiality, but here we are back to what I said before: when the people are in a situation of possible inertia, they are already inert.

The integral accident

JA: You said before that 'modernity will only come to a halt within the ambit of the integral accident' ...

PV: Indeed, the accident has always fascinated me. In fact, I am currently preparing my end-of-the-century book, the one for the year 2000, which will be on the integral accident, although I am writing another book before that. The integral accident is the one that integrates all others.

JA: Could you elaborate on the concept of the integral, or, generalized accident, a little further?

PV: Let me put it this way: every time a technology is invented, take shipping for instance, an accident is invented together with it, in this case, the shipwreck, which is exactly contemporaneous with the invention of the ship. The invention of the railway meant, perforce, the invention of the railway disaster. The invention of the aeroplane brought the air crash in its wake. Now, the three accidents I have just mentioned are specific and localized accidents. The *Titanic* sank at a given location. A train derails at another location and a plane crashes, again, somewhere else. This is a fundamental point, because people tend to focus on the vehicle, the invention itself, but not on the accident, which is its consequence. As an art critic of technology, I always try to emphasize both the invention and the accident. But the occurrence of the accident is being denied. This is the result of the hype which always goes together with technical objects, as with Bill Gates and cyberspace, for instance. The hype in favour of technology dismisses its negative aspects. It is a positive thing to have electricity, it is a wonderful device, but at the same time it is based on nuclear energy. Thus what these three types of accidents have in common is that they are localized, and this is because they are about relative velocities, the transport velocities of ships, trains, and planes. But from the moment that the absolute velocity of electromagnetic waves is put to use, the potential of the accident is no longer local, but general. It is no longer a particular accident, hence the possibility arises of a generalized accident. Let me stress the point by giving you two examples: the collapse of the stock exchange and radioactivity as result of a nuclear conflict. These examples mean that when an event takes place somewhere today, the possibility arises that it might destroy everything. A virus in an electronic network, an atomic leakage in Chernobyl – and that was not much, compared to a massive nuclear strike. Today's collapse of the stock exchange is a nice icon for the integral accident, in the sense that a very small occurrence changes everything, as the speed of quotations and programmed trading spreads and enhances any trend instantaneously. What happened a few weeks ago in [South East] Asia is an integral accident, well, almost an integral accident.

The aesthetics of disappearance

JA: In works such as *The Aesthetics of Disappearance* (1991a [1980]) you argue that modern culture is not simply characterized by speed but also by what you call the 'aesthetics of disappearance'. What is the relationship between speed and the aesthetics of disappearance?

PV: These are the cinematic effects, which are characteristic of the contemporary arts, and stem from film, television, video, etc. Let me explain: in ancient societies you had an aesthetic of *appearance*, which means that there was an enduring material support to the image: wood or canvas in the case of paintings; marble, in the case of sculptures, etc. Save for music, most aesthetics-related phenomena were phenomena of appearance, of emergence. Painting enabled the emergence of a figure on the canvas, which was subsequently 'fixed' with a varnish, for example, Leonardo's *Mona Lisa*. The image had appeared, as it were, through the medium of the canvas. The same could be said of Michelangelo, shaping *Moses* out of a block of marble, and that block of marble, suddenly *becoming* Moses. Persistence had a material basis. But with the invention of photography, of the photogramme, that is of instant photography, and of cinematography, from that moment onwards, one enters into an aesthetic of disappearance. At that stage, persistence is no longer material but cognitive, it is in the eye of the beholder. Things owe their existence to the fact that they disappear, like they do on a screen for instance. They are there, they appear, and are in motion, *because* they vanish afterwards. Quite different, therefore, from frescoes, paintings, etc. It is a sequential phenomenon. In the first phase, there was a cinematic effect of painting: if you take snapshots of an artist at work, you see that the painting develops in stages. But this is a very slow cinematic phenomenon as opposed to the film where we are talking about 24 frames per second – even up to 60 frames per second with special effects. So, this is the aesthetics of disappearance, it means that most of the art has vanished. Hence, by the way, the current crisis in contemporary art. Hence, too, 'the art of the motor'. When I write about *The Art of the Motor* (1995 [1993]), I mean that there has been a motorization of art. And, by 'motor', I mean the French cinematographic word '*moteur*', for 'action'! This motorization of art is a very important phenomenon, and you cannot come to grips with the current crisis in the contemporary arts – I am thinking of *documenta* in Kassel, among others – without it [Joly, 1996]. All branches of the arts are involved in this motorization, that is, in acceleration.

JA: So, you are arguing that the crisis in the contemporary arts is the direct outcome of motorization? ...

PV: Yes, it is the result of the motorization of images. Let's take ships, for instance, and compare the grace of a sail-boat with a motor vessel:

you're not talking about the same kind of marine vessel any longer. The same holds true for figurative images: whether they are from paintings, or from photo stills, or the cinema, or video: it's not the same. You must see that. Meanwhile, photography and cinema have influenced painting. They have also influenced the theatre, and other realms too. Motorization has exerted its influence over art in general. Every time there is a gain, there is a loss too. By losing the slow pace of the revelation of things, we have lost one sense of time in favour of another. Let me give you another example: the moment we acquired the mechanical lift, we lost the staircase. It became the service or emergency staircase, and was no longer the magnificent grand staircase of old. But we gained in speed – as is always the case. When transatlantic air services were invented, we incurred the loss of the ocean liners. This holds true in all possible realms.

Foucault and Baudrillard

JA: Much of your recent work is concerned with cyberspace and imaging technologies of various kinds such as VR. However, it appears to be less influenced by Jean Baudrillard's writings on the nature and impact of *Simulations* (1983) and 'hyper-reality,' and more by Foucault's work on surveillance in *Discipline and Punish: The Birth of the Prison* (1977 [1975]). Why is this?

PV: *Discipline and Punish* is the source, obviously. Let me remind you that when Foucault published *Discipline and Punish*, one of his collaborators – he had quite a few of them at the time – was Jacques Donzelot. And Jacques Donzelot happened to sit on the examination board of one of my students who was doing research on prisons. We were working on prisons together, on the Panopticon and so on, as part of the college curriculum at the time, and that was before *Discipline and Punish* came out. The proof of that is that the illustrations provided in Foucault's book can be directly traced to my student's thesis! His name, incidentally, is Carthoux, and his thesis – for the Ecole Spéciale d'Architecture – was entitled 'The Place of Detention'. So, whether there is mutual influence or not, there are, again, clear parallels. Another link is of course my work about war and its particular field of perception.

Now, as far as Baudrillard is concerned, there is for sure something about his work that I have never liked at all, and that is his concept of simulation. I do not believe in simulation. To me, what takes place is substitution. Seminars have already been convened on this theme. The reason why is that I believe that different categories of reality have unfolded since the beginning of time, from the Neolithic Age to the present day. This means that reality is never given, but is the outcome of a culture. And thus we have a category of 'class I reality', and then there is a simulation of that reality, through a new technology, such as photography, or some other thing, or VR, for instance, and then you have a fresh substitution, a second reality. Hence simulation is a mere intermediary phase, without import. What is important is substitution; how a class I reality is substituted by a 'class II reality', and so on, up to the 'nth' reality.

JA: For you, then, one class of reality is continually substituted by other realities?

PV: Well, reality is produced by a society's culture, it is not given. A reality that has been produced by one society will be taken over, and changed by another, younger society, producing a fresh reality. This happens first by mimicry, then by substitution, and the original reality will, by that time, be totally forgotten. Take, for instance, the reality of the ancient Egyptians, of the Chinese of thousands of years ago: we cannot make any sense out of it, we are clueless about what it looked like, about what it sounded like.

JA: You talked before of the 'disappearance aesthetic'. At the same time, Baudrillard suggests that the advent of simulation and hyper-reality have led to the 'disappearance of the social'. Isn't there some kind of connection between your work and his?

PV: Absolutely none whatsoever. As I have said and repeated often: there is a nihilistic dimension in Baudrillard's writings which I cannot accept. It is quite clear to me that Baudrillard has totally lost faith in the social. To me, this is sheer nihilism. I have not at all lost faith in the social. First of all, I believe that the social eludes the so-called social sciences, and always has – that's why I am not a sociologist! So I am disappointed, and very much so, about politics, but I am not disappointed by the social. You need only to go into the streets, and meet the poor: they're extraordinary, superior people. The social drama leaves the stunts of the political class far behind. The power and resilience of individual people in the streets puts the intelligence of today's political leaders to shame. And as far as the social scientists are concerned, the less is said the better!

Technological culture

JA: Would you say that your work on the aesthetics of disappearance is characterized by a disenchantment with the modern world? Do you advocate a return to some kind of religious sensibility, one that might place limits, for instance, on the social effects of cinematic disappearance?

PV: I believe that, without some religious culture, it doesn't matter which, one will never be able to understand technological culture and cinematics. I believe that a society, a society which has moved to such an extent into virtuality, will not be able to advance further, without an appreciation of moral virtues, that is, of mystical thought. I mean by that all that has been contributed by philosophers and theologians, of all religions, not only Christianity. The new technologies bring into effect the three traditional characteristics of the Divine: ubiquity, instantaneity and immediacy. Without some cultural familiarity with these themes, mediated by Christianity, Protestantism, Buddhism, Judaism, Islam, etc., they remain incomprehensible. One cannot come to grips with the phenomenon of cyberspace without some inkling of, or some respect for, metaphysical intelligence! That does not mean that you have to be converted. I believe that the new technologies demand from those who are interested in them that they have a substantial measure of religious culture – not merely some religious opinion. I may emphasize that all this has nothing to do whatsoever with 'New Age', and the like ...

JA: Don't you think that some people invest technology with a mystical dimension already?

PV: Yes, of course. 'Transhumans', New Age types, cyberpunks and the like. There are plenty of them in the United States, you need only to read Mark Dery's book.[15] I think this is a scary development, leading up to the Heaven's Gate sect, whose members committed suicide in order to depart for the stars. But this is not the sort of thing I am talking about. My point is simply that without a knowledge of the history and philosophy of religions, one cannot come to grips with what I have termed 'technological fundamentalism'. Which is the possibility of a *deus ex machina*. Just like there is a Jewish fundamentalism, or an Islamic, or Christian one, you have also now got a technological fundamentalism. It is the religion of those who believe in the absolute power of technology, a ubiquitous, instantaneous, and immediate technology. I think a balance is needed to remain free *vis-à-vis* technology, a balance which consists of a knowledge of religion, even if this entails the risks of fundamentalism and intolerance. Without this knowledge one is without balance, and one cannot face the threats of technological fundamentalism, of cyberspace and of the extreme lunacy of social cybernetics.

The war model

JA: To many people, your work in *Bunker Archeology* and later is associated with what has come to be known as 'the war model'. Could you explain this model?

PV: Well, as a child of the Second World War, a 'war baby', you may say that the war was my university. I learned to know the world through the fear brought about by war. So for me the archetypal war was the Second World War, which lasted from 1939 to 1945. This war produced both Auschwitz and Hiroshima – in fact I keep a stone from Hiroshima on my desk. The war model is a method of total control over a territory and of a population. The aim is to have total control of the population, to bring a whole region or a continent into subjection, through radio, telephone, and a combination of both of these was already very much there during the Second World War. Hence my work is about defining total war as a conflict model, in all realms, not only in the realm of the military, but also in the realm of the social, and in what I would call 'colonization'. Colonization is already a model of total war. To quote [Jules] Michelet, the nineteenth-century French historian: 'Without a powerful navy, there are no colonies.' It is the power of technology which makes colonization possible; maritime power is one. Later, other forms of colonial power followed. Thus it is clear that my writings on the war model are linked to the history of the colonial empires, that is, to the times of colonial imperialism and ideological totalitarianism.

JA: Does the notion of the war model flow only from the Second World War? Or, is it linked in some way to your resistance to the Algerian war? Or both?

PV: What is for sure is that, as far as my approach to war is concerned, I have passed through three stages in my life: I suffered from the Second World War as a child; I was called into military service during the Algerian war and served six months in Algeria – in the Aurès, the mountainous region south of Constantine. And I opposed nuclear war, that is, the total war *par excellence*. So the three wars that have moulded me, we could say, are the Second World War, the Algerian war, and the epoch of nuclear deterrence. These wars, of course, carry the seeds of their followers, especially the Malvinas [Falklands] war and the war in the Persian Gulf.

The war of images

JA: In the early 1980s you produced one of your most well-known books, *War and Cinema: The Logistics of Perception* (1989e [1984]). In this book you discuss the use by the military of cinematic technologies of perception. Why is the analysis of the relationship between war and the cinema so important for you?

PV: Because images have turned into ammunition. Logistics deals in the first place with the supply to the front-line of ammunition, energy and so on. The front-line is constantly being replenished with ammunition, energy and foodstuffs. Now, from the end of the First World War onwards, but especially with the Second World War, the front-line is also being fed with images and information. That means that a 'logistics of perception' will be put in place, just as there is a logistics of fuel supplies, of explosives and shells. For instance, one can observe that the First World War was fought on the basis of maps. Maps were being drawn, lines were sketched on them and height-lines established, whereupon the artillery was told where to fire. But at the close of the war, maps were being displaced by aerial photography, shot by planes and then assembled on tables like mosaics – I did that kind of job myself, when I was a HQ staffer. How did that come about? Well, because the destructive power of artillery is such that the ordinary topographical landmarks simply disappear – here, again, the aesthetics of disappearance at work! Only film or photography keep the memory of the landscape as it was, and as it is constantly being reshaped. The film substitutes for the ordnance survey and, at the same time, architecture goes underground. It buries itself in the soil, in bunkers, in order to escape control from the skies. If you look at the Second World War, there was no bombing without photographs of the planned bomb site being taken back, being scrutinized with specialized equipment. Images thus become a product of extraordinary strategic importance. And if we switch to contemporary military conflicts, what you get are video missiles, unmanned miniature planes or 'drones', observation satellites and more wondrous things. War has morphed into images, into the eyes ...

JA: According to you, war is now a war of images?

PV: Absolutely. It is impossible to imagine war without images. And, if possible, 'live' images.

Cyberwar in the Persian Gulf

JA: Your reflections on the so-called 'cyberwar' in the Persian Gulf were published as *L'Écran du desert* (1991c). What, for you, are the qualitative differences between conventional warfare and cyberwar?

PV: First, about the book's title. It is very important because there were three phases in the Gulf War. Two are well documented, and the third has been named by myself: 'Desert Shield', 'Desert Storm' and then, '*Desert Screen*' – the latter is my invention. You may say the title is 'War TV'. The Gulf War was truly a war of images. This is because it was fought out, on one hand, with drones, that is, with flying cameras on unmanned planes. On the other hand, one also saw Cruise missiles, which were making surveys all the time about where they were flying, with televised bombs which were streaming into Saddam's bunkers, with video missiles. A jet fighter pilot turns on his screen, fires a missile equipped with a camera, and the missile lights up what is on the horizon, while the pilot sees *beyond* the horizon. And, as soon as he sees an adversary, he directs the missile towards him. We have, therefore, now entered a type of war which is about directing images, hence the invention of C^3I – a type of war management which means command, control, communication and intelligence – a kind of (film) director's way of running a war, with images and information coming up from everywhere at once. One observes that in the very first armed conflict after the Cold War, the image is right in the middle of the mechanism. The war is being directed straight from the USA, through communication satellites which are guiding the Patriot missiles. There is a kind of video game war going on. This perfectly illustrates what I wrote seven years before in *War and Cinema*. In fact, quite a few friends told me that they couldn't make anything out of my book in 1984, but now, after the Gulf War, they tell me that they have got the message – seven years too late. So when there is talk today about the 'new war', the 'info war', the war of information, well, now we are in quite an uncharted territory.[16] It is quite clear that the USA is currently entering a period of great upheaval in military affairs. This means that the command of 'globalitarian', or total information, by the last remaining Big Power, leads to a repositioning of its powers. What we now see happening in its relations with Iraq goes a long way to show the limitations of this war of information, as far as the 'how-far-to-go', 'what-to-do', issues are concerned. It is very difficult to make pronouncements about these developments, save to say that 'cyberwar' manoeuvres have already taken place in Germany, and have been witnessed by my friend James Der Derian.[17] Here we enter a realm of electronic gamesmanship of which very little can be said. It's still quite tricky, and confidential. I am presently working on that, of course, but there is simply not very much open information about this war of information. What is certain is that the locale of war is no longer the 'geosphere', military geography, the realm of geostrategy, but the 'infosphere', cyberspace. We have entered a new world.

The war machine: Deleuze and Guattari

JA: Before we leave the subject of war, could I ask you about your relationship to Deleuze and Guattari's philosophy and politics of desire? Their 'Treatise on Nomadology: The War Machine,' in *A Thousand Plateaus: Capitalism and Schizophrenia* (1987 [1980]) is obviously influenced by your writings about pure war, military space, speed and power. But what, if anything, have you learnt from their writings and how has it influenced your thinking?

PV: I do not think there is influence here, but, rather, convergence. If you care to look in *A Thousand Plateaus,* I believe there are twenty-seven references to my work. That's not nothing. Now, I am not stating this in order to claim as my own the qualities of Deleuze and Guattari, whom I have loved very much, but to emphasize that, here again, there were parallels at work. However, I felt rather closer to Deleuze than to Guattari because I am totally devoid of any psychoanalytic background or culture. Guattari and I were, though, on extremely friendly terms, and we did things together. You see, Deleuze was, like me, a man of 'the event', someone who not only worked with the concept of the event but who also rose to the occasion when an event occurred and who reacted with feeling, as befits a phenomenologist. Hence, to me, the interest of *A Thousand Plateaus* lies chiefly in its liberating effect from a certain kind of academic discourse, one which belonged to the end phase of structuralism. I am not talking about Foucault here. I am referring to [Claude] Lévi-Strauss, to [Louis] Althusser and so on. Here, again, liberation took on a kind of musical hue. For me, *A Thousand Plateaus* is also a form of, shall we say, '*ritornello*' [a recurring couplet or refrain in a folk song], as they called it themselves. So what I like about Deleuze and Guattari is their poetic language, a language which enables them to convey meanings that cannot be conveyed otherwise ...

JA: Do you mean that Deleuze and Guattari have a poetic understanding of the world, as opposed to a prosaic or an analytical one?

PV: Yes, but even better, a 'nomadological' understanding of the world – they have that word of their own after all – stemming from the fact that the world is constantly on the move. Today's world no longer has any kind of stability; it is shifting, straddling, gliding away all the time. Hence their ideas about superimposition, strata, layers and cross-currents. Ours is a world that is shifting, like the polar ice-cap, or 'Continental Drift'.[18] Nomadology is thus an idea which is in total accordance with what I feel with regard to speed and deterritorialization. So, it is hardly surprising that we clearly agree on the theme of deterritorialization.

The gaze of the machine

JA: Your interest in the acceleration and automation of perception was further developed in *The Vision Machine* (1994b [1988]). What was your central aim in that book? ...

PV: There was, for me, this crucial development, of which nobody, once again, seemed aware. Everybody was talking about Orwellian remote control and surveillance, with cameras all over the place, scanning the city. I agree, it is scary, the Orwell scenario, police cameras everywhere. But there is something worse, which gives its title to *The Vision Machine*: a device to see with. For it means that an inanimate object now can see *for itself*. A remote camera, for example, is for the use of a policeman or a security guard. There is someone behind it who does the viewing. Nothing special about that and nothing to worry about. But behind the vision machine there is nobody. There is only a micro-receiver, and a computer. A door can 'recognize' me, as it were. This set up without a human spectator means that there is now vision without a gaze. And let me remind you that the research on the vision machine – that is its official name, I did not invent it – was for the Cruise missile! Cruise missiles were equipped with detection radar and built-in mapping systems. They had maps charting their course towards Teheran or Leningrad. The device was constantly surveying the ground with radar and checking it against the map to make sure the missile was on course. No need for a vision machine here, the radar does the work. But, at the final approach stage, a vision machine is necessary, in order to film the target and choose the window to enter the building or the door to the bunker. These vision machines are an improvement on what are called 'shape recognition devices'. They are like those industrial machines that punch holes in metal sheets. They come equipped with a microchip that enables them to recognize the shape of the sheet they are supposed to punch holes in. This is termed contour recognition, which is not fully fledged vision yet. A further development has led to the devising of highly sophisticated vision machines for Cruise missiles. This means that Cruise missiles are endowed with a gaze even though it is an automatic one ...

JA: But all this is not being carried out for the machines themselves. It is being carried out by, or at least on behalf of, human beings, even if none are directly involved? ...

PV: No, nobody is there. Well, ultimately, yes, of course, but when you've got a camera, you make a film, and then you view it. Here the object is looking *for itself*, the Cruise missile looks for itself. To me, something like this is an unheard of event. Imagine this table we are sitting around starting to look for itself!

The transplant revolution

JA: In *The Art of the Motor* (1995 [1993]) another shift seems to take place in your thinking. For, in that work, you focus on the invasion of the human body by technoscience. Could you explain your interest in what you call 'the transplant revolution'?

PV: Oh yes, this is the 'Third Revolution'. In the realm of speed, the first revolution was that of transportation, the invention of the steam engine, the combustion engine, the electrical motor, the jet engine and the rocket. The second revolution is the revolution of transmission, and it is happening right now in electronics, but it began with Marconi, radio and television. The third revolution, which is intimately linked to the miniaturization of objects, is the transplantation revolution. By this term I mean that technology is becoming something physically assimilable, it is a kind of nourishment for the human race, through dynamic inserts, implants, and so on. Here, I am not talking about implants such as silicon breasts, but dynamic implants like additional memory storage. What we see here is that science and technology aim for miniaturization in order to invade the human body. This is already true of the cardiac stimulator, a device I am especially interested in, since much of my work is about rhythms and speed, and the cardiac stimulator is what *gives* the rhythm to the life of a human patient. I am writing about that in my next book, and about the case of those twin sisters, which were prematurely born, and who had a cardiac stimulator implanted in them practically from birth: their life-rhythm, thus, is that of a machine, a stimulator. Here is an icon of the transplant revolution, of the human body being eaten up, being possessed by technology. Technology no longer spreads over the body of the territory, as with railways, motorways, bridges and large factories, but now enters the innards of the human body ...

JA: And, in your view, this is a negative development?

PV: It is absolutely scary. It means that the machine enters into the human. It is no longer a prosthesis, it is a new eugenism in fact ...

JA: Nonetheless, this is a difficult position to maintain with someone whose life may depend upon the insertion of a cardiac stimulator?

PV: Well, here again you see how the indisputable is always put forward in order to foster extremely dubious measures. It all starts by saying how great those things are for people who need them, and then comes the day when it is being forced upon people who don't need or want them. There lies the problem.

JA: Is this the basis of your criticisms, in *The Art of the Motor* (1995 [1993]), of the Australian performance artist Stelarc?

PV: Yes. This is because Stelarc has opted for 'eugenic suicide'. Instead of committing plain suicide, he does so by grafting himself into various gizmos, so that in the end, there will be no Stelarc left, pffuuut!, gone! Only a pure automaton will remain. That being said, his work is absolutely fascinating.

JA: How does the transplant revolution relate to your concept of 'endo-colonization'?

PV: First, endo-colonization happens when a political power turns against its own people. I have lived through this during the Second World War. Totalitarian societies colonize their own people. You cannot understand Nazi Germany without accounting for the fact that it had been deprived of colonies and embarked on a programme of colonization at home. So Germany's colonization was a programme of colonizing the East (*ostkolonization*), inclusive of Poland, Russia and France for that matter. But, by necessity, Germany's colonization was also a logic of endo-colonization, that is, to force upon its own population the fate that the British – or the French – had forced upon the Aboriginals in Australia or the Blacks in South Africa, or, in other words, brute force. And, in the case of the transplant revolution, what takes place is an endo-colonization of the human body by technology. The human body is eaten up, invaded, and controlled by technology ...

JA: Are you suggesting that the idea of the transplant revolution is identical to the concept of endo-colonization?

PV: Yes, it is, but on the person, on the human body. There is no colonization without control of the body. We are here back to Foucault, evidently. Every time a country is being colonized, bodies are colonized. The body of the Negro, of the slave, of the deportee, of the inmate of the labour camp, is a *colonized body*. Thus technology colonizes the world, through globalitarianism, as we have seen earlier, but it also colonizes bodies, their attitudes and behaviours. You need only to watch all those nerdy 'internaut' types to see to what extent their behaviour is already being shaped by technology. So we have this technology of absorption, or as the Futurists used to say: man will be fed by technology, and technology will colonize human behaviour, just as television and the computer are doing, but this last form of colonization is a much more intimate, and a much more irresistible form. This is scary! It is neo-eugenism, endo-technological eugenicism!

Cyberfeminism

JA: In *Open Sky* (1997 [1995]) you make reference to 'cyberfeminism', a movement which some see as one of the most important theoretical and political developments in the past decade with regard to our under-standing of the human body, technology and subjectivity. Could you describe your response to these developments?

PV: Well, I have become very interested in the notion of 'cybersexuality'. Even if it is still at the gimmick stage, it is a well-known fact that re-search is very advanced in the field of 'tele', 'remote', or cybersexuality, especially in Japan. And thus, I am quite baffled to see feminists – far from opposing, like I do, the conditioning of the female body, or the male body for that matter – projecting themselves as followers of cybersexuality. I cannot understand it. I cannot understand why oppos-ing machismo does not also imply opposing cybersexuality. Do the cyberfeminists really believe that cybersexuality is going to liberate them? Come on … Give me a break!

JA: Are you arguing that feminists have much more to lose than they have to gain by embracing cybernetic technologies?

PV: I believe that the question of technology is predicated upon the ques-tion of sexuality, be it male or female. If cyberfeminists do not want to understand the replacement of emotions by electrical impulses – be-cause that is what we are talking about – the replacement of emotional involvement by electrical impulses, it is clear that they will never be lib-erated. Instead, they will become the servants of a new type of sexual control. Remote or tele-sexuality is by definition machine-controlled sexuality.

JA: The American cyberfeminist Donna Haraway (1985) has stated that she, 'would rather be a cyborg than a goddess'. What is your reaction to such claims?

PV: [*laughs out loud*] I want to be neither a God nor a cyborg! I want to be man. It suffices to be a man – or a woman. As I said before, 'Man is the endpoint of the wonders of the universe'!

Georgio Agamben

JA: One final question. Are there any other cultural theorists writing today whose work you admire?

PV: Hm, this is a difficult question to answer, but, yes, there is one book which I've just reviewed, and liked very, very much. It is Giorgio Agamben's *Homo Sacer: le pouvoir souverain et la vie nue* (1997). In ancient Roman law *Homo Sacer* means a human being whose life is considered worthless, meaning someone whom one could kill without committing homicide, and who is also unfit for sacrificial purposes. Such a man stands condemned to summary execution. Killing him is no worse than squashing an insect. I must say I have a boundless admiration for Agamben. I was asked by several papers to give my choice of the best books of the year and I mentioned *Homo Sacer*. It is a remarkable book, and one with which I could not agree more.

Translated by Patrice Riemens.

Notes

1. This interview was conducted on 27 November 1997 at the École Spéciale d'Architecture in Paris. I would like to thank Mike Featherstone for his encouragement, Ken Harrop for personal and institutional support, and Mark Little for practical help in setting up the interview. However, I am also heavily indebted to Magali Fowler for interpretation and to Rob Turner and Patrice Riemens for translating numerous letters, tapes and texts. Lastly, I am especially grateful to Paul Virilio for giving his time and energy so freely to this project.

2. See, for example, Kerrigan (1997: 14–15).

3. Gestalt psychology is a body of thought which springs from the experimental studies conducted by German psychologists like Max Wertheimer and Kurt Koffka around 1910. Briefly, the Gestaltists argued that philosophical, artistic, scientific, perceptual and aesthetic configurations endowed with qualities as a whole could not be characterized simply as the totality of their parts.

4. 'Hypermodernism' is a term I reserve for a forthcoming book on Virilio.

5. Here, Virilio is referring to Daniel Halvéy (1872–1962), an anti-clerical radical French historian and well known 'Dreyfusard'.

6. Paul Dirac and Werner Heisenberg were both instrumental in developing Einstein's theory of relativity and quantum mechanics in the early part of this century. For a recent and accessible introduction to this fascinating but complex field see Milburn (1996). Henri Bergson (1859–1941) founded a philosophy based on 'creative evolution' and, like Virilio, was much preoccupied with questions relating to the nature of knowledge, time and religion. See, for instance, Bergson (1910).

7. Abbé Pierre is a figure held in high regard in France for his championing of the poor.

8. See, *inter alia*, Marcel (1950) and Ellul (1965).

9. Sir Francis Galton coined the term eugenics in 1883. Eugenics is, of course, the 'science' which purports to 'improve' humanity through the application of genetic policies.

10. Robert Morris (1931–) is an American minimalist sculptor and Land artist. However, in recent years he has turned increasingly to figurative painting. For a general overview that includes Morris's work, see, for example, Lucie-Smith (1995: 74–133).

11. Archigram is the name of an English utopian architectural group, founded in 1960 by Peter Cook (1974). It disbanded in 1975. Paulo Soleri (1919–) is an Italian architect who, since the 1950s, has worked in the USA on alternative planning schemes at the Cosanti Foundation in Scottsdale, Arizona (see Wall, 1971). The science fiction-inspired Metabolic Group in Japan was initiated by Kenzo Tange (see Kurokawa, 1972).

12. For a somewhat different explanation of the break up of *Architecture Principe*, see, I. Scalbert and M. Mostafavi, 'Interview with Claude Parent', in Johnston (1996: 49–58).

13. See, for instance, Mandelbrot (1977).

14. As indicated in the references below, *Pure War* (1997) is the title of a recently revised book-length interview with Virilio conducted by Sylvère Lotringer. The English edition of *Popular Defense and Ecological Struggles* (1990 [1978]) does not contain an Introduction.

15. Virilio is referring to Dery (1996).

16. 'Info War' is the title of the Postscript in the new edition of *Pure War* (Virilio and Lotringer, 1997: 165–86).

17. See, for example, Der Derian (1992).

18. 'Continental Drift' is the title of a chapter in *Open Sky* (1997 [1995]).

References

Agamben, G. (1997) *Homo Sacer: le pouvoir souverain et la vie nue*. Paris: Seuil.
Baudrillard, J. (1983) *Simulations*, trans. P. Foss, P. Patton and P. Beitchman. New York: Semiotext(e).
Bergson, H. (1910 [1889]) *Time and Free Will: An Essay on the Immediate Data of Consciousness*, trans. F.L. Pogson. London: George Allen and Unwin.
Cook, P. (1974) *Archigram*. London: Klotz.
Deleuze, G. and Guattari, F. (1987 [1980]) *A Thousand Plateaus: Capitalism and Schizophrenia*, trans. B. Massumi. Minneapolis: University of Minnesota Press.
Der Derian, J. (1992) *Antidiplomacy: Spies, Terror, Speed, and War*. Oxford: Blackwell.
Derrida, J. (1973 [1967]) *Speech and Phenomena, and Other Essays on Husserl's Theory of Signs*, trans. D.B. Allison. Evanston, IL: Northwestern University Press.
Derrida, J. (1976 [1967]) *Of Grammatology*, trans. G. Spivak. Baltimore, MD and London: Johns Hopkins University Press.
Derrida, J. (1984) 'No Apocalypse, Not Now (Full Speed Ahead, Seven Missiles, Seven Missives)', trans. C. Porter and P. Lewis, *Diacritics*, 14 (summer): 20–31.
Derrida, J. (1996 [1995]) *Archive Fever: A Freudian Impression*, trans. E. Prenowitz. Chicago, IL: University of Chicago Press.
Dery, M. (1996) *Escape Velocity: Cyberculture at the End of the Century*. New York: Grove Press.
Ellul, J. (1965) *The Technological Society*. London: Jonathan Cape.
Foucault, M. (1977 [1975]) *Discipline and Punish: The Birth of the Prison*, trans. A. Sheridan. London: Penguin.
Gibson, W. (1984) *Neuromancer*. London: Victor Gollancz.
Haraway, D. (1985) 'A Manifesto for Cyborgs: Science, Technology, and Socialist Feminism in the 1980s', *Socialist Review*, 80 (2): 65–108.
Johnston, P. (ed.) (1996) *The Function of the Oblique: The Architecture of Claude Parent and Paul Virilio: 1963–1969*, trans. P. Johnston. London: Architectural Association.
Joly, F. (ed.) (1996) *documenta. documents 1*. Kassel: Cantz Verlag.
Kerrigan, J. (1997) 'When Eyesight is Fully Industrialised', *London Review of Books*, 19 (20): 14–15.
Kurokawa, K. (1972) *The Concept of Metabolism*. Tokyo: Architectural Foundation.
Lucie-Smith, E. (1995) *Art Today*. London: Phaidon Press.
Lyotard, J.-F. (1984 [1979]) *The Postmodern Condition*, trans. G. Bennington and B. Massumi. Minneapolis: University of Minnesota Press.
Mandelbrot, B. (1977) *The Fractal Geometry of Nature*. New York: Freeman.
Marcel, G. (1950 [1949]) *The Mystery of Being*, Volume 1: *Reflection and Mystery*, trans. G.S. Fraser. London and Chicago: Harvill Press.

Merleau-Ponty, M. (1962 [1945]) *Phenomenology of Perception*, trans. C. Smith. London: Routledge.

Milburn, G. (1996) *Quantum Technology*. St Leonards: Allen and Unwin.

Venturi, R., Scott Brown, D. and Izenour, S. (1977) *Learning From Las Vegas*. Cambridge, MA: MIT Press.

Virilio, P. (1986 [1977]) *Speed and Politics: An Essay on Dromology*, trans. M. Polizzotti. New York: Semiotext(e).

Virilio, P. (1989a [1984]) *War and Cinema: The Logistics of Perception*, trans. P. Camiller. London: Verso.

Virilio, P. (1989b [1986]) 'The Museum of Accidents', trans. Y. Leonard. *Public 2: The Lunatic of One Idea*, Special Issue of *Public*, 2: 81–5.

Virilio, P. (1990 [1978]) *Popular Defense and Ecological Struggles*, trans. M. Polizzotti. New York: Semiotext(e).

Virilio, P. (1991a [1980]) *The Aesthetics of Disappearance*, trans. P. Beitchman. New York: Semiotext(e).

Virilio, P. (1991b [1984]) *The Lost Dimension*, trans. D. Moshenberg. New York: Semiotext(e).

Virilio, P. (1991c) *L'Écran du desert*. Paris: Galilée.

Virilio, P. (1994a [1975]) *Bunker Archeology*, trans. G. Collins. New York: Princeton Architectural Press.

Virilio, P. (1994b [1988]) *The Vision Machine*, trans. J. Rose. Bloomington and Indianapolis: Indiana University Press and British Film Institute, London.

Virilio, P. (1995 [1993]) *The Art of the Motor*, trans. J. Rose. Minnesota: University of Minnesota Press.

Virilio, P. (1997 [1995]) *Open Sky*, trans. J. Rose. London: Verso.

Virilio, P. (1999 [1990]) *Polar Inertia*, trans. P. Camiller. London: Sage Publications.

Virilio, P. and Lotringer, S. (1997 [1983]) *Pure War*, revised edn, trans. M. Polizzotti, Postscript trans. B. O'Keeffe. New York: Semiotext(e).

Wall, D. (1971) *Visionary Cities: The Arcology of P.S.* New York, London: Praeger.

PART TWO

ON ARCHITECTURE

2

PAUL VIRILIO AND THE OBLIQUE

Interview with Enrique Limon

EL: In the 1960s you theorized architecture/urbanism while working on several projects. Did you have any formal training in architecture? How did your interests develop in the field of architecture and urbanism?

PV: I don't have any training in architecture whatsoever. I came to the question of the city through the question of war. I am a child of the war. I was born in 1932, and I lived through the trauma of full-scale war, the destruction of cities, like Nantes, where I lived and where eight thousand buildings were destroyed. It was this relationship with war which led me to become interested in the city and in architecture.

Let me try to explain. First of all, my interest in architecture has been an interest in the ballistic. Military architecture is not static and is not concerned with the resistance of materials. It is an architecture of ballistics: gazes, masks, screens and other means of deflecting shots. Which is to say that the act of destroying is part of the construction. Architecture opposes destruction. It does not oppose rain, climate, habitability, but it is supposed to withstand destruction. This has been an important element for me. Without the bunkers of the Atlantic Wall, without the Second World War, I would not have been interested in architecture at all. This is crucial. What interested me is to what extent a full-scale war is a totalitarian space, and to what extent the organization of war went beyond the organization of a front-line. In the Second World War the whole continent was organized for war, with anti-airstrike defence, with defence against landing operations (Atlantic Wall). Basically I became interested in architecture because of war, through the destruction of cities and the awareness that there was a totalitarian space. I lived through this totalitarian space. Let me give an example: When the Germans invaded France, I was in Nantes. We switched on the radio and we heard that the Germans were in Orléans. There are 400 kilometers between Orléans and Nantes. We thought, 'They are still in Orléans. We have got time to pack.' After the meal though we heard a weird noise out in the street. I rushed out (I was only 8), and I saw the enemy already there. This was the *Blitzkrieg*. Thus I experienced this conjunction of speed and war which led me to issues such as the influence of technology on the organization and development of territory.

I am a war victim. A lot of people of my generation, whether in Germany, France or England went though this childhood trauma of war. Today in Sarajevo there must be a lot of Virilio kids watching war like voyeurs. A kid is a war voyeur. He watches the atrocities through a keyhole. That explains *Bunker Archeology*.

EL: In the mid-1960s there was a group of artists and architects in Paris and Europe that formed Groupe Espace. What was your involvement with Groupe Espace, especially with Claude Parent and André Bloc?

PV: André Bloc was at the time the editor of *Architecture d'Aujourd'hui* which was the most important French architecture journal. Together with architects and sculptors he set up Groupe Espace with Claude Parent. André Bloc asked me to join them. I went along to one meeting which I remember took place in the café Chez Zimmer next to the Châtelet Theater. We had dinner and chatted about architecture but that was it. In other words Groupe Espace ceased to exist when Groupe *Architecture Principe* started.

In the 1960s we were talking about multidisciplinarity, about the necessity for mingling of the arts. Painters, sculptors and architects got together to invent a sort of cultural 'melting pot'. This was definitely linked to architecture/sculpture, with which I was not involved. To make a living I was doing stained glass for painters. Through this I worked with some great talents: Braque, Matisse, Le Corbusier and Rouault. In the early sixties I gave up painting and began to get involved in architecture. While I was painting I got my real education from having the chance to hear some of the most significant thinkers in France: the philosophers Vladimir Jankelevitch, Raymond Aron... In Germany I began to get interested in Gestalt theory through Wolfgang Kohler and Kurt Koffka from the Gestalt school. I was also interested in phenomenology of perception. I was a student of Merleau-Ponty. So my interest in painting ran parallel to my interest in philosophy, and it all eventually led me to architecture.

I find in Gestalt theory the same elements that I find in war, which I dealt with subsequently in *War and Cinema*. The battlefield is a field of perception, of camouflage; the camouflaging of objects in order for them not to be recognized is a '*Gestaltung*' phenomenon (of Gestalt theory). For me the ballistics of the gaze is a very important element.

EL: How did your interests in perceptual psychology (Gestalt theory) affect your research on the oblique function?

PV: Weight and gravity are key elements in the organization of perception. The notion of up and down linked to the earth's gravity is just one element of perspective. The Quattrocento perspective can't be separated from the orientation effect of the field of vision caused by gravity, and also by the frontal dimension of the canvas which is never at a slant. Both painting and research on perspective have always been conducted on a frontal dimension.

As soon as one starts to incline planes and to get rid of the vertical, the relationship with the horizon changes. Gravity does not come into play in the perception of space in the same way at all. When one stands on an inclined plane the instability of the position changes the relationship with the horizon. The idea is that as soon as a third spatial dimension (the oblique) is brought into the relationship with regard to space and weight changes, the individual will always be in a state of resistance – whether accelerating as he is going down, or slowing down as he is climbing up, whereas when one walks on a horizontal plane weight is nil (or equal). The idea was to work with gravity in a new way; to create a vision of instability while the perspective is stable. You see this clearly in the case of drunkenness – when you are drunk and start to move around the whole world starts moving, perception is moving with the body. Here the structure of the ground moves...a gravity or gravitational drunkenness! You could call it a kind of 'eroticization' of the ground.

When I did some research on the Atlantic Wall in the 1950s there were a lot of bunkers which had toppled over. Once the sand was gone I got into these inclined spaces. I got into the habit of taking photographs of unstable spaces. Here I was standing on the sea-side on inclined dams. When I was a child I used to play in these bunkers. I became very familiar with this landscape, this bunkerland. The idea of the oblique comes from such inclined bunkers.

EL: Was this angular geometry for sculptural space in direct opposition to Le Corbusier's Right Angle?

PV: Completely. It is a critique of orthogonality. It is a critique of large blocks of flats that were built at the time like sugar lumps. The intention was to go beyond orthogonality, beyond Euclidean geometry, towards an architecture based on a non-Euclidean geometry, on topology.

The oblique function is the architectonic implementation of topology. Leaving Euclid's grid surfaces for the oriented surfaces of topology (Moebius band, Klein bottle, etc.). The function of the oblique is the application of topology to architecture as a whole, and not only to parking garages or to the Guggenheim Museum. It's like saying: 'Euclidean geometry has built architecture from early history until modernity. Tomorrow we will build with topology.'

Later, I became friends with Gilles Deleuze who published *Le Pli* (1988), he was working on folds, on topology, on oriented or skewed surfaces. 'Pli' is the etymology of 'complication,' of 'complexe'. In this book Gilles Deleuze referred to Leibniz. I was interested in topology, a way of pleating the ground. We were moving in the same direction.

What Groupe *Architecture Principe* tried to say was: 'We are going to build topologically. No more cylinders, no more spheres, cubes, pyramids, etc. ... No more plane surfaces. Let us replace them by oriented surfaces whose angles will be defined by the architect.' He does not program the angle in an orthogonal dimension; it is always a given.

Obviously, I don't care if the plane is a triangle. What comes into play is the elevation and everything that works in elevation. So I want to program an angle in elevation. One can use undulating surfaces, but theoretically we have to break them up before working on them. It was very hard to work with the materials that we had at the time. There was a search for constructive possibilities which was not made easier because of the idea of unevenness. We were working on what is called the threshold of recovery, with slopes in all directions. The idea is clearly to have free surfaces.

EL: How did the oblique function relate to the larger context of urbanism?

PV: The oblique function is radically linked to urbanism because its purpose is to define a third urban order. The first urban order (villages, land population) is mainly based on horizontallity. The second urban order based on verticality ended with megastructures: first the New York skyscrapers in Manhattan, then the Japanese projects to build a 2000 meter-high tower, Wright's project of a 1500 meter-high tower, etc. ... This is outrageous. In my opinion, the vertical order has come to an end.

The idea is to lead architecture and urbanism into the third urban order, to claim that a city can expand both linearly but primarily through topology, through oriented surfaces which allow the ground not to be covered. There will be bridge structures and megastructures, but which use the oblique. So we are aiming for both a linear and oblique urbanism. Here we come back to the Russian 'desurbanists' and that kind of visualization/perception of space. The third urban order and all the *Architecture Principe* issues put the vertical city on trial. At the time, towers were being built everywhere, on the banks of the Seine and elsewhere. The tower was the most exalted type of architecture. Our opposition to towers was absolute. Verticality was absurd because it did not allow communication. It only caused concentration, stacking. Verticality is a ghetto. When people talk about racial ghettos we reply: 'Yes, these are horizontal ghettos.'

EL: Because the oblique function was a critique of the vertical and horizontal norms in architecture and urbanism at the time, would you consider this 'political' space?

PV: A political space is a geopolitical space. 'Political' means nothing. A
political space applies to a piece of land, whether small (a city) or large
(the nation-state). It is geopolitical in the 'political geography' sense,
but also in the 'geometry' sense. There is a political geometry. Bentham's
Panopticon for instance is a police-state political geometry. Foucault
analyzes it in *Discipline and Punish*. In Bentham's Panopticon one man
can control all the inmates from one main central spot thanks to transparency. This is geopolitics, i.e., political geometry, not political geography. A space is always political through geography and geometry.
Geostrategy and war brought me to this conclusion. For the military
only strategies matter. The Gulf war was a geostrategic war. Within 'geography' there is 'geometry'. When you build a tower from which you
control a city (the Hilton in Beirut for instance), men will fight in order
to occupy and control it. This is political geometry, but also geostrategy.
So there you have it: the work of the child of the war who saw it all.

EL: How would you situate your work during this period amongst the work
of other radical groups of the time such as Constant's 'New Babylon',
the 'plug-in' cities of Archigram, the unitary urbanism of the Situationist International, influenced by Henri Lefebvre? And did you have
any connection to the work of Yona Friedman in Paris?

PV: We were very much interested in Constant's 'New Babylon'. We invited
Archigram to exhibit for the first time in France at the Claude-Nicolas
Ledoux salt mines. So we had exchanges with Archigram, they invited us
to Folkestone. We read the Situationists a lot. I have many issues of the
International Situationist review and of course the idea of 'urban dérive'
interested us very much. In fact my architecture was called 'des sites de
dérivation'. What drew our attention to the Situationists' approach was
the concern with the first urban riots, which we analysed as early signs
that the modern city was bursting out (for instance the Los Angeles
'Watts riots' in the 1960s; riots in Chicago, Detroit). We wanted to go
out there and talk with the people who were rebelling in the ghetto, not
about racial issues but about their living environment, about urbanism.
Like the Situationists we feel that urban riots have several dimensions:
racial, economical but also urban. There is an issue of space, of political
geometry, of geopolitics. We worked with Henri Lefebvre. I had less
contact with Yona Friedman, although I invited him to the École
Spéciale d'Architecture (ESA) to teach as a visiting professor.

EL: You mentioned that your affiliation with Claude Parent ended in the
midst of May '68?

PV: During that time I was very interested in what was going on in Germany, with the Situationists in Strasbourg and the Provos in Amsterdam. When I went to Germany to take photographs of the Berlin Wall I met a group of 'alternative' people who criticized the idea of the city. Through Weber from the Communist League I heard about Rudi Dutschke who was about to come to France in May 1968. First of all Rudi Dutschke was a Christian (Protestant). We had a lot in common. We were supposed to meet, but Rudi was injured in a bomb attack and did not come to Paris. I was not a communist myself. I was both Christian and anarchist. You look surprised, but that is the truth: 'Paul Virilio was an anarcho-Christian!' When the uprisings began I obviously became involved. Parent did not. He went to the right, and I to the left.

When the uprisings came to an end in August of 1968, I fled and hid in Brittany in order not to be arrested. At this point Parent and I split for good – he treated me as though I were a revolutionary – and consequently Groupe *Architecture Principe* disappeared.

Many students of the ESA had heard about me and they asked me to teach there. So then I started teaching at ESA and have been there since.

Before the events, in 1966, I had written at the entrance of the Sorbonne the phrase which subsequently became famous: 'Imagination takes power'. When the Sorbonne was occupied by the students in '68, I made a huge poster with this phrase. So you see, it was not so much the 'red' dimension, but rather the situationist, anarchist, romantic dimension of May '68. I am not a Marxist. I never have been. But of course I am left-wing. But that's now an old story. Everything has changed since then. I still believe that the events of May '68 signify something quite different to what it is popularly supposed they were about, which for the moment remains invisible.

EL: Has this political change and your theoretical work of the early sixties had any impact on your current writings on aesthetics, time, politics and virtual space?

PV: During the sixties I was working on geopolitics, on geometry, on actual space, on topology etc. In '68 I realized that one could not interfere with space without taking power. So I dropped the issue of space completely to focus on topics like time, speed, dromology, which have been the center of my work for the last thirty years.

Groupe *Architecture Principe* was about space and politics whereas the issue of speed is about time and politics, which opens a whole new vista of research. All the relevant documents will be republished next year for the thirtieth anniversary of Groupe *Architecture Principe*. But for me, that was a kid's game. It's over. I was 35. Today I am 64. It's a long time, thirty years.

3

THE TIME OF THE TRAJECTORY

Interview with Andreas Ruby

AR: That architecture is predicated by time in the same measure as it is by space is something that has been recognized every now and then in the past. But it is only recently that it has again become the subject of serious reflection. This might be because the most fundamental time-related aspects of architecture are expressed in an extremely slow, almost indiscernible time: time as given by the age or the physical life span of a building. Now, however, this kind of historical duration has accelerated considerably. For example, while the Egyptian pyramids at Giza are over four thousand years old, the existence of the French Pompidou Centre in Paris is threatened after a mere twenty years! What has happened in the meantime to shorten our sense of duration?

PV: The acceleration of history that we have witnessed in so many aspects of life has of course not made an exception with regard to the life span of buildings. In contrast to previous epochs, a building today is not built to last forever. Just as the vehicle in the course of 'progress' has been continuously gaining speed, the life span of buildings has also accelerated, something that is manifest in their early ageing and swift deterioration. An eloquent example of this is found in the fact that, whereas up to now, a construction permit was enough to put up a building, nowadays in the United States, and soon in France too, you also need a demolition permit. The transient duration of a building is therefore being projected in advance by the planners. A building has ceased to be something lasting, something eternal, as it used to be. As its life span is now limited to fifty or hundred years, it has become something of a moment in time, a three-dimensional image that will vanish before long.

AR: It is as if the building had been issued with a temporary 'residence' permit?

PV: Precisely. Just as in many other walks of life, architectural duration has also been disqualified. It has been limited in advance. You see the exact parallel happening today in labour relations in the shape of short-term employment contracts. I believe that the concept of duration cannot be separated from the idea of solidity. Something that is solid is something that is going to last. In the early days of European architecture, this relationship was expressed in the complementarity between a building and its location. Whether the building was of a religious, political, or a military nature, it was always basically an appendage to the location, which was taken as everlasting – as in the case of a rocky promontory, or a desert, for instance. The architectonics of a building complemented the tectonics of its location, and took for all practical purposes its life span from it, and which was considered timeless. In the course of history, new materials have lent a new mobility to architecture. The thought of settling on a location for a long period has evaporated, and in its place came the campus, the colony. Now, one of the first axioms of urban planning is the durability of a building's location. But today some people think about moving Tokyo to some other location. Durability is no longer something that is taken for granted. For instance, during the Second World War, after the terrible air raids on Hamburg, Hitler wanted to have the city rebuilt somewhere else. Le Corbusier had similar plans with Caen, particularly after the Allies destroyed the town after the D-Day offensive. Both projects remained unrealized. However, such architectural projects demonstrated that, today, the city is considered something that can be moved around.

AR: Besides this ontological relationship, architecture also has a phenomenological relationship to time, which manifests itself primarily in our sensory experience of space. It is a time that materializes in fact only at the level of individual experience, and therefore little of it is to be experienced from books.

PV: It is absolutely true that space can be measured in at least two ways: one is with a meter and another is with a clock. The spatial and temporal use of a building is linked to the question of movement. The acceleration of a body inside the home is of course quite limited, but even there the body is a body in motion. Velocity is after all not necessarily speed. But this dromological, or 'speed-space', becomes noticeable only at the level of really large spatial constructs – in airports, factory halls, or hospitals for instance – where there is a functional need to move quickly from one part of the building to the other. But in general, architecture is far too little concerned with the sort of time that is engendered by the use of a specific place. Most architects conceptualize space only in terms of height, volume, floor-to-wall ratio and so on. Consequently, I have thought about it with my students and pondered whether it might not be useful to look for some inspiration in the realm of choreography, in the notation of movement, and in the conception of space in terms of time. I believe those established notations like plan, section and elevation have lost their general validity. One should search for a time based notation system that would permit us to factor in the time of the built environment.

AR: Could simulated spaces, such as the ones one encounters in contemporary virtual spaces, lead to such a notation system?

PV: This is certainly a possibility. It is too often forgotten that the technology of Virtual Reality has been developed, not only in the realm of military oriented research into the flight-simulators of the US Air Force, but also in that of architecture, and in order to produce virtual models of buildings. Nicholas Negroponte advanced this research. Negroponte founded both the 'Architecture Machine' group and, later, the Media Lab at the MIT. In a virtual architecture model, space is no longer separated from the trajectory; the relation to that space is precisely defined by this 'navigation', and this relationship creates a kind of behavioural ballistics. In that respect, the virtual architecture model offers, contrary to the more common representations of space, the possibility to include the activation of space by virtue of the trajectory into the design process. The trajectory is an element that springs from the relationship between the object and the subject. There is, for instance, a trajectory of the body, and of the gaze. And I believe that a future architecture, indifferent to whatever uses it will be put to, will also need to have a 'trajective' conception of space.

AR: But haven't there been a few architects in the past who have shaped their spaces in such a way that they gave the impression of constant change, and according to the movements of their users? I am thinking in particular of Vasari's Uffizi buildings in Florence, and of buildings by Bernini.

PV: Another example would be Chambord Castle on the Loire. When one leaves the estate by car and looks at it through the rear window, one gets the impression that the castle is ever so subtly rising. Of course, we perceive the castle from the perspective of contemporary vision. But the automobile has only accelerated the effect of viewing it from the rear of a horse carriage, a view that was to be seen at the time the castle was built. It is an arresting representation of power that is only made possible by the fact that the castle is encircled at some distance by a low wall that at close range hides the bottom part of the building. So as one moves away from the castle, the viewing angle becomes better and better and one gradually gets to see more of the building. But you are right, the Uffizi buildings are also examples of spaces that are precisely defined in time. Those long covered galleries, which are running alongside the interior passageways of the Uffizi, have something of the stationary railway carriage about them, and their windows frame and therefore expose the landscape. Architects have laboured this theme repeatedly and often in surprising ways. A walk through a mediaeval convent would summon up the exact opposite effect. Here the covered galleries and the arcades are inward looking and direct the spectator's gaze to an inner courtyard, which is empty, since monks are not supposed to let themselves be distracted by the outer world, but should concentrate exclusively on their intimate communion with God. By contrast, the emphasis of Renaissance architecture was on the outer world, as can easily be seen in landscape paintings of the period. Of course, the Renaissance was also the time when the fortified walls and other forms of defence were opened up to the outside, so as to let the human gaze scan across the expanding landscape. However, this development was not linked to the seeking out of potential adversaries but to the sheer pleasure of looking out at the world. The addition of roofs finally transformed the promenades into galleries and the effect when one walks through them is similar to that of the effect of a railway carriage, where the landscape passes by our eyes. The difference between the two is that in the example of the Uffizi the flow of the landscape is caused by the movement of the people whereas in the example of the train the flow of the landscape is caused by the movement of the train itself.

AR: Doesn't that mean that movement transfers space into another existence without necessarily destroying it, as Heinrich Heine or Victor Hugo described the effect of railways?

PV: Precisely. This is why I understand speed as an environment. It is not a coincidence that I have called myself an urbanist for so long or that I have taught at a school for architecture for over thirty years. For me, speed is an environment, as that word is understood in the natural sciences. Speed is a domain with specific properties. Speed is not simply a matter of time. Speed is also space-time. It is an environment that is defined in equal measure by space and time. In addition, architecture too, whether it is moving or not, is defined by the speed of movements in space.

AR: But such a trajectory, such a quality of space, can only be displayed by an architecture that understands the human body as a space-determining element?

PV: Yes, but in a completely different manner from the way it was under-
        stood in the past. The Vitruvian body, and also Le Corbusier's Modula-
        tor, takes the body as a given mass in order to transfer the idealized
        proportions of the human body into the dimensions of architecture. But
        today, it no longer makes sense to view the body only from the angle of
        its proportions. Today one must assume an energized body, that is, a
        body with reflexes and anticipatory qualities, a body that is constantly
        in-becoming, just as some choreographers and modern dancers do
        already. For example, when my friend William Forsythe introduces me
        to the most beautiful female dancer in his company, he doesn't say: 'Is-
        n't she cute?' This is because, for him, the human body is first an unbe-
        lievable motor. And when he finds this dancer, this motor beautiful, he
        does not think so much of her breasts or buttocks, but of the dynamism
        of the motor, of its vitality. The beauty of a dancer is for him not that of
        Nike of Samothrace or that of Venus of Milo. It is not the beauty of a
        statue. And I too am of the opinion that an architect should no longer
        understand the body as a statue, but as something dynamic.

AR: Do you discern people working along these lines in contemporary
        architecture?

PV: No, not really. In fact, I tend to think that they have lost the dimension
        of the body that Vitruvius or Le Corbusier had but without gaining any-
        thing new in the process. To a large extent, contemporary architecture is
        taking flight into abstraction. An abstraction of deconstruction, of the
        combinatory principle or an abstraction of materials, which in most
        cases does not go beyond mere formalism. In any case, I do not get the
        impression that the body is playing a leading role in contemporary
        architecture; but that is rather in accordance with an epoch where the
        body is doomed to disappear. The contemporary human being is a use-
        less redundancy that is increasingly being replaced by machines. Archi-
        tects, for instance, are working more with machines than with people
        these days. And to the dynamics of space provided by the body we can
        add the changes in our relationship to space that is being provided by
        the new real-time technologies. Just as the introduction of the gallery of
        mirrors in the Palace of Versailles or in the coffee-houses of Paris modi-
        fied our relationship to space, so the screens of telecommunication will
        further modify our relationship to space.

AR: Just as the transportation revolution in the nineteenth century altered
        our spatial perception of cities …

PV: … Whereby it turned out that, with increasing speed, control over the
        cities also increases. The increasing velocity that has been brought

about, first by the railway, but mostly by automobiles and later by planes, dictates a higher level of control. The time-space of a city needs to be anticipated. In the beginning human vision was adequate. Later, cameras came in. The anticipation of space is a physiological reaction of our perception facing increasing velocities. The faster one moves, the more one must anticipate what is coming. The focus of our gaze is being consequently pushed forwards. This is being confirmed by research into the experiences of both Formula One racing drivers and competition skiers. It is no different in the city. The more the speed of a city increases – through automobile traffic, but also through telecommunications – the more it becomes necessary to anticipate appearances. This is a form of totalitarian control that relates to the contemporary transparency of architecture.

AR: You mean a transparency that articulates itself spatially as this anticipation of space?

PV: Of course, since in order to see one needs to clear the horizon first. One cannot anticipate in a mediaeval city because of the completely labyrinthine layout of the streets. Conversely, the Hausmannian boulevards of Paris have cleared the horizon of the city in order to make it predictable. But this also applies to architecture. The glass architecture of the modern era was also predicated upon the will to clear the field of vision.

AR: In a certain sense, this already held true for Le Corbusier's window frames, which were supposed to open up a simultaneous vision on the landscape.

PV: Exactly. Architecture is constantly becoming more optical in nature, and therefore becomes more and more part of the logic of surveillance. Transparency in architecture is to me a pathological sign of the acceleration of movement and information in the city. From this point on, one is no longer far removed from the kind of architecture without duration we were speaking about at the beginning of this interview. It is an architecture that constantly renews itself, and is in this way able to keep up with the swift changes of fashion. Whereas a specific and valid style of architecture used to endure – at least in part – for several centuries, today such endurance is limited to a decade at the most. One needs only to look at the functionalism of the 1960s, at postmodernism and deconstructivism as examples of this trend. In a certain sense, then, the cinematics of the audio-visual realm have spread out over the urban landscape too. The façades of buildings have been turned into time based images.

AR: That is the reason why Rem Koolhaas no longer designs façades, because he thinks they will be exchanged after ten years anyway. Now he concentrates more on the interior spaces.

PV: A reaction that it cannot be denied has a fair amount of logic to it. If you go one step further, then you discover what is the real project of today: the 'media building', where the facades have morphed into screens. For example, in Shanghai there is a skyscraper that is covered on all four sides with screens showing non-stop advertisements, films and videoclips!

AR: A three-dimensional urban television set you could say. This way, the age of the media – the era of real time and suspended time – also enters the built environment, and is superseding the traditional chronology of past, present and future.

PV: It is a demultiplication of time, and one that also affects reality itself. As, for instance, with football stadiums equipped with giant screens, where the spectators can experience the real presence of the players, but without having to forfeit the mediated vision and other features they've got accustomed to from watching TV such as time-loop and instant replay.

AR: These media engendered notions of time are simply becoming more and more part of our 'real' experience of time. This cannot leave architecture and urbanism untouched.

PV: On the most general plane, one can no longer understand cities in terms of separate entities, defined by some kind of specific location, but only as a global network, because all these once separate cities are now in a constant state of exchange with each other. Architecture will have to come to terms with the problem of 'hosting' virtual space within its concrete spatiality. Just as, in the seventeenth century, it absorbed the fictitious spatiality of mirrors, it will, in the twenty-first century, absorb the far more fictitious, and yet very real presence of virtual spaces. Productive work will simply not take place otherwise, and in parts, that is already the case today.

AR: And so, for architects, what is at stake can no longer be to reclaim the slowness of the past, however they conceive it, but to learn to handle real time.

PV: There can be no doubts about that. Up to the present day, architects have only worked with real spaces. From there stemmed the importance of geometry, structure and materials. But in the future, architects will also have to deal with real time. The virtual and the real city will exist side by side. The task ahead, however, is to make them truly co-habit.

Translated by Patrice Riemens.

Note

This interview originally appeared in 1996 in the German architectural journal *Der Arkitekt*, 3: 171–73 1996. This is the first time it has been published in English.

PART THREE

ON SPEED-SPACE
AND CHRONOPOLITICS

4

SPEED-SPACE

Interview with Chris Dercon

CD: An idea that comes up again and again in your books is that of the TV screen, the TV screen looking out on the world like a portable window. Enlarging on this idea, one could say the world is merely retransmitted by screens and satellites. What do you mean by this idea of the portable window?

PV: I used this term in reference to architecture, because the problem in architecture is first and foremost one of doors and windows. It is not the wall which encloses, since a structure that cannot be entered is not a structure for man.

There are three windows. There is the French window (door) which serves to effect an architecture, a place where man lives, be this a city or an apartment. There is the window which renders itself autonomous, the window as a place of light or looking – here we have an extraordinary invention related to a religious problem, the problem of the cult of light, through the claustra, solar calendars, etc. The third window is the television screen ... So when I speak of a window, I mean this third window. I am speaking also of another constructed space, that of telecommunications and the new technologies. Another point concerns cutting out: you only have an image if there is cutting, for nothing is ever seen in its entirety. Everything is always perceived through a frame, and it's certain this frame existed from the moment the first eye opened upon the visible field. This process continued with the framing of paintings, the frame of the photograph, and the frame created by the television camera eye. I believe when you talk of a third window, you are talking about a new frame, a sidereal frame, since with communications satellites and live re-broadcasts, the problem of the window becomes a macrocosmic phenomenon. But, this all stems from the very first window, the porthole drilled in the megalithic tomb. In these tombs there was a tiny hole to let the sun shine in. All this goes back to the beginning of time. That's why I call it the continuation of a story, the aftermath of that first sighting.

CD: The view through this third window might represent a catastrophe of perception, because as seen through it, reality becomes blurred. We are living in this loss of the real, because we only perceive reality through images. How should we react to this third window, how should we question it?

PV: As a first step we spoke of space; I think here we should speak of time. The contemporary image is a time-image, even a speed-image. The first pictures were space images, and that's what I refer to when I speak of an aesthetics of disappearing. I think we may come back to that in order to answer your question, but it really won't be an answer. Until the invention of photography, there was only an aesthetics of appearance. Images only persist because of the persistence of their medium: stone in the neolithic era or in ancient times, carved wood, painted canvas. ... Those are an aesthetics of immersion, of the appearance of an image which becomes permanent. The image is sketched, then painted and coated, and it lasts because its medium persists. With the coming of photography, followed by cinematography and video, we entered the realm of an aesthetics of disappearance: the persistence is now only retinal. Despite the film used in photography and cinema, there is no longer any real 'support'. The sustaining medium is retinal persistency because there is a persistency of the image in my eye that is this image in motion. Let's never forget that. So I believe an aesthetics of disappearing is another world, another link to the real. It is a link to the real as fleeting, as uncertain. The real in an aesthetics of appearance consists of being the solid, durable, hard real – hard in both senses of the word, i.e. hard and aggressive. So I believe that reality was a reality of solidity, of real presence, as they say. With cinematography, with photography first of all and now with infography, reality is shown as fugacious, but I think that we, too are fleeting.

CD: You have mentioned fugacity. Another very important concept in the almost real functioning of the magnetoscope is that of establishing a program of absence. What is the relationship between the idea of fugacity and the idea of a program of absence?

PV: I think the old image, the old reality, was a reality that can be presented as a space-time reality. Man lived in a time system of his actual presence: when he wasn't there, he wasn't there. Today we are entering a space which is *speed-space*. Contrary to popular belief, the space we live in is a speed-space. This new other time is that of electronic transmission, of high-tech machines, and therefore, man is present in this sort of time, not via his physical presence, but via programming. We program a computer or a videotape machine to record a telecast in our absence, to be able to watch it the next day. Here we have, I think, a discovery: the olden space-time was an extensive *space*, a space where duration of time was valued. Whatever was short-lived was considered an evil – something perjorative. To last a short time was to not be present; it was negative. Today we are entering an era of *intensive* time: that is to say that new technologies lead us to discover the equivalent of the infinitely small in time. In previous times we were conscious, with telescopes, of the infinitely large, and with microscopes, of the infinitely small. Today, high-speed machines, electronic machines, allow us to comprehend the same thing in regard to time. There is an infinitely long time which is that of history, of carbon-14, which enables us to date extremely ancient artifacts. Then, we have an infinitely short time, which is that of technology's billionths of seconds. I think the present finds us squarely between these two times. We are living in both the extensive time of the cities of stories, of memories, or archives, or writing, and the intensive time of the new technologies. *That's* the *'program of absence'* that's how we program our definitive absence, because we'll never be present in that billionth of a second.

No human being can be present in the intensive time that belongs to machines. Man is present in the average time situated in the long duration of historical phenomena and the short duration of his reflexes, of the 'twinkling of an eye'. We can say the same for the cinematographer. Beyond 60 images per second you can no longer perceive anything. Here again, you see, the problem of space is central. The new space is speed-space; it is no longer a time-space, a space where time is manipulated. What we are manipulating is no longer man's time, but machine's time, which I call speed-space, or the dromosphere, meaning the sphere of speed. In conclusion, from my point of view, speed is not a means, but a milieu – another milieu, and one that tends to escape us. When we think of speed, we say it's the means of getting from here to there fast, it's the means of seeing the Antipodes live when there's a game, or of watching the Olympics in Los Angeles. But I say no to this. It's a milieu, and a milieu in which we participate only indirectly through the videotape machine after recording, through information science and 'robotized' systems.

CD: You have spoken of the relationship between dromospheric space – of speed-space – and an aesthetics of disappearance, in connection with *the machinery of war*.

PV: Yes.

CD: For you, one of the most important factors in this new time-space concept – let's call it speed-space – is the strategic or stratifying development of war.

PV: Yes, insofar as war has always been the laboratory of the future. Because of the necessity to survive, and to face the possibility of sudden death, be it in ancient or new societies, war has always been the laboratory of techniques, of mores. I really believe this, and we must not forget it. War has also been the laboratory of speed. When Sun Tzu, the old Chinese strategist of several centuries ago, said that 'promptitude is the essence of war', he said it at the time of the cavalry. Now it is obvious that this saying is still true: witness the debate over euromissiles in Europe just a year ago. So, war is in fact the laboratory of modernity, of all modernities. And it is in this sense that it has been a subject of permanent study for me. It is also because I myself have experienced it. I lived through a war in my childhood, and it affected me deeply. Thus, war is not merely an amoral phenomenon, it is an experimental phenomenon inasmuch as it reverses productivity relations. War produces accidents. It produces an unheard-of accident, which is upsetting the traditional idea of war. Substance is necessary and accident is contingent and relative! That is the traditional story of the return to the accident. In war time the opposite is true. Here accident is necessary and substance relative and contingent. What are war machines? They are machines in reverse – they produce accidents, disappearances, deaths, breakdowns. I think war in this sense conveys something which at present we are experiencing in peacetime; the accident has now become something ordinary.

CD: You have spoken elsewhere of the relationship of cinema to modern techniques of war. As you know, it is said of Viverstein's films, and of all the products of Nazi cinema, that they were made especially for propaganda purposes. Is it not interesting to view these productions according to Jean-Marie Pienne's theory that technology is built upon the idea that there is no such a thing as death? So here's an immediate connection between technology and the idea of heredity. Let's not for the moment consider this idea of propaganda and this idea of the strategy of the image from the viewpoint of atavism. Let's say that there is a paradox: technology and atavism, an atavistic technology.

PV: I'm having trouble grasping your idea of atavism. I understand the word but I can't grasp what you mean by it. This being said, I think we can talk of propaganda. During the Second World War, the German army with the American army – the French army was less advanced on this score – was to develop the 'Peca' companies, the cinema companies created to follow the divisions. Films were regularly brought into headquarters to provide a direct vision of the front. This was because television, though it already existed, wasn't ready to do this yet. The camera operators of the land army and airforce served as on-the-spot reporters where the war was actually taking place. But it is certain that the Second World

War was essentially a radio-telephone war for the whole population. Nonetheless, we see Nazi regime dignitaries conducting research into colour as opposed to Technicolor. At the beginning of the war, Agfa-colour pictures were earthy and yellowish in hue, whereas Technicolor reds and blues were already bright. You have the Germans of the era saying, 'Ah, those colours are distinctly better than ours, and we're going to have to get ours to look much more lifelike.' I think this is important, especially for propaganda.

CD: Is there a difference between the idea of developing the cinema and the statues of Arno Breker? Technology is based on the idea that there is no such thing as death. It's the same thing as Arno Breker's statues. At that point, technology becomes atavistic. There is a paradox in cinema production.

PV: Well, here I'll begin with an anecdote about General Macarthur. When he was leaving his post in Korea, because he had planned to use nuclear arms but was refused and demoted, he said in his last official words, 'Old soldiers never die. They just fade away.' I think this expression is very cinematographic and very 'disappearance-aesthetic'. It is true the new technologies allow the dead man to live again, allow the duration of what has disappeared. There is a sort of universal conservatory, when you watch an actor on TV. You can see Mussolini, Hitler, Jean Gabin, Claude François, live again. It is in fact a form of conservation. I've always been amazed to see to what extent cinema is a sort of temporal porthole, as if there were a porthole in time. To be able to write 'War and Cinema', I was looking at the archives of the Army Cinematographic Services at Fort d'Ivry, and I had asked to see films of the 1914–18 war. I was chiefly interested in the fact I'd be seeing soldiers of that war in their youth, in their vitality, in their illusion – and they couldn't see me. As if it were a time-porthole which reverses the arrow (the direction) of time. So I said to myself that now, perhaps, in looking through this lens, we'll see people who do not yet exist. I have to ask myself that question.

Yes, I think cinema is a sort of porthole into the past, and this porthole is through the camera lens. Recording myself today is, I believe, to make myself particular to a time which will not be my own. Through this viewfinder, this porthole, people yet unborn will see me, but I have no way of seeing them. The arrow of time is reversed. And indeed we have here an event of the cinema, an event of this speed-space. We are no longer in time-space. It is, in fact, an illustration of what I was talking about earlier. We are in a speed-space: it is the recording capacities of a machine which will allow people of the future to see me. I had the privilege of seeing myself twenty years after, in my friend Eric Rohmer's film

Le Marbre et le Cellulo. I had been interviewed in 1965 and I saw a projection of this film in 1985. It had an awful effect on me, because to see this man who had existed twenty years before, to see him again today, was in a way frightful. It wasn't a problem of the beauty of youth, it was a problem of identity – it wasn't me. Not at all. That man quoted the word time-space continuum even, and that was the only word which allowed me to connect myself to him, for everything else – the clothes, the tie, the hairstyle – everything was wrong. If I had known twenty years ago, I would certainly have said something else!

CD: There is also another reversal, that of day and of night. Is there a link to be made between the day–night relationship and the night bombings of the Second World War and the idea of night as a black hole, in 'Star Wars' [The Strategic Defense Initiative]?

PV: There is much to be said here. It is certain that technological war allowed us to continue to make war at night, in other words, we're performing theatre. Then, after that, in 1914, 1925, those same projectors were used to pick out the planes coming to bomb in order to shoot them down. So here we have a whole light-war; tracer-bullets will be used to make night-time shooting possible, and flares to light up the troops' night chargers (flare revolvers and rifles). And I myself saw those special effects in the Second World War. During the bombings of the city of Nantes I saw those projectors, those tracer-bullets, those rocket-parachutes tossed out of bombers to light up the bombing zone. It was a fabulous show of unheard of and even tragic beauty. It was Rome burning. So it's certain the use of new technologies extended war to the totality of time, not only as in the past wars in summer time, but also war in wintertime. In antiquity war was waged starting in March, and then stopped in September–October. The new technologies have allowed us to wage war year round. But up until 1914 no one made war at night, they stopped at nightfall. Now, with the new technologies, not only do they make war all the time, in all seasons, but non-stop, day and night. We have a totalizing phenomenon that is also a phenomenon we experience daily with live broadcasts from the four corners of the earth, which allow us to watch a festival or a ballgame. There is therefore a cancellation of the daytime. In the same way that there is a cancellation of time-space, there is a cancellation of daytime as a way of dividing up time. Daytime is no longer the astronomical day, it is the day of techniques. With astronomical daytime, chickens went to sleep when Man did. Today, chickens continue to go to sleep when the sun goes down, but men no longer do. When the sun goes down, electric light and television go on. It's another time, another day beyond the solar day. I think that's new.

CD: Now that war takes place beyond the horizon, can we still speak of war
or of a war?

PV: Indeed, now they are talking of a trans-horizonal weapon – the term is a
technical one. But I believe that war has never been linked to the horizon. It always was, even when geographical, a war of time. Its territory
was always temporal. When Sun Tzu said, 'Promptitude is the essence of
war', he meant war is not simply a problem of hills, valleys and mountain
passes which have to be defended, it's a problem of time; hence, the
invention of the cavalry. Cavalry was its strike force, the strike force of
that time. Afterwards, it was the artillery which replaced this strike
force. Every war is a war of time, and I think there have been profound
changes, changes which brought about the invention of new weapons
and which today are reaching a limit. 'Star Wars' is also a war of time,
but it is no longer the time of decision. If you take the history of decision
in war, war was first delegated to commanders, great captains of the
Middle Ages, then afterwards, with the invention of headquarters, the
decision was concentrated in individuals – the ministers of war, chiefs of
staff, who concealed the decision. There was a phenomenon of concentration – the dispersal, the diaspora, of decision disappeared. Then, with
the Second World War, there was the creation of the general headquarters, a headquarters of armies and groups of armies, whose great strategist was Eisenhower. Here again you had a phenonemon of retention of
power over a chief of general headquarters who made the decisions concerning a half a continent or half a hemisphere. With nuclear weapons,
this retention of the time of war, of the time of decision, became even
more concentrated in one lone individual, the head of state. Presidentialism in France is connected with nuclear power, the strike force.
Presidentialism in the US is similar, even if its origin is not exactly the
same. Nuclear weapons demanded there be just one decision-maker.
This, moreover, is one of the major handicaps to the creation of Europe:
if we want a nuclear Europe, there will be no Europe, because we'll
never manage to agree on a President.

In fact, this moment is in the process of disappearing too. The
supreme decision-makers, François Mitterand, Reagan, Gorbachev
himself, are in the process of disappearing. Why? Because now with
'Star Wars', transhorizon and transcontinental weapons, the decision-
time to fire will drop to a few milliseconds. With laser weapons that
work at the speed of light, 300,000 kilometres per second, there's no
question of saying, 'Mr President, it seems that some rockets have taken
off on the other side of the Atlantic'. No, they would already be there
before you could say so. So now the formidable idea is taking hold in
the US and the USSR, around the 'Star Wars' debate, of the automatic
responder, meaning the idea of a war-declaration machine. Why?
Because man's time is no longer the time of the speed of light. Man

cannot intervene: he may have been elected and hold supreme political and military powers, but he does not have the power to act at the speed of light. Today a drama is being played out. But no one is talking about it, despite the demonstrations I participate in, despite Clifford Johnson's court case, which has been launched in the US. A computer expert at Stanford says, 'the new concept of firing on alert is a mad concept, for it delegates the declaration of war to a machine'. Now, constitutionally, the commander has no power to delegate. Reagan does not have the power to delegate the decision to declare nuclear war to a machine. For what reasons? Quite simply because a computer breakdown cannot be identified as the free act of an individual head of state. I think that between the commander of the Middle Ages and Reagan or Gorbachev today, and finally the automatic responder, it's clear that promptitude is the essence of war. That essence of war eliminates man from the system. First the big battalions are replaced by materials, then big materials are replaced by very small, sophisticated materials (satellites or MX missiles), and finally man, the supreme decider, is eliminated in favour of a responder which will, of course, be coupled to another responder.

CD: Will the idea of speed-space instead of time-space influence the means of representation in the cinema and the artist's image?

PV: I think it's already had an influence. We witnessed the shift from extensive to intensive time with cinema. We experienced it first with cinema of 16 images per second, then 24 images per second, then tracks, then reels; we had films which lasted a few minutes – I'm thinking of Meliese's films – then we had films lasting half an hour, then films one and one half to two hours, which is the average length at 25 frames per second. With the new machines today we are in fact playing with the subliminal. We are in the process of reducing the length of films to half or three quarters of an hour, but projected at 60 frames per second. We are going from the extensive films of Abel Gance and Eisenstein, whose films lasted up to ten hours, to the intensive film – the video clip or half-hour film. I think that there's a movement here; more goes into speed-space, 60-image per second films than went into time-space, 24 frames per second films, but we are at the limits of the subliminal. We know that beyond 60 images per second there will be no more viewers, since nothing more will be perceived. Here, again, intensiveness is confirmed – the shift from extensiveness to intensiveness. It's certain that artists, be they film-makers or video-makers, use this. They play in this dromospheric space, in speed-space. I think special effects are one of the most interesting areas in cinema. I remember coming back when *Alien* was released. It was made and shown before *Star Wars*. I remember viewers, young people, coming in and saying 'fasten your seat belts'. What they were coming to see wasn't a story. It was a movement. They wanted to be carried away in the special effects. They were disappointed. Though *Alien* is a good film, it's not one where you fasten your seat belts. It's another film which tells a story about monsters, whereas *Star Wars* was a film where you fastened your seat belt. Now it seems to me cinema is fastening the viewer's seat belts, via video clips, special effects and through infography and synthesized images. We saw this in *Tron*, and other films. There is a cinema beyond the 24 frames per second one, a speed-cinema, which is no longer a time-cinema, a tale. I don't think that's bad. What is bad is that we lack a Meliesse. Meliesse was the inventor of telescopic effects, of montages of different temporalities. Today, it is unfortunately too commercial, and I regret the lack of a Meliesse of electronic effects.

CD: You say that we lack a Meliesse, but the story has become less and less important. Therefore, we also lack a Roland Barthes, since without one, we can't go on telling tales. What are the consequences of this?

PV: That's the moral position I've always wanted to avoid. It's true that speed is a drunkenness, a drug – there's no doubt. It has the same effects. You vomit, you get a headache, just as when you get drunk or take other drugs. That's the negative aspect I've developed in my books. But I don't think that anything's ever totally negative. The world is not so simple. At one and the same time, it is dreadful, in that it causes us to lose the relationship to the subject. But it also teaches us about our fragility, our fugacity. That is perhaps the moral lesson of that which has no moral.

CD: Then special effects become a homeopathic means, a vaccine. Is that why special effects have been so exaggerated, and that an artificiality beyond artificiality has been created?

PV: For the moment, it's indeed the commercial system and therefore a system of facility. As for me, my preoccupation is that, behind speed-space, another relationship to the real is hiding. It's just as humanistic, just as moral or ethical as the other. Only no one has yet been behind that mirror. For the moment they're playing the way they played with the first cinema, the first films. It wasn't cinema, it was effects, effects you'd see at a country fair. They showed films at fairs. I think this is just a stage.

CD: What remains to us is the idea of editing, of arrangement. The idea of original creation no longer exists, no longer counts. In that case, when we are editor–arrangers, do we have to create or exaggerate the artificiality, as we would the story?

PV: The model is the speed composition. Now there is a very old model of speed composition and that's music. Music has confused speeds in harmonics in an extraordinary fashion for a very long time, to use only Western references. Speed-compositions were very well developed, through Bach, Handel, Mozart etc. in the universe of sound. Intervals of time were extraordinarily well developed and utilized. In the optical system, it hasn't happened yet. Abel Gance hoped for it. He hoped to make the music of images, but I think the means of his time did not permit this. Transparencies and superimpositions were not sophisticated enough. Today I believe we are about to enter a time of compositions in optical speed and special effects. These are the rather spectacular aspects of this music of the eye. For the moment we just have vulgar things, but there's a possibility here, which will or won't be realized. We see the video clips being used for ads, and the films being made with fantastic special effects, but, alas, for the moment, we are not moving towards the realization of that potential. But it could happen, and I believe there will be a [Guillaume de Nacho] or a J.S. Bach able to do the same thing with pictures and light. The new techniques allow it.

CD: Another consequence: in video and cinema, we're seeing more and more violence and hard-core pornography. I'm thinking of the English expression 'video nasty'. Isn't there a desire for images which still have this notion of reality?

PV: Yes, absolutely. Pornography is an example of retrogradation. The body only appears through obscenity. Now there exists this retrograde vision of the body. Personally, I think the word 'obscenity' corresponds to its etymology, which we often forget is 'ill omen'. It is curious to see that Sun Tzu – who I quote a lot, as I believe his is the only philosophy of war – says 'weapons are tools of ill omen'. I'd like to say that through unrestrained pornography, there is a return to the body, which is a lost body. This obscene body is not a body to come, it's a lost body. It's the equivalent of a cadaver, the putting to death of the body. I admit it bothers me profoundly. What shocks me in pornography is that in it, boredom is weeping. There are the tears of boredom, not those of pleasure.

CD: Listening to you, you seem to be attached to the idea of the 'Immaterialists', of Lyotard – the possibility of developing a new idea of the material, of material representation. Do you think that the use of the term the 'immaterialists' is correct?

PV: I've used that term for a long time, saying that war went from the material of war to the immaterial of war. That seems completely coherent to me. I feel we have indeed tended to forget everything that's invisible. Now, with the aesthetics of disappearance, we are obliged to care about all things invisible. In the past, the invisible was present through religion and mythologies. When we read in the third epistle of St Peter the sentence, 'One day is ... as a thousand years, and a thousand years as one day', we have a vision of relativity that was the vision of the whole of antiquity. Even if here it is expressed through Christianity, this vision of relativity was present in ancient history – the invisible peopled the world. The invisible world was an important element of reality. With the onset of materialism, of the Age of Enlightenment, of the political history of the nineteenth century, the invisible was, I would say, censored. It signified the old customs; it was an archaic vision. The visible and the material were priviliged to the detriment of the invisible, as the deeds of society are not all visible.

CD: This notion was also to change the idea of the essence of being.

PV: Certainly. Besides, it isn't by chance that we are seeing a powerful return of religious ideologies. Personally, I'm religious, I am a Christian. You are obliged, as I've often said to non-believing friends, to reintroduce only the question of God, not the answer, which is a personal problem. If not, don't speak of the immaterial. You cannot speak of the 'invisible and immaterial' if you continue to censor the question of God. When you talk of the Big Bang, of the creation of time and space through the theory of the Big Bang, you're talking about the question of God. So, let's call a spade a spade: the Big Bang is about God who has come back among us. And in fact here I think it's one of the positive aspects of the new technologies. They reintroduce the question of God, and I mean The Question and not Khomeni's or anyone else's answer.

CD: You were saying that it's important to ask questions. When does one see this change of solutions toward questions?

PV: I think it's our generation. Our generation has to return to questions. Why? Because the preceding generation had all the solutions – the economic solution through capitalism and the consumer society; the political solution through Marxism or capitalism; the military solution through dissuasion. All the solutions were there. Now we've seen the results and are experiencing the drama of these solutions, so I believe our generation must again find the questions, and that's not easy.

CD: The last question: what are the consequences of this dromospheric space, speed-space, for the workings of the city? I'm thinking especially of the difference between urbanity and suburbanity. Does it still exist?

PV: It's important to return to the city. To return to the city is to return to politics or to the political people. It's not by chance that in Greek the city is called the '*polis*'. The city was created in a relationship to territorial space. It is a territorial phenomenon, a phenomenon of territorial concentration. Old villages are spread over a territory which is not a territory but a field, in all senses of the term. There is creation, from the old villages, through what has been called kinesis, of an urban territorial unit – the Greek city-state, to take a well-known reference. Since politics and the city were born together, they were born through a right: the creation of a territory or of an estate by right, being established, the right of autochthonism. There are rights because there is territory. There are rights and therefore duties – he who has land has war, as the people of Verde said. He who has rights in an urban territory has the duty to defend it. The citizen is also a soldier-citizen. I feel this situation survives up to the present; we are experiencing the end of that world. Through the ups and downs of the state, the city-state, the more or less communal state, and finally, the nation-state, we have experienced the development of politics linked to the territory; always down-to-earth. In spite of railroads and telephones, we experienced a relationship to the soil and a relationship to a still coherent right. There was still a connection to territorial identity, even in the phenomenon of nationalistic amplification. Today, as we saw earlier with the end of time-space and the coming of speed-space, the political man and the city are becoming problematic. When you talk about the rights of man on the world scale, they pose a problem which is not yet resolved, for a state of rights is not connected with a state of place, to a clearly determined locality. We can clearly see the weaknesses of the rights of Man. It makes for lots of meetings, but not for much in the way of facts. Just take a look at Eastern European countries or Latin America. It seems to me that speed-space which produces new technologies will bring about a loss, a derealization of the city. The megalopolises now being talked of (Calcutta, or Mexico with 30 million inhabitants) are no longer cities, they are phenomena which go beyond the city and translate the decline of the city as a territorial localization, and also as a place of an assumed right, affirmed by a policy. Here, I'm very pessimistic. I feel we're entering into a society without rights, a 'non-rights' society, because we're entering a society of the non-place, and because the political man was connected to the discrimination of a place. The loss of a place is, alas, generally the loss of rights.

Here, we have a big problem: the political man must be reinvented – a political man connected to speed-space. There, everything remains to be done, nothing's been accomplished. I'd even say the question hasn't been considered. The problem of the automatic responder we were talking about earlier, the legal action which Clifford Johnson is taking against the US Congress, is in my opinion the trial of the century. The problem of rights there is the right of the powerful man, the last man, he who decides. Now, he too will no longer have the right, if he delegates his right to an automatic machine. We truly have here a political question and an urban question, because at present the cities are undone by technology, undone by television, defeated by automobility (the high-speed trains, the Concorde). The phenomena of identification and independence are posed in a completely new way. When it takes 3 hours to go to New York, and 36 to New Caledonia, you are closer to American identification than to Caledonian or French identification. Before proximity, there was territorial continuity. We were close because we were in the same space. Today we are close in the speed-space of the Concorde, of the high-speed train, of telecommunications. Therefore, we don't feel conjoined to people, the compatriots of the same people – the Basques or the Corsicans. We no longer have the time to go to Bastia, because practically, we are closer to New York, because you can't go by Concorde to Bastia. We have here a phenomenon of distortion of the territorial community that explains the phenomenon of demands of independence. Before, we were together in the same place, and could claim an identity. Today, we are together elsewhere, via high-speed train, or via TV. There is a power of another nature which creates distortions. We are no longer in space, but in speed-space. Because of speed-space there are fellow countrymen participating in the same non-place who feel close, whereas one's own countrymen in Corsica or New Caledonia are in reality so far away in speed-space, so beyond 36 hours or 10 hours, that they are strangers and therefore desire their autonomy. There's a logic there, and it's a logic which poses problems.

Translated by Daphne Miller.

© 1986 *Impulse* and Paul Virilio. Interview with Chris Dercon, in *Impulse*, 12 (4), 1986. © 1986 translation by Daphne Miller.

5

PERCEPTION, POLITICS AND THE INTELLECTUAL

Interview with Niels Brügger

Perception

NB: During the Gulf War, you wrote a number of newspaper articles on the war. Reading these articles, I was under the impression that the course of this war had already been predicted in your books from the 1970s and 1980s. I would thus like to ask you to do a kind of 'anamnesis' of these books by speaking about your position today through your earlier works and with the Gulf War as the current point of departure.

In *War and Cinema: Logistics of Perception* (1989 [1984]), you base your analyses of our perception of the world in general on war. What are the consequences for perception when geographical space becomes less important, when vision and action become simultaneous, and when speed turns into the speed of light?

PV: First of all, one can no longer speak of space or time without speaking of speed. Philosophically, but above all physically, to speak of a space is instantly to speak of the relationship of time to this space. Thus to speak of time is to refer to the time of displacement and the time of perception. Clearly, in war, which for centuries has essentially amounted to wars of movement, wars of displacement (based on assaults, attacks), one must start implementing greater, more decisive speeds in military confrontations. This tendency is of course evident in assault techniques (cavalry, tanks), but it becomes even more manifest in telecommunication techniques, that is, techniques of perception and information. In this sense, a war is always a reorganization of space. A new war reorganizes the space of society by its means of assault and by its means of information. This was clear in the Gulf War in an exemplary and, in my view, definitive way because it concerned an extremely limited local war that could only be won so quickly because it was controlled on a global scale.

The technologies of real time that still weren't perfected with the invention of the telegraph and the telephone since a delay remained (due to the coding and transmission of the message), have attained their maximum scale. It is now possible for us to act, to tele-act, in real time and not only to gather information and perceive by satellite. As I have often said, we can distinguish between three decisive actions, each tied to a certain period: tele-audition (telephone, radio), television in differed time, and finally tele-action, that is, the possibility of tele-acting instantaneously regardless of the distance. I stand rather alone in insisting that speed is clearly the determining factor. In my capacity as social analyst, I do not wish to deliver monologues but to partake in a dialogue. For the past twenty-five years, my work has nevertheless been solitary. To say that speed is a determining factor in society requires proof, an effort that is starting to exhaust me. Thus, in my view the Gulf War was a kind of confirmation of what I announced seven years previously in *War and Cinema*.

NB: A book that could almost be regarded as a kind of screenplay for the Gulf War?

PV: Absolutely. But you see, when I published this book in 1984, people said 'But what does it mean?', 'The pictures are being used to wage war, the pictures are ammunition, and this is not a metaphor, it is concrete,' and so forth. In this respect, the Gulf War unfortunately ended up illustrating this situation. But the true problem is that we still have not understood that we are no longer in the world of Newton, but in the world of Einstein. I have said this numerous times and shall repeat it because it is so obvious that I don't understand how one can fail to acknowledge it. Up until Newton, the world was characterized by time and space being absolute, and all of history was determined by this situation until Newton. But since Einstein, who was capable of giving a physical form to this theory of relativity, it is speed that predominates. All of my work, whether on war, urbanism, social relations or economy – all of it simply aims to rephrase the question of this final absolute. I don't think people are able to understand much of what I've written if they don't understand that my work is not driven by one subject – war, transportation, urbanism, and so on – but by treating the question of installing speed as the categorical imperative of the modern world – including in everyday life.

NB: In other words, what you have called the law of dromology, a law that gives rise to dromological pollution?

PV: It goes without saying that if the three terms currently function together (space, time, speed), speed is the determining element, the absolute element. Relativity means that space and time are relative to speed, which is absolute; it is very simple, but it is fundamental. Taking this as our starting point, it becomes increasingly evident that we live in a world no longer based on geographic expanse but on a temporal distance constantly being decreased by our transportation, transmission and tele-action capacities. Thus, all of our technologies lead to a final kind of pollution, no longer atmospheric or hydrospheric – the pollution of the air and water – but dromospheric: the total area of the world is being reduced to nothing. Tomorrow, in one, two, three generations, the world as a geographic expanse and duration will have disappeared. This is a considerable event, a drama, a tragedy, but one that results from the production of our technologies, which since the dawn of mechanics and even since we started taming animals, has unceasingly endeavoured to attain greater speeds. We would never invent a machine to decelerate, to slow down. The world is thus destined to be exhausted as a spatial and temporal expanse because the world is finite and because speed has become the absolute speed of light.

Allow me to illustrate what I mean by telling you about my journey to Japan. I'm almost 60 years old and up until two years ago I had never been to Japan. As far as I was concerned Japan was on the other side of the world, the farthest away one could get. Of course, I had travelled before, but never so far away, and going to Tokyo in 14 hours, flying over the world in such a short span of time meant that Japan no longer seemed exotic to me but had become endotic, that is, 'domestic'. In a sense, this journey shrank the world for me. It is of course only a reflex, but when a journey like this becomes as ordinary as travelling to the Mediterranean or North Africa, it naturally provokes an effect of confinement, an unbearable claustrophobia. I knew Foucault when he was working on imprisonment, and one might say that what he developed at the level of society, I developed at the level of imprisonment in speed, that is, the end of the outer, exotic world.

NB: So instantaneity reigns, which, by the way, we saw during the Gulf War, where there were two kinds of instantaneity: instantaneity on the battlefield and instantaneity in transmission (even if there weren't any transmissions from the battlefield).

PV: Absolutely. The Gulf War was managed from Washington, the Pentagon and Atlanta, where the centre for calculating the missile paths is located. So in a certain sense what happened in the Middle East, in Iraq and in Kuwait, was tele-guided from geostationary satellites located just above the battlefield that instantaneously sent information either to Maryland, the Pentagon, or Atlanta. And these instantaneous perceptions made possible the incredibly precise weapon guidance that won the war without war, so to speak, in that besides the bombardments there was almost no war. So this Gulf situation was actually the start of this contraction. It was a world war that took place locally, but a world war because it made use of the entire world.

NB: And it was the first war in real time?

PV: Yes, it was even the war of real time. Real space was infinitely less important that real time. In previous wars, even in Vietnam, the territory played an extraordinarily large role: they had to fight in rice fields, traverse deserts and fortresses, which took a very long time. In the Gulf War, everything was controlled instantaneously and in only five weeks.

NB: The problem of this disqualification of territory leads me to another crucial point related to perception: immateriality. By this, I'm referring to the immateriality of the battlefield and immateriality in general.

PV: Any battlefield is above all a perceptual field, because the primary act is that of aiming, of attaining an objective. Once we have seen something, we have already started to destroy it. As long as something is invisible, it is protected by its invisibility. Whether it is arrows or stones people throw at each other, perception is the determining factor of war. Something my mother used to say always comes to mind: 'It isn't polite to point at people.' This statement surprises me because it suggests that pointing at people is a threat. So, in a certain sense, each war reorganizes the perceptual field; for instance, by the conquest of elevated sites: the higher up one is, the farther one sees, the more one fore-sees. Before the telephone, people went up to the highest points. Next balloons were invented to see from above, even when the battles took place on plains, and it stands to reason that the invention of airplanes equipped with cameras during the First World War was an attempt to reorganize the perception of the world.

Allow me to cite an example: survey maps lost their interest to the advantage of film. We should be aware of the importance of cartography in history, even philosophically – a map is a method of writing. But suddenly, with the First World War, all of this changes in favour of photos, photo mosaics, then film, and finally television. Today of course, satellites have assumed this important role, now more important than survey maps or films shot from airplanes. So the immateriality of vision becomes a crucial factor, even to the detriment of explosives and weapons. If aiming is more important than the weapon itself, it is understood that one day deterrence will no longer be caused by weapons but by the gaze. Think of a weapon, a revolver, for example. If I stick a revolver in your face, first of all you don't know if it is loaded or not; it may not be loaded, but when I say 'give me your money', you are going to give me your wallet, and I don't even have to make use of my weapon, maybe there aren't even any bullets in it. So this power of deterrence is one of the determining factors of a weapon. A weapon is not so much a means to kill, to injure, than it is a means to deter action, to forbid an action and cause someone to surrender. All weapons always have an active dimension (they can actually kill) and a passive dimension – but also active – deterrence. But up until and including the atom bomb, deterrence was caused by weapons. Someone says 'I have a great big bomb', okay, you surrender and reach an agreement. This is what happened between the Soviet Union and the United States. But today our visual capacities are surpassing the very capacities of the atomic weapon, and the Gulf War was the first time in history that the capacity of perception prevailed over the capacity of destruction. And with this we arrive at the third kind of supremacy in weapons. Three types of weapons have succeeded each other in history: weapons of obstruction, weapons of destruction and weapons of communication. Weapons of obstruction are, for example, all kinds of shields, helmets, ramparts, or bunkers. Weapons of destruction include arrows as well as missiles. Weapons of communication are, for example, spies, smoke signals, messenger pigeons, satellites and spy airplanes. As mentioned previously, the faster speed dominates over the slower speed – there are no longer horses on the streets, there are cars. Today missiles no longer possess the greatest speed (they don't fly particularly fast, only a few thousand kilometres an hour), but instead means of communication (radar or satellites of all kinds that function at the speed of light); so they are superior because they pose the threat of destruction. For the first time, the Gulf War places the supremacy of weapons of communication above the supremacy of weapons of destruction, including nuclear destruction. This does not mean that tomorrow there will no longer be nuclear arms; it means that we are witnessing a revolution in how the world is perceived, as was the case with the conquest of summits and the construction of towers.

NB: Perhaps it should be emphasized that this revolution in perception affects vision in a profound way, insomuch as direct vision has lost some of its importance. Despite the fact that people, especially journalists, were forbidden to approach the battlefield, even before this prohibition they weren't allowed on it. Due to the revolution in perception, it was impossible to see the battlefield directly; it could only be seen through machines, prostheses, screens. Direct vision seems to have disappeared.

PV: First of all, direct and indirect vision are linked to optical mutation. From the invention of photography until the invention of television, of course, we have progressively moved from optics to electro-optics. There are two kinds of optics: a direct optics, that of my eyes or even of my glasses, and an indirect optics. For instance, when I am able to see in real time what is happening 1,000 kilometres away due to the speed of waves, I am experiencing electro-optics. These two kinds of optics mean that perception occurs in two registers. The soldier, but also the civilian, is in two spaces: in that of direct vision and at the same time in that of indirect vision, created, for instance, by 'live' television or surveillance cameras. And here I'm not referring to television shows, but to technique.

From now on, there will thus be two new kinds of light. Before there were two kinds of light: natural light and artificial light, sunlight and electrical or candle light. Now there are two other kinds of light: a direct light (candles and electricity, which are the same kind of light – one is natural, like the sun, the other is artificial, as is electricity, but both of them are direct) – and an indirect light (that of electro-optics in real time, which illuminates what is happening at a distance by virtue of a camera and a monitor, that is, by virtue of the speed of light). If we had seen what happened in the Gulf with a delay of two years, for instance, it would not be a question of optics, but a piece of history, an account. So this problem of two kinds of light – direct and indirect – leads to the problem of two transparencies: the transparency of real space – that of the air, of the atmosphere, of glass – and indirect transparency, which I call trans-appearance. What is trans-appearance? It is the transparency of appearances instantaneously transmitted across great distances. It is a new transparency, indirect, electro-optic and no longer optic, but still a transparency. And these two kinds of transparency are henceforth contained in each other. From now on, we will be endowed with double vision. At the same time – still referring to real time – there is double vision, and it goes without saying that this conditions social relations, politics, strategy and so on; and today the Soviet Union and the United States are certainly the strongest because they are the only ones who possess these strategies. We of course have satellites in Europe, but we don't control this indirect transparency, this capacity to attain an objective, to attain information immediately.

NB: Your comments on transparency make me think of the horizon: are there two horizons?

PV: Yes, there is one horizon that is the direct horizon: a line. It is the horizon line that allows us to limit the perceptual field (for example, the 40 kilometres of the horizon line when one looks out across the sea). It is the horizon of real space. And there is a horizon of real time, which means that there are also two perspectives: on the one hand, one perspective of real space with a horizon line and a vanishing point, and on the other hand the perspective of real time, in which the horizon is no longer a line but a screen. This is a critical event. Currently I'm working on a book on the perspective of real time in order to try to see how these two perspectives function together.

NB: This problem of the horizon is a problem that you have already treated in an article entitled 'L'Horizon au carré' (*Liberation*, 29 September 1990). I really like this title because the expression 'au carré' can both mean on the screen and 'squared', that is, a kind of doubling.

PV: Yes, that is true: 'au carré' has both meanings, although I was actually only thinking of a screen. If we consider the pilots of today, for example, they have two kinds of vision: looking up and looking down. When they look up, they see the panorama, and when they look down, they see the screen that gives them tele-vision; this also involves a kind of doubling.

NB: To conclude our discussion of perception, I would like to address a final theme: the relation between speed and vision, or rather between movement and vision. Is it possible to say that the ultimate means of transportation today are the machines that transport vision without transporting the body?

PV: It goes without saying that speed is a way of visualizing the world. When I walk at the speed of 4 kilometres an hour, I have a certain vision of the world. When I stop to look at a tree, it is immobile. When I start walking again, the tree seems to pass by. This passing by is tied to the speed of the observer. If I pass the tree quickly in a car, the tree will become indistinct, and if I pass it very quickly, I won't see anything; I'll only see a blur, a fog.

So speed is always a way of seeing the world differently. Means of transportation are not only a means of displacing oneself from one point to another. I have often used different vehicles for the mere pleasure of seeing the speed; for example, in the beginning I often took the TGV [high speed train] to see its effect on the countryside, and I wrote about what I have called dromoscopy, that is, the vision of speed, which implies a major philosophical question: which tree is the true one? The tree that is only a frozen image whose branches and every single piece of bark I can describe in detail, or the blurred tree that passes by? We know very well that both trees are true. Yet in Newtonian rationalism (space and time are absolute and speed is relative), the true tree is the frozen, immobilized tree. The true man is the statue; the canon of the statue, as Michel Serres would say. But I believe that we are heading in the opposite direction, where the genuine tree is the tree that passes by, because we are always moving: my eyes move, I move even if I'm sitting down. So in a certain sense, our relationship to reality has been affected by the Einsteinian era, in which speed is essential, absolute, while space and time are relative; the tree can no longer be the same.

NB: This is precisely the problem you described in *The Vision Machine* (1994 [1988]) in connection with the discussion between Auguste Rodin and Paul Gsell.

PV: Indeed. Rodin's comment is very interesting. Paul Gsell says to Rodin: 'a photographic instant is truth'. And Rodin says: 'No, it is false because in reality time does not stop'. And he is absolutely right because the photograph is but a frozen image. Besides, we should not be speaking of the photograph now; we should be speaking of frozen images. But Rodin is right in respect to the photograph; in a way he anticipates the cinema. It is not photography that is false. He says: 'Photography is false and my art is true.' But it is not the photograph itself that is false; it is only false because it is halted. And this leads us toward the question of the relationship between movement and vision. Just as airplanes and weapons are becoming outdated in respect to means of communication, means of transportation are becoming outdated in respect to 'means of vision'. It is no coincidence that videos are set up in elevators and movies are shown in airplanes. I'm convinced that just as cars have replaced horses, cars themselves are in the process of disappearing in favour of highly sophisticated transmission techniques, of which data-suits, virtual reality and cyberspace are the first signs. The dominance of speed certainly seems to point in this direction.

NB: But when the means of transportation become means of transmission, what happens to the body?

PV: This implies what could be called the third revolution. The notion of revolution to which I'm referring is tied to the law of proximity. The law of proximity is the law of the least effort, or the law of the least action. Allow me to illustrate: when people have to go to the third floor and an elevator and an escalator are both available, everybody takes the escalator. This is related to the law of proximity. Previously the law of proximity was mechanical but now it is electromagnetic. When it is possible to communicate instantaneously by telefax, people don't send letters, which is already starting to happen. This marks a considerable change.

The first important revolution in the order of proximities is the revolution in the means of transportation of the nineteenth century with the train, the car and the airplane. The revolution in transportation is now being completed with the TGV and the hypersonic airplane, which have almost attained their maximum speeds. The second revolution under way is the revolution in the means of transmission, where speed is no longer the relative speed of the train, the car or the airplane – not even hypersonic (this is a relative speed) – but rather the absolute speed of electromagnetic waves: informatics, television, cyberspace, and so on. Now there is the additional possibility of this revolution in transmission becoming incorporated in the human body itself. Already with data-suits, a kind of technical outfit, certain techniques external to the body may be put into it. But prostheses already exist that are directly integrated into the body, such as the pacemaker and other technical transplantations (not organ transplantations, but transplantations of robots). The last territory left to technify is therefore not the territory on which freeways, railways or airports are constructed, but the human body, in which prosthetic techniques are implanted. And while these prostheses are being implanted internally, there is nothing to prevent biotechnologies from being swallowed in the future, or the body from being nourished technically, just as we have chemical nourishment today.

NB: That is, from the automate toward the animate?

PV: Exactly. This idea of the animate might explain people's taste for narcotics, sleeping pills, and so on. As though society were already designing this revolution in transplantations whereby the body itself is equipped and not external objects. My work on this subject is based on the law of proximity, for it is this law that allows me to say what I'm saying. I'm not the one saying it, it is not a fiction, it is that the law of proximity keeps us from regressing: a higher speed always eliminates a lower speed. If there are no longer horses in the streets it is not because someone decided this, it is because the law of proximity required it. This law is a kind of physics of politics. Whether it is on the left or the right, we cannot oppose it. This is what Lenin means when he says that communism is Soviet Power plus electricity. Today one might say that advanced capitalism is capitalism plus electronics. It is a question of the physics of politics, which is not taken into account, and when I speak of dromocracy, of dromology, I'm referring to this physics. Certain people have said to me 'but you're speaking of war,' and my response is 'no, war serves to illustrate the situation because this is where it is most obvious; it is my laboratory, nothing else.' I've often said that if these cutting-edge technologies were useful to agriculture, then I would be a specialist in agriculture.

Politics

NB: In *War and Cinema* you spoke above all of war and perception, but you don't deal with the relationship between perception and politics, which you had already treated seven years earlier in *Speed and Politics* (1986 [1977]). I would therefore like to ask you the following question: how should or how can we address politics today? How should we reformulate the stakes in politics now that perception has been transformed in the profound manner we just discussed?

In *Speed and Politics*, your starting point is that every city is a war machine and that politics is born within the ramparts of the city. Could you please elaborate on this idea about the relationship between the city, war and politics?

PV: To say that the city and war are linked is a euphemism. The city-state, polis, is constitutive for the type of conflict called war. Just as war itself is constitutive for the political form called the city-state. Although the nomads' tribal confrontations characterized a tactical antecedent of the conflict organized by sedentary societies, it is not until the rise of cities that true war emerges from the historical development of the city-states. Actually, political conflict lies not so much in the actual perpetration of war, but above all in its economic preparations. I would even say it is a strategic forewarning (the mayor of the polis is a strategist). This kind of military anticipation was primarily tied to the development of a 'theatre of operations': the training ground where the war would actually take place.

Just as the hunter's traps anticipated the movements and the bringing down of the game, so the war anticipates the soldiers' movements, their clashes, and finally their halts. This is why the urban territory, its borders and means of access are so significant as a 'training ground' within this strategic thinking that has been interwoven with the political thinking linked to the 'city leader' from the very beginning, he being at once the mayor and military leader in the antique city-state.

There are three major epochs in the history of real war: the tactical and prehistoric epoch, characterized by tumults and limited clashes; the strategic epoch, which is historical and purely political, and finally the logistic epoch, which is contemporary and transpolitical, where science and industry play a determining role in the destructive power of the armed forces. Likewise there are three major kinds of weapons that have succeeded one another in importance throughout the ages, in the military duel between 'offensive' and 'defensive': weapons of obstruction, destruction and communication. And to each of these types of weapons corresponds a certain kind of military confrontation: siege warfare, mobile warfare and blitz or total warfare, respectively.

NB: In respect to this close connection between the city, war, and politics, it would be interesting to reintroduce the problem of speed. Since the disappearance of the fortified castle played a crucial role in the fall of feudalism, one might wonder what happens to politics when speed is increased to the speed of light in the technologies of war, in the construction of the city, and in the constitution of political space. Is politics going to undergo just as profound a change today as that which caused the fall of feudalism?

PV: Until now societies have only used relative speeds: the horse, the ship, the train, or the automobile, the airplane. From now on, they will make use of the absolute speed of electromagnetic waves. There is thus the risk that the fall of feudalism will in the future be succeeded by the fall of democracy. The question is whether we can actually democratize ubiquitousness and instantaneity, which in fact are the prerogatives of providence, in other words, absolute autocracy? Today the tyranny of a dictator is being replaced by the tyranny of real time, which means that it is no longer possible to democratically share the time it takes to make decisions.

But let's go back in time, to the origin of the Greek city-state. Athenian democracy is also a dromocracy, a hierarchy of speed and not just of wealth. In 'The constitution of the Athenians,' a text dating from *c*. 430 B.C., it says that in Athens the people and the poor matter more than the noble and the wealthy, which is fair in that it is in fact the people who make the ships sail and who thus give the city-state its power. In contrast to Sparta, this is a maritime democracy, the power of Athens being primarily supported by ships and less so by infantry. Athens is, then, democratic, but also dromocratic, since those who make the ships sail are the ones who control the city. As opposed to traditional autocratic regimes, the sharing of power in Athens goes hand in hand with the physical power of displacement – which was never the case for antique knighthood, in particular *equites romani*. Likewise, in Venice both the spoils and speed were shared. Thus, the considerable political and cultural power attained by these two great historical cities literally stems from the propulsive capacity of a population completely involved in the great accelerating movement of history. Athens and Venice are both cities where civil rights are linked to the population's capacity for propulsion, while in land-based societies, where the cavalry predominates instead of the ship, it is the nobility that is dominant. And cavalry implies knighthood and feudalism, or the rejection of democracy. It is very surprising to see that of two vehicles, one animal and the other technical, one brings about democracy and the other forbids it. There are no democratic knights in the history of our societies.

But what exactly is democracy? Democracy is sharing. The sharing of what? It is not the sharing of money, it is the sharing of the decision from the beginning: we have the right to share the decision. But in contemporary societies decisions are made within incredibly short time limits. Once again, the revolution in the means of transportation and transmission brings about a speed in decision-making beyond democratic control. So today the question of democracy is not that it is threatened by some tyrant, but by the tyranny of technique. Allow me to exemplify this: the crash on Wall Street. What exactly is the automation of the quotations on Wall Street? The installation of an automatic quotation system that functions without human assistance and in real time poses the problem of decisions no longer being shared, since it is the machine that decides. This is an example taken from the stock market, but it is an example that indicates that a democracy in real time is almost impossible. Is democracy at all possible, that is, the control and sharing of a decision, when the time in which to make the decision is so short that there is no longer time for reflection? This is the big question today. In former societies and up until today, the possibility of sharing decisions existed because the societies were based on relative speeds. But as soon as societies start being based on the speed of light, what decision will remain to be shared if time can no longer be shared? Allow me to present another example. In the beginning there were supreme commanders. In democratic societies, there were captains, generals, and so forth, each with his own responsibility in war time. Little by little, as the time available for decision-making became shorter, the general staff was invented. And then with the atomic bomb, who is it that decides? Gorbachev and Bush are the final decision-makers in the end. Tomorrow these two men won't even be necessary, as the response will be automated, given by computer. This analysis demonstrates the degree to which using absolute speed instead of relative speeds threatens the very essence of democracy.

NB: Just a moment ago we spoke about a kind of immateriality in space. What is the relationship between politics and the immateriality of space. Is it reasonable to speak of the immaterialization of politics?

PV: Politics is the art of the possible – you must know the expression. But what is special about these technologies is that they are technologies of the impossible, of that which is impossible for humans. Humans may be considered to control them by implementing them, by conceiving of them, but once they are implemented they can no longer be controlled; the very speed of their operations eludes human control. This is why I protested so strongly against the picture of the Cruise missiles being fired and the people applauding. To me this is an insane picture.

   Returning to the expression 'politics is the art of the possible', this is about the connections between all of us, and here too proximity is

essential: in this expression it is still a question of a kind of fabric hold-
ing society together, and the real space of geography still predominates.
Then, suddenly, a world-wide society is conceived; the first major railways are commenced in Europe and later in the colonies, several isth-
muses have been pierced, the Suez and Panama canals, for instance.
This political utopia may be said to begin with the nineteenth century –
with the great theories, great megapolitical visions, including total war –
until the confrontation between East and West, or atomic deterrence
(which was no longer political). But the increasing importance of local
politics and the return of urban politics today is certainly a result of
technique having separated us too far from the political materiality of
real space in favour of the transpolitical immateriality of real time.

The intellectual

NB: In the 1980s, there was a lot of talk about the death of the intellectual,
and Lyotard has even written an epitaph for the intellectual. If I'm not
mistaken, at one of your conferences you yourself said that Sartre was
the last intellectual. Apparently, the role of the intellectual has undergone certain transformations. Why has this role changed? Can it be
explained by the fact that, that which has legitimized the intellectual –
Marxism and the idea of emancipation – seems to be compromised
today? This is Bernard-Henri Lévy's position in *Les Aventures de la
liberté* [1991]. Or should we look toward the themes we just discussed:
the profound transformations in perception and politics?

PV: When I say that Sartre is the last French intellectual – to remain in the
French context – it is because he is the last political activist. Contrary to
what most people think, in my opinion the intellectual was killed or dis-
credited by political activism. I think that the term intellectual was
invented at the time of the Dreyfus affair, that is, in respect to a particular issue. In my view, the intellectual did not start with the Dreyfus
affair, that is, with the intellectual as political activist, who defends an
individual, like Voltaire in the Calas affair. In order to do this it isn't
necessary to be an 'intellectual'. A political activist doesn't need to be an
intellectual, which has been evident for the past 200 years. Thinkers, be
they major or minor, have disqualified themselves by becoming enclosed
in political activism. To me the work of a thinker consists of his work, not
his opinions. To me opinions are nothing. So to consider opinions of primary importance is to disqualify the work. I could name many examples
of this. At the time of Voltaire, the work was of primary importance and
opinions were secondary; the Calas affair is not about what Voltaire did,
even if this is important. The decline of the intellectual stems from
the fact that he started considering his opinions to be of primary

importance, to the detriment of his work. In my opinion, the great intellectuals are Kepler, Copernicus and Galileo. I mention these names because I do more work in the field of physics than that of philosophy. So to me Galileo is a true intellectual, Einstein is a true intellectual, but not Sartre. And perhaps Sartre is in fact not a great enough philosopher and too great a political activist. Hence the decline. But Sartre is without doubt a great political activist, just like Raymond Aron, of course.

NB: But hasn't the intellectual always had a certain affinity with politics?

PV: But the work is political! Galileo's work is political. Copernicus's work is political. Einstein's work is political. Politics is not voting for, being against, giving moral lessons, no, it is the work. A true philosophical work is political. In this, we recognize the decline of politics: it is merely a game of meanings, a humanism in the most elementary sense. This is the true question. In my view, Galileo is a true politician; Copernicus is a true politician. They weren't just astronomers. To change our view of the world is to change politics.

This is also why I often avoid participating in various actions. I have participated, but I often avoid them by saying 'no, it is what I do that is political'. Reread *Speed and Politics*, it is more political than signing a petition. I hate those professors of crowds like Sartre, who position themselves on street corners and start speaking. I can give you a recent example of what I do. At the start of the hostilities between the Slovenians and the federal troops in Yugoslavia, a Slovenian student doing a research project on my work asked me if I would sign a petition. I said I wouldn't, after which he asked me if I would do an interview, which I didn't mind doing. So I was interviewed on the war, and the interview was published in a Slovenian newspaper in July 1991. I told him 'I'm not going to tell you what's right or wrong; first I'm going to talk about war and then about the civil war, and then you can do as you please. I'm not going to make any moral lessons, do as you please. If you want to destroy one another – do as in Beirut, Lebanon, and Ireland – that's your problem. I'm going to say something about war. I'm going to explain that the kind of war you make serves no political end, it has no real political objective; we are no longer in the epoch of Clausewitz, war is no longer the prolongation of politics by other means. That chapter is over, as the means surpass politics, invalidating it in a certain sense!' That is all I said, which is not political activism but part of my work. In other words, this is my kind of political activism, which is often misunderstood. Of course, I have an opinion, but I consider my work on war to be of primary importance. If, however, one signs a petition, certain people are going to make use of it to kill others. I believe this is one of the issues on which I have the most difficulty with my contemporaries; in our world opinions prevail over the work, over the interpretation; an interpretation is far more productive than an opinion. An interpretation based on consistent work, not something decided in five minutes and under the influence of one's emotions.

NB: So there are two kinds of political activism: street activism and conceptual activism?

PV: To be a conceptual activist means to produce concepts. This is true political activism.

Translated by Stacey Cozart.

Note

This interview originally appeared in 1991 in the Danish journal *Slagmark*, 18: 145–160. This is the first time it has been published in English.

6

THE INFORMATION BOMB:
A CONVERSATION

Interview with Friedrich Kittler

Speed, war and politics

PV: At the moment, are we not witnessing a tremendous hype around the Internet, cyberspace and the virtualization of everyday life? Concepts such as 'tele-shopping', for example, mean that people will no longer meet face to face, as in the city centres of old, but, instead, stay at home and shop from there. How do you respond to such developments? For me, as an urbanist, it is all profoundly disturbing.

FK: Such developments look like the outcome of a very remarkable and hidden strategy, one that is only now coming to fruition, after having been in the preparation stage for well over fifteen years. 1982, for example, saw the distribution of the first personal computers. That was their name even then. 'Lonesome cowboys' you'd put on an office table. However, they could do only one thing: write text. I emphasize the latter because somehow these devices have become better and better over the past few years and now they're going to swallow up all other media: the telephone, the telegraph, the fax, and, before long, images, sound and CDs too. And on top of that, you can wire them all together, worldwide, thanks to those wonderful networks. Thus, that very modest investment that sits on every third desk in the developed countries metamorphoses in a flash into a global information network. That's a really big spider and scares all other media to death.

PV: But doesn't the emergence of global information networks also mean that we have reached, in all possible senses, the frontier velocity of electromagnetic waves?

By this I mean that we have not only achieved the escape velocity that enables us to shoot satellites and people into orbit but also that we have hit the wall of acceleration. This means that world history, which has constantly accelerated from the age of the cavalry to the age of the railway, and from the age of the telephone to the age of radio and television, is now hitting the wall that stands at the limit of acceleration. The question is what happens to a society that stands at the limit point of acceleration? In past societies, for example, progress was predicated on the nature and development of their acceleration. Acceleration was not only related to speeds of memory and calculus, but also of action.

Today, though, one can no longer speak only of 'tele-vision.' One must also speak of 'tele-action'. To be 'interactive' means to be here, but to act somewhere else at the same time. And yet, I doubt whether the questions I am concerned with are being raised at all today. How many people, for instance, realise that a global historical accident has been triggered as consequence of this situation? For every time a new type of velocity is invented a new type of specific accident occurs. I'm always stating that when the railway was invented, derailment was invented too. Ships, like the *Titanic*, sink on a given day at a given place. However, since the invention of 'real time', we have created the accident of accidents, to speak with Epicurus. That means that historical time itself triggers the accident, as it reaches the frontier of the speed of light.

My impression is that what is being bandied about as the progress of communication is in fact merely a step backward, an unbelievable archaism. To reduce the world to one unique time, to one unique situation, because it has exhausted the possibility to devise new systems of acceleration, is an accident without precedent, a historical accident the like of which has never occurred before. Indeed, this is what Einstein called, very judiciously, 'the second bomb'. The first bomb was the atomic bomb, the second one is the information bomb, that is, the bomb that throws us into 'real time'. I believe that what people say about the performance of computing also applies to the faculty of looking at the world, to the faculty of shaping the world, of steering it, but also of living in it.

FK: Then probably the two dangers described by Einstein go hand in hand, historically and systematically. For instance, one of the trendy ideologies at the present time is that the new information technologies like the Internet are good for fast, efficient and global communication. But the truth is that both computers and atomic bombs are an outcome of the Second World War. Nobody ordered them. It was the strategic and military situation of the Second World War that brought them into being. Hence, they were not devised as communication tools but as a means of planning and conducting total war. And yet, none of this is currently admitted by the cyberspace ideologists in the USA, Europe, or Japan.

Even so, unlike you, I do not believe that the limit of acceleration has already been reached. For me, the catastrophe, so to speak, lies in the fact that while the current speeds of transmission and calculation cannot be upped much further, it is still possible to extract strategic and economic advantage from the possession of a system that is faster than one's competitor's. There is still a difference between secret machines and the machines sold on the market, and this difference is about performance and velocity. And it is still unclear where things are headed. The speed of light is indeed an absolute limit. But that is in a vacuum. However, in real existing technologies, electricity goes much slower than in a vacuum. Consequently, there still lie huge battles ahead in the realm of acceleration, with optical circuits replacing silicon and so on. These developments are going to mean acceleration with a factor of millions. Hence, I have some difficulty in seeing the accident develop already.

Yet I do believe that time as a relevant input is indeed eluding some people. To me, the urgent question is: how are culture and politics going to react to the slow demotion of their power? For both are predicated upon everyday speech and the normal human nervous system, which are both slow. However, neither speech nor the nervous system can be handled any more without machines preparing, assisting, and, in the end, even assuming some of their decision-making processes. How does one react to these developments, as a philosopher, as a politician?

Interactivity, information Chernobyl and imperialism

PV: You are totally right in pointing out that the origin of these technologies lies in the Second World War. Indeed, one must state that with the invention of the atomic bomb, something completely different got invented too, something that is presently in crisis by the way, and that is nuclear deterrence. Should we not say the same today in connection with the information bomb? Should we not say that interactivity is in some way a form of radioactivity? This is not a mere metaphor; it is a very concrete thing. Should we therefore consider a different form of deterrence for the next century? I don't mean military deterrence, which was about preventing the use of the atomic bomb, but social deterrence, which would be about preventing the damage caused by the progress of interactivity. Why? Because, for me, a global society founded on 'real time' is simply unthinkable ...

And yet, isn't interactivity already happening, so far as our working and home environments are concerned? Should we not attempt to prevent the consequences of this immediacy of action and information exchange? How will it affect the poor and the weak? Is a social deterrence of the global information society conceivable? For me, such developments carry the same risks as a Chernobyl-like catastrophe, with damaging consequences for people's way of life and for social relations. Aren't there signs already today of social disintegration? For instance, isn't structural unemployment an effect, or a type of fall-out following the explosion, of the information bomb? And this is only the beginning. What is your opinion on these social dimensions of the information bomb?

FK: Sure, the present mass unemployment is caused by the automation of production. I just have this vague feeling that sociologists and politicians are also to blame for the fact there is so much unemployment. For example, information technology is the only technology I know of that is radically reprogrammable. That is, it can constantly turn out new things, as opposed to the assembly line Henry Ford erected in Detroit, where one single make of automobile passed through for dozens of years. Thus, with this basic technology, which was really invented for the purpose of innovation, one could invent all the rest. However, our current conceptions of society and education mean that many people are systematically denied access to this technology. There is, then, an endemic computer illiteracy being created in society, through propaganda, advertising, and marketing strategies, and these prevent many people getting access to the technology. I am sure that today's hackers would not be able to find a job.

But that is an incomplete answer to your question. As far as an information-Chernobyl is concerned, it might already have happened once, in a primitive version, with the crash of the stock market in 1987. For such crashes show what the consequences are of the fact that, today, business takes place on a world-wide information network. To counter such developments measures are, of course, being taken. But what all this means is that the good old days when everybody could do whatever they wanted with their own computers are now firmly behind us.

We are all being controlled through our machines, and the more networked these machines become, the stricter the mechanisms of control and the safeguards will get. And this also holds true for the bureaucracies that are built into that system. At best, the Internet will remain a space of freedom for a year or two, but, within a few years, it will most probably have fallen into the hands of big capital, and then the controls will be put in place. The other danger is that, along with the control mechanisms, the informational bureaucracies – precisely in order to avoid an information Chernobyl – will also expand. Thus, together, big capital and the informational bureaucracies may well simply scuttle the liberalization of information. In other words, it is highly likely that a new hierarchy will be set up as counter to the danger of system collapse, and it will be structurally the same as the one that currently exists between the computer literate and the computer illiterate. Consequently, on one side there will be those who understand the codes, like the cryptographers and cryptologists in the Second World War. But, on the other side, there will be the masses in their billions who are shut out for security reasons.

PV: Of course, and every time technologies have been made speedier, economic accumulation and concentration have also taken place. Today, for example, we are witnessing a conglomerate gigantism, whether it is in the form of Time Warner or Bill Gates. We see monopolies arising from the demise of anti-trust legislation, and all these developments contribute to the centralization of command. At the very moment we are being told that the Internet is bringing us freedom in terms of place and time, we see that by sheer coincidence information trusts are emerging, world-wide conglomerates, which, incidentally, are no longer simple multinational corporations.

I am also wondering whether it is not the case that through this illusion of information-induced freedom a new uniformity is being implanted in a masked form. Something that, thanks to its multiformity, its way of thinking, and its culture, is implanted very easily. We know, for instance, how the medium, in whatever circumstances, devalues the information in the transfer from written text to screen text. We also know that the computer is making us poorer in spirit. For example, whether we want it to or not, the computer synthesizes information. Now, anyone who uses a synthesizer in music – let us say as a stand-in for a violin – knows very well that a real violin has a completely different sound from that of a synthesized violin. And yet, the computer is nothing but an information synthesizer. The content of information is being semantically reduced, something cognitivists know very well, by the way, and this, it seems to me, is something we should take note of. Unfortunately, these things pass unnoticed.

As usual, everything negative remains untold, yet it is, interestingly enough, always there, in an embryonic form. How is it possible to state that technologies are being developed, without any attempt being made at learning about the very specific accidents that go with them? And while this obviously holds true for the television, it holds true for multimedia technologies too.

FK: Probably one should act as Bill Gates does and sell things as if they were not what they are. You sell computers, but you tell people that they are desks, or desktops, or you tell them that they are television sets, the television sets of the future. That way, you can throw a thick mist around these devices and their system-specific shortcomings, and sell many of them. This is very much an American marketing strategy, and one may surmise from it that the drive towards trusts and conglomerates is possibly the last historic chance available for the Americans to maintain *Pax Americana* on the technological road. For example, after it had looked as if the technological advantage had moved to Japan in the 1970s, America succeeded in the early 1990s. But only by virtue of its edge in electronics and computers, and most prominently in its efforts to define the standards under which we are now communicating over the Internet and with other networked machines. The question is: are these standards the best in a human or a mathematical sense? These are two very important aspects. For example, standardization and unification are absolutely in tune with globalization, and it is quite baffling that nobody in Europe – no expert, no industry – is attempting, even in a small way, to question these new standards which are coming the way they do, and as they are, over the big pond.

Territory, time and technology

PV: For me, the new technologies make space disappear into a void, in its extent and in its time. This is a profound loss, whether one acknowledges it or not. There is also a pollution of the distances and time stretches that hitherto allowed one to live in one place and to have relationships with other people via face-to-face contact, and not through mediation in the form of tele-conferencing or on-line shopping. What is your opinion about this profound loss? Are we not calling an end to ourselves and to the spatial and temporal dimensions of the world this way?

FK: There is indeed a loss of space, because everything now takes place in the diminutive spaces of electronic circuits. But the ironic thing about all this is that I still have difficulty in realizing it, the fact that time has definitely contracted. One of my favourite games is to play with computer graphics. I take a small piece of the world, a very simple central perspective, write a program, and let it run. One picture, which takes a photographer the famous one-thirtieth of a second, will take 5 or 6 minutes of computation time on a very advanced computer. That is, it's only after those few minutes that the next picture will appear. The simulation, or synthesis of the images of the world is still not taking place in 'real time' at all. Look at the problems facing people who produce computer-generated films: they need 20 hours of computation time for one dinosaur, and then the thing walks across the screen for a measly 3 seconds. Here time is still very much a problem, and the historic moment, where the time of the world will really have been overtaken lies far, far ahead. That's what all these controversies are about.

As for the loss of proximity, I could live with that, in time. Let's take an example from real life again. It's no fun to spend your life with just three commands under the MS-DOS operating system, so you open directories, move them around and delete them. But as soon as you're under UNIX, from the start you're merely one person amidst 300 programs, of which you know ten at best. So during the first few months you get to know twenty programs, then forty, finally 100. You then discover that you're not alone any more. Rather, you live with 100 programs, of which you only need twenty, and then you also find that there are two or three programs you never needed to learn, because they're running in the background. These programs are called 'daemons', by the way, and they have a very bizarre proximity to the user. You never see them, and yet they're constantly doing something for you, like the angel in the mediaeval *Angelo Loci*. Indeed, I have this feeling that we should slowly let go of that old dream of sociologists, the one that says that society is by nature made up only of human beings. Today – and tomorrow – the term 'society' should include people and programs. There are, I think, already possibilities of proximity. Programs are not stupid. After all, it's why they were written in the first place. They are often more intelligent than your neighbour around the corner.

PV: Yes, but every new technical advance involves a loss of something. For example, the loss of social bonds is linked to the demise of the proximate human being. That is, someone who has a material existence, someone who might even smell bad, who might even be a boring nuisance. Now, though, one can simply zap such people away. The loss of proximity is one of the causes of the current crises in our cities. And yet there is always an actual place where one lives. But, today, it is not what is near that is privileged but what is far away. Indeed, it seems that the person on the computer screen is preferred to the person who is close at hand. This even extends to marriage. In so-called 'living apart together' relationships, for instance, men and women live in separate houses, as if they were already divorced. And the children get to learn, as a kind of aside, how to commute constantly between their mother and father. And that is only the beginning. Through 'cybersex' one can now have intercourse at a distance too. But aren't all these examples metaphors of decay? Are these not already an effect of the information bomb? This is how it seems to me, even if I am exaggerating. But who wouldn't exaggerate when faced with such developments?

I am convinced that, as with pointillism and divisionism in the arts of the nineteenth century, nuclear physics, the decay of matter, and, of course, fractal geometry have social consequences. That is, the decay of matter not only affects the social structure of the individual but also the reflexive relationship of the couple, the latter of which is the true basis of the evolution of human history. Why? Because demography is the founding element of history. This is significant, isn't it? I do not object to computer programs, but I wish the programmers would speak more of men and women. What is your opinion?

FK: Fractal geometry was invented with the aim of making Euclidean geometry somewhat more complex. Suddenly, we have a world that is no longer made up exclusively of straight lines and circles, but one consisting of curvatures and clouds. And all these beautiful things are very similar to human flesh, unlike, for example, the angular buildings of Le Corbusier or the somewhat complicated lines drawn by Phidias of Athens. However, although fractal geometry has always existed in principle, it only became calculable after the invention of the computer. Nevertheless, its complexity is nearer to human beings than Euclidean geometry.

Euclid's ideas resemble the process described by Foucault and yourself, in which young recruits were drilled and formed into battle lines in the eighteenth century. However, the new mathematics of chaos might very well turn out not to be a model that will necessarily break up couples but, rather, attend to the complexities of the individual. Similarly, the feedback theory could, potentially, attend to the relations within couples. Put bluntly, it seems to me that Freud's theory about the relationship between men and women is sillier than the theory Bateson elaborated on the grounds of feedback-chains. To be able to show that a two-way conversation is infinitely malleable seems to me to be a considerably more sophisticated description of social linkages than a description that relies on internalized images involving an incessant and lifelong struggle. Thus Bateson's feedback-based description of informational relations is evidently grounded in the techniques of message dispatching. And, when it was first advanced, it could not be derived from psychology.

The models that are available nowadays to describe complexity are better than the previous models. But why people – and I include myself here – would rather sit in front of a computer than do other things such as have a conversation is difficult to explain. Perhaps it is a fascination with power? For example, in earlier times, some people directed their love away from their wives and families and directed it instead towards an image of Jesus or Mary. Today some people direct their love toward new technologies. But whether it is the technology itself that sucks away our Eros, our libido, or whether it is the handiwork of the people who market it I am not so sure.

Technological fundamentalism, integration and social cybernetics

PV: I believe that a caste of 'technology monks' is being created in our times, and that there exist monasteries of sorts whose goal it is to pave the way for a new kind of 'civilization'; one that has nothing to do with civilization as we remember it. The work of these technology monks is not carried out in the way that it was in the Middle Ages. Rather, it is carried out through the revaluation of knowledge, like that achieved for Antiquity. The contribution of monks to the rediscovery of Antiquity is well known. But what is not well known is that we now have technology monks, not mystics, but monks who are busy constructing a society without any points of reference. Indeed, we are confronted with what I call 'technological fundamentalism'. That is, fundamentalism in the sense of a monotheism of information. No longer the monotheism of the Written Word, of the Koran, of the Bible, of the New Testament, but a monotheism of information in the widest sense of the term. And this information monotheism has come into being not simply in a totally independent manner but also free from any controversy. It is the outcome of an intelligence without reflection or past. And with information monotheism comes what I think of as the greatest danger of all, the slide into a future without humanity. I believe that violence, and even a kind of 'hyper violence', springs out of technological fundamentalism.

For example, at present, there is a lot of talk about the problems posed by the resurgence of militant Muslim fundamentalism. Bombs are planted and so on. But I believe that at the same time almost as much work is going into the development of the information bomb; a bomb that will have the same destructive effects on society's capacity to remember its past, a past that has a structure of its own and shapes the present. We are merely the product of what was. And whoever forgets the past is condemned to live it anew, as the saying goes. And yet this is exactly what is happening with new information and communications technologies. That said, I am not at all inimical to information. It is simply that there is not enough debate about the totalitarian dimensions of information. On the other hand, I do not think that it is appropriate to blame the technology monks for the sins of technological fundamentalism just because no one else takes responsibility for them. The technology monks do not always know about these sins. What's your opinion on the fundamentalist dimension of information?

FK: I totally agree. Of course, the people who are programming the whole thing are blissfully forgetful of the history of Europe, and the invention of printing and modern calculus which made it all possible. Both came more or less contemporaneously into being around 1450–1500. Book printing made it possible to copy and disseminate everything, and algebra made it possible to calculate everything. But these two things did not happen together. What was written still had the need of police action or the force of love to compel people to do what was described. But when you program, a real kind of 'integrism' appears. One does not simply write: what one writes, the program performs – period. And the final coming together of the promises of the printing press and those of modern mathematics, after 500 years of latency, represents infinite power: a true kind of integration in that all previously separated technologies – metallurgy, semiconductors and electricity – now merge together. It is difficult to say whether there is a limit to these developments. Indeed, I think this is the burning question of the moment.

Basically, there are but a few far-seeing scientists who say that the principle of digitization in itself is quite wonderful, but that there are inherent limits to its performance, which, therefore, gives the lie to all the marketing hype. These limits consist in the unremarkable fact that nature is not a computer, and that, therefore, a number of highly complex human phenomena, by their very nature, fall outside the scope of the current processing paradigms. This is, in fact, the only rational hope

I have that we have not arrived at the end of history. Because if the digital calculators did not have a kind of internal limitation, they would truly bring world history to an end, in all the aspects that you have mentioned: time would no longer be human time, space would no longer be human space, but merely a corridor within the circuits of these wonderful little machines. But if these little miracles themselves have constraints, then we can envisage without difficulty a twenty-second and a twenty-third century in which the principles of digital machines would not be discarded, but would instead be complemented by some sort of new – yet to be invented – principle.

PV: Isn't it time for those who build these machines, and who praise their merits, to get together and examine the damaging effects of information monotheism? For example, in 1888, the inventors of the European railway system met in Brussels. Why? Because the development of steam engines was progressing apace, and because the performance of locomotives was increasing rapidly, and the engineers were building more and more fantastic tunnels and more and more stable metallic bridges. But there was a problem: the train dispatching system could not keep pace with the increasing performances of the machines. That's why they met in Brussels and also why they created what is nowadays called controlled traffic management. The so-called 'block system' was devised there. Thus, if the TGV [high-speed train] runs smoothly nowadays, it is because there is an automatic block system and because the position of the signals is repeated in the train driver's cab. This means that there are hardly any train accidents any more. The starting point of the discussions in Brussels was on the negative, on what did not function. Contact switches and signals were devised, and these became the basis of a very sophisticated form of data management. But why are there no conferences nowadays on the damaging consequences of unemployment? On the wrong turns taken by urbanism? On the obverse side of technical progress? Why don't we busy ourselves today, just like the engineers of the nineteenth century did, with the specific accidental risks of the railways, that is, the derailment. Why don't we busy ourselves with the specific – albeit, I admit, immaterial – danger posed by the data networks and the arrival of social cybernetics? If I am not mistaken, I think that both Alan Turing and Norbert Wiener feared the application of cybernetics on society? And now we are being told by politicians like Ross Perrot that social cybernetics is not only progress but the apex of democracy!

It seems to me that it is about time that the people who are working on those programs start implementing a counter-program also, in order to put a limit to these sorts of developments. Why, for example, don't they apply their intelligence to the negative aspects of technological development? Why do they always conceal the original sins of these techniques, whereas shipbuilding was furthered by making ships water-proof, and the aeronautic industry was furthered by making engines and the monitoring of air space more reliable. Why don't we have such people in the realm of digitization?

FK: I have only one answer and it is a totally idiosyncratic one. As is often revealed when accidents take place, many firms are made up of one-half engineers and one-half non-technical sales people, such as marketing executives and lawyers. The spokespersons for such firms are always attorneys, with a smattering of MIT professors every now and then. I do not know of any large company where things are in the hands of the people who devise the computer program. Thus the people who devise the program, and who also know what is wrong with computer systems, are basically treated as program slaves. I am sorry to use this term but that is what they are called in the industry itself. However, the people who are in charge of corporate propaganda, the people who actually own the firms, like Bill Gates at Microsoft, have written maybe five pages in the last twenty years, and that is it. This social division precludes discussions about negativity. The people whom you quoted earlier are in fact free academics. They think like physicists but they don't work for the computer industry. Nevertheless, it is very important to discuss these matters with the people who plan, build and operate computer systems.

Information, catastrophe and violence

PV: Why not discuss them in Brussels then? After all, the block system conference took place in Brussels. I think that you have put your finger on what this is all about: commercial enterprise. But information cannot be allowed to become a commercial enterprise. It is the stuff the world is made of. For example, what we are doing right now has nothing to do with entrepreneurship; it is a dialogue, a conversation. How can one possibly limit the question of information to the realm of the commercial enterprise? Worse still, to enterprises that are evolving into absolute monopolies? We are facing the tyranny of real-time information. But information should be a product of everyday usage, like electricity. We are a phenomenon of matter, of its mass and energy. That is, we constitute, *sui generis*, history and existence. To be is to speak. Is not the Latin word for infant 'the one who does not speak'? Now, information is being turned into a product of global enterprises. It is a tragedy that is being sold to us as progress. It makes me angry, especially when I think that Europe is not taking any action on these issues at the moment. For instance, when those who are responsible for the licensing of new computer products met in Brussels in 1994 they were totally enthusiastic for the new systems and products. And those who went there in order to plead for a more sceptical approach were treated as if they were a nuisance. And that happens in the place where European information policies are supposed to be created and implemented.

FK: That is the catastrophe. For are we not talking about the amalgamation of an old definition of copyright, dating from the times of Goethe, with the property rights of intellectual products which have arrived with the invention of the new digital machines? In fact, this most recent definition of copyright not only does away with any kind of author's right but also with any form of 'spiritual' property. Why? Because the new machines can imitate any other machine, and that includes us, in so far as they can imitate our thinking. Thinking machines were of course a gift from England and invented shortly before the war by Turing. His ideas were then imported into the United States, and the big question there was: how can we make a profitable proposition out of this? Well, it looks like they have been tremendously successful over the past fifty or sixty years.

The most scandalous piece of news that has reached me recently is that it has become possible in the US to patent mathematical equations. For 2,000 years such acts were prohibited. Indeed, mathematics was the freest of all sciences and fell outside the scope of patents. But if American concerns succeed in having the European 'author's right' modified to suit their own ends, then exactly the opposite will have been achieved than what was intended by people like Turing. This is a real menace. Information cannot be allowed to be privatized. However, I do not believe that the privatization strategy will hold out in the long run. This is because the machines are proliferating out of control. Consequently, the software cannot, in the end, be protected by patents. And nor should it be in the long run. So far as the hardware is concerned, the machines as such, well, everybody knows that the manufacturing costs are going down all the time. The result of this will be that, in ten years time, what are now the absolute top-notch machines will be had for almost nothing. In short, we may not get informational democracy right away, but we may get zero-cost property soon.

PV: Perhaps, then, instead of looking at these issues from a pessimistic standpoint, we should conclude our conversation by looking at them from a more optimistic one? But this is difficult. For have we not attempted, amidst all the current enthusiasm for tele-technologies, to formulate our critical thinking about their future? However, let us not focus here on the future of the marketization of these products, or on the future of information monopolies, but, rather, on the future development of the machine. Why? Because its development does not run parallel with the sale of computers but with the evolution of its own performance. And the evolution of machine performance, as you said, is predicated upon the recognition of the damaging effects of negativity. We should therefore warn people against the archaic instincts of those who pretend to create a global realm of information without bothering to analyse to what extent the reduction of content has destructive consequences. Of course, these consequences not only impact upon small firms and on the millions of people who remain unemployed. They impact upon the actual creation and historical development of human beings themselves, not to mention the development of social thought. And therein lies the key regulative element. For the human memory is not merely the dead memory of the computer hard drive but the living memory of human beings. And without living human memory there is only the violence revealed by the explosion of the information bomb ...

Translated by Patrice Riemens.

PART FOUR

ON ART, TECHNOCULTURE
AND THE INTEGRAL ACCIDENT

7

PAUL VIRILIO

Interview with Jérôme Sans

JS: Your approach to reality is mediated by the concept of 'dromology', which would appear to lie at the center of your work.

PV: Dromology is the science or the logic of speed and you're quite right to see it as the core of my work since the problem of speed opens our way into the entirety of the contemporary world and offers a key for reading it; the notion of speed is an incomparable analytic instrument for dealing with its political, strategic and social situations, and with others as well. When I wrote 'The Logistics of Perception' [*War and Cinema*, 1984/1989], where I talk about war and cinema, people thought that I went outside the field of my subject by bringing up cinema, which is a question of the cinematics of the image, just as I'm interested in the cinematics of the automobile. I am just as much interested in motorized vehicles – automobiles, planes, armoured cars, or motorcycles – as I am in the audiovisual speed of cinema, video and tomorrow's infography: in everything where you find the phenomenon of acceleration. In our situations of televisual experience, we are living in nothing less than the sphere of Einstein's relativity, which wasn't at all the case at the time that he wrote it since that was a world of trolley cars, trains and at most the rocket. But we live today in a space of relativity and non-separability. Our image of time is an image of instantaneity and ubiquity. And there's a stunning, general lack of understanding of speed, a lack of awareness of the essence of speed.

JS: With respect to our notions of duration, instantaneity has today re-placed the idea of chronology and thinking in terms of centuries …

PV: As I see it, we've passed from the extended time of centuries and from the chronology of history to a time that will continue to grow ever more intensive: infinitely tiny partitions of time contain the equivalent of what used to be contained in the infinite greatness of historical time. The entirety of our history is now being written at the speed of light, which is to say in nanoseconds, picoseconds and femtoseconds whereas the organization of time was previously based on hours and minutes. We no longer live even in a world of seconds; we live in a world of infinitely tiny units of time. And this passage from an extensive to an intensive time will have considerable impact on all the various aspects of the conditions of our society: it leads to a radical reorganization both of our social mores and of our image of the world. This is the source of the feeling that we're faced with an epoch in many ways comparable to the Renaissance: it's an epoch in which the real world and our image of the world no longer coincide. The world has already experienced epochs of transition, and I believe that we're in the midst of another one.

JS: Would you agree that this new notion of time contains a feeling of urgency, a little like the idea in *L'Homme pressé*? [1941 Paul Morand. Paris: Gallimard]

PV: Yes, except that Paul Morand is first of all concerned with automobile speeds, the speeds of the dandy who's in love with speed. That's not a world of stress. But the world we actually live in is a world of violent collisions and a universe of audiovisual speeds, no longer simply the speed of the automobile. To put things simply, we can say that there are four kinds of speed: the metabolic speed of the body, the emotions and the reflexes (we could also call it animal speed); then there's technological speed; we also have the automobile speed of the motors that come to replace the modes of transport where we make use of animals; and I'd say that audiovisual speed comes to replace human perception and human reflexes. And, of course, there are couplings between metabolic speed and automotive vehicles and all the problems of cognition and feedback. We can also talk about the coupling between audiovisual speeds and the instantaneity of reflexes and all of the drug effects that aren't simply a question of chemical hallucinogens but rather of hallucinatory effects connected to television, video clips and the acceleration of the passage of image sequences (60 images per second ...). You see it again in economy: all of these monetary fluctuations are connected to a constant impacting and telescoping of values that can never be stabilized because the entirety of the world is everywhere co-present. It's enough to see how the recent crack on the New York Stock Exchange has to be connected with the famous technique of 'program trading' where programmed computers are doing automatic buying and selling.

JS: Would you say that this rupture between image and reality implies that there is not one reality, but several?

PV: What's certain is that our current troubles of perception – which we experience both individually and at the level of what Baudrillard would speak of as transsexual or transpolitical mores – result from the fact that reality and our images of reality no longer connect with one another. But some people argue that reality no longer exists and other people table a debate on the disappearance of all images of reality. And that, as I see it, is where the situation looks ugly. I think that there are generations of realities – just as there are demographic or cultural generations – even if they succeed each other less rapidly. There is no longer any single reality that we can think of as given once and for all. Even if a mountain is always where it was, and even if stone is still stone, the ways in which we perceive them have been constantly changing since the beginning of time. So generations of realities are connected to generations of images, starting from the prehistoric cave paintings up until hyper-realism and the painting of the present, passing through Picasso along the way. It's clear that we are currently in a period of substitutions. One generation of reality is in the process of substituting itself for another and is still uncertain about how to represent itself. And we have to understand that it is very much connected to real-time images. It's not a problem of the configuration or the semiotics of the image, but a problem of the temporality of the image. When Walter Benjamin talks about 'the image in the era of its technical reproducibility', I adopt his idea of 'technical reproducibility' in a way that's different from what he intended. He was talking about the serial production of photographic images, or about series of photographs, but I find it necessary to think about photograms, or film frames, or about videograms, which participate in extremely short units of time that no longer have anything to do with photography and posing, nor even with snap-shots. I'm talking about the times and images that have been created by cinema. But no one is any longer satisfied by any of the possible representations; we have a crisis of reality itself, which in any case has turned into something transitory.

And my position is very different from Baudrillard's since what I see isn't simulation but substitution. Let's take light for example. The discovery of fire and the invention of electricity were thought of as spectacle and as a simulation of the sun. But is there anyone today who thinks about the sun when he sees an electric light? All of the phenomena of representation – video and even infography and holography – will end up being banalized in much the same way and will no longer rank as instruments or elements of art. This explains my interest in a video-maker like Michael Klier; in films like *Le Géant* he gives us back-to-back mountings of images of airports or empty streets, and it seems less a question of cinema than of lighting. And what you've got your hands on is a phenomenon of substitution that's equivalent to the replacement of natural light by electric light in farm economies. I work with substitutions, which is to say with series, and I'm not at all interested in hero-worshipping the sublime or in having any similar sort of attitude to simulacra. Here I don't at all see eye to eye with Baudrillard. Since I'm an urbanist as well as a war specialist, the things I take seriously are phases rather than objects. And perhaps because the military question has long since come to terms with the problem of the simulacrum: those demonstrative war threats that so often slip over into tragic replacements of themselves with the real thing. This is to say that reality is never simply given and is always generated by the technologies and modes of development of a society at any given moment of its history. And in this respect, speed is an element of representation: it serves functions of vision and not of forward motion. A particle accelerator is thus the equivalent of a telescope.

JS: But one could also say that the speed with which images succeed one another in our present universe doesn't at all serve the purpose of helping us to see, and helps us in fact to avoid it.

PV: That's because we haven't given proper attention to the phenomenon of substitution, which is to talk about the esthetics of disappearance as opposed to the esthetics of appearance or emergence that lies at the origins of art, at the origins of representation. Figures emerge, solidify and grow fixed. A sculpted stone is finally fixed into something static, and into the persistence of its materials. The same thing is true of paintings, photography and works on paper ... But starting in the nineteenth century, and most of all, generally speaking, from the invention of instantaneous photography – which was to create the possibility of film, or of the photographic film frame – our esthetic has ceased to be the esthetics of retinal persistence. This is a phenomenon of substitution, and we have a passage from something material to something that isn't: we move into the area of the mental persistence of the image. Things exist all the better and are all the more animated to the degree that they disappear. Their disappearance is responsible for their presence, just as their power was formerly a question of their stability and solidity and of the persistence of the materials of which they were made. For an example, we can think of the pyramids.

JS: But what's the vehicle for these images?

PV: Images are no longer something to be interpreted. Just as artifical electrical light has been ousted from all artistic function so as to assume another function that's practical and elementary, images have become a new form of light, but it's a question of lights that we can't yet understand since we're still attracted by their spectacularity. And that's particularly true for video, television, and even for cinema, which is now in its death throes for precisely this reason. These images are the vehicle of something that we haven't yet analysed: the final stage of artificial light. We're still taken in by all the little broadcasts, whereas the only broadcasting that corresponds to what I'm talking about, and that ranks as something *avant-garde*, is Ted Turner's Cable News Network, which is 24 hours a day of live information broadcast by satellite and without even so much as a pretense of interpretation. You can't think of it as a newspaper. It's a window, what I've referred to as 'the third window'. You have to be something of an architect to say a thing like that, an architect who has also worked as a glass cutter. I'm aware of just how little the discipline of architecture, in the truest sense of the term, can exist without a mastery of light. And it's clear that these new images have functions of illumination. That's why I'm now working on architecture and images taken together.

JS: All the same, I still have the feeling that it's impossible today to talk about images without talking about blindness.

PV: Yes, that's quite true. Darkness, or obscurity, is what I talk about as 'image block'. No image can exist independently of others, and this sense of sequentiality is something I find interesting. Images are always interconnected: there's the mental image, the ocular image, the optical image, which is the one you correct with glasses, and then the graphic or pictorial image as well as the photographic, cinematographic, videographic and infographic image. These eight images constitute an entirely opaque block that totally conceals reality since we haven't sufficiently investigated what they are. The interconnections between these images have never been dealt with. Film-makers, video-makers, people in graphics, artists and infographists are all off working in their separate corners. Each group finally manages to catch a particular little image in its teeth, but without understanding that this whole block of images is what forms the new world and all the new unknowns, and that we absolutely have to face up to it if we want to see what it's about. We need serious analyses through means that belong as much to the physiologist where mental images are concerned as to the new technological chemistry of hallucinations ... This blindness comes less from images – which in their own way are certainly blinding – than from our blindness with respect to their interrelations. I have never admitted that when I advance towards a tree, the tree seems to advance towards me. That's the very basis of dromoscopy. It's clear that one has already touched a mystery here, and it's something that holds for all images. So there's a need for real analysis instead of all these quarrels about hyper-reality, abstraction and graffiti-ism ... That sort of thing may be worthwhile for art dealers, but there are better things to be involved with and to do. The image has become the world. That's why I talk about a block. They make up the world, and they're on the way to shutting it down. Thanks to the satellites, the surface of the world is now totally known to us, but the images that serve us by allowing us to look at the world have become just as unknown as the unveiled world itself. The unknown has shifted position: from the world, which was far too vast, mysterious and savage, it has not moved on to take its place among these images, which have grown far too large and disturbing ... The explorers who are ready and able to analyse them are very rare, even though you can spy out the beginnings of something. Scientists, artists, philosophers ... we find ourselves in a kind of 'new alliance' for the exploration of the nebular galaxy of the image. Images always and necessarily exist in relationship to a recognized reality. And a reality is a language that people share. People with different realities can't communicate with one another. It's the image that allows the sharing of a reality. But now we have this great opaque block that no one can share. Everybody has a piece of it. Nobody understands that he has to put his piece in a common pot, and that he has to try to enter that sphere of reciprocity and intelligence that made for the phenomenon of the Renaissance, in which everyone could participate. Even before being a question of the organization and geometrical perfecting of the city, the Renaissance was first of all a question of organizing a way of seeing. It's enough to read *L'Oeil de Quattrocento*.

JS: You also talk about the decline of writing and see that this benefits orality and the image.

PV: Yes. You get into the sphere of a kind of pathology of the image as a result of the blindness you were talking about before, and that too is pathological. It's clear that the greatest damage yet done to reading and writing is that contemporary readers have now generally become incapable of forming mental images on the basis of the written word. They're in the habit of having images that replace interpretation. These are images without interpretation and they stun you like a blinding light, so they have damaged people's ability to create mental images, to make their own cinema in their heads. There's a defect in literary representation: its images don't constitute figures. And the decline of writing comes principally from the fact that graphic, photographic and videographic images have replaced mental images.

JS: You frequently take part in discussions of the new technologies, including infography ...

PV: I simply try to be something of an equivalent to Apollinaire in his meetings with painters, except that I don't pretend to have his talent. I try to get film-makers and video-makers together … and I take the floor for the ones who are absent. This seems to me an urgent thing to do. What I'm trying to show is the really powerful character of the images that are produced just about everywhere around us and that nobody is analysing. Because images have become munitions. Their delivery and their impact have the same speeds as the impact of a bullet. The arms of the future will much more resemble a TV than a mortar. An electron cannon is very close to the kinds of cannons of charged particles that are likely to get installed for the 'Star Wars' [SDI] program. Images don't at all disarm me. Quite the contrary. I think I've made a certain contribution to the demystification of militaristic cinema, the films like *Apocalypse Now, Platoon*, or the most recent film by Kubrick, these various films that I have written about. The essential question, however, has nothing to do with the genre of the war film, which is just as *passé* as the western; it's rather a question of the ways in which war is fought by means of cinema or video, or with the infography of tomorrow. Simply to have given realization to something doesn't yet mean that you know what it is. An engineer is fooling himself if he says, 'I built that object from top to bottom, therefore I have mastered it.' That's the essential philosophical question, and it's what we're talking about when we talk about the problem of the image.

JS: You have written, 'After the nuclear disintegration of the space of matter, we have finally arrived at the territory of the time of light.'

PV: You've found the most important phrase in the whole text. And it's not a metaphor. We're absolutely in touch with the question of relativity, and of quantum non-separability. We live in a world where everything is always copresent, a world without determinisms, where before and afterwards no longer make any sense, and where our gaze, the very fact of observation, is what creates effects. For the physicist of quantum mechanics, there is no longer any possibility of reaching the reality of matter since measuring it means necessarily to disrupt it. The simple fact of looking into a test tube means to modify what takes place inside it. We have a world of mysteries and enigmas. And the same thing that happens with the test tube takes place with television, where there's the problem of telepresence and live broadcasting. Live or direct television broadcasting is a quantic phenomenon. The notion of real time brings us into the midst of a revolution of the image. Live broadcasting is one of the greatest enigmas of present time and of reality in general. What can a tele-reality at a distance amount to? One is no longer simply a spectator; that's already old hat, one is also a tele-actor. That's an unheard-of phenomenon, a fissional phenomenon like the splitting of the atom, but here what's being split is reality. All the same, this isn't to say that one won't be capable of reconstructing a reality through the new images of tomorrow. It's enough to read that remarkable book by the physicist David Bohm, *The Plenitude of the Universe*, where he talks about the possibility of a non-Copernican representation of reality.

Translated by Henry Martin.

© 1988 *Flash Art* and Paul Virilio. Interview with Jérôme Sans, in *Flash Art*, International Edition 138, January–February 1988. © 1988 translation by Henry Martin.

8

PAUL VIRILIO

Interview with Dominique Joubert
and Christiane Carlut

DJ: How does the poster fit into the city?

PV: The city and the poster work together just as public images work with public spaces. The idea of 'public' and the corresponding idea of publicity are interconnected. This is an important theme today. Just as there exists a logistics in military thinking that is used to reach targets,[1] there is also a logistics in urban perception, i.e., with the effect of the message: the city declares itself through its monuments, but also through signs, inscriptions and posters. Public areas need to be marked and signposted, and I think that the problem of urban signposting is a fundamental element of a city. There are no signs in the countryside, there are just different atmospheres; I was going to say moods. As Amiel wrote, 'A landscape is a mood'. On the other hand, the city needs signs for orientation. It is a labyrinth. How to get around? There are the names of the squares, streets, and of course, large printed panels, which also include publicity. In Tokyo, for example, publicity comes as a welcome sight, because there are no other references for us. We do not understand the language, we don't recognize the signs or the numbers, but we still need to have some references. During the invasion of Czechoslovakia, the citizens of Prague undertook the first non-violent defense of the city by removing all the street signs and building numbers so that the foreigners could not tell where they were. Residents have a mental image of their city; they don't need signs. Foreigners, on the other hand, invaders, need these signposts. By obliterating these, they were defending the citizens. We can thus see the indicative function of a city, a function inherent to the urban environment and I would say to the citizens also. And this leads to democracy. There is no democracy without information. And no business without communication. I mean business in the widest possible sense, not just in terms of sales, but also in terms of the business of communication between individuals.

We see this today with the problems of television, with the risks of abuse and manipulation of opinion. Withholding information, excess

information and misinformation can damage democracy, but an excess
of publicity can, I would say, ruin business, in other words, ruin the
message.

DJ: And your personal experience in poster art?

PV: When I was young, 16 or 17 years old and needed money, I painted
movie posters. At that time, I became interested in the great poster
designers of the period: Paul Colin, Cappiello and Cassandre. For me,
these poster designers were mural painters.

Another important element that marked me: I saw the Affiche Rouge
in Nantes during the war. I saw it with my own eyes and I have not forgotten it. This brings up the question of war. War is also declared through
propaganda and through mobilization. For me, the poster was an indi-
cation, not only in terms of space, but also of time. The time of peace
was over; the time of war was about to begin, with all its atrocities.

Now we were moving towards publicity, image and graphic design.
Mural paintings were starting to be widely used. We could see the older
walls with advertisements for shoes and health products, with 'Lion
Noir' wax and 'Bébé Cadum' soaps. The newer paintings referred to the
automobile. Today, we no longer see this revolution in transportation;
we are now living in the era of transmission: Sony, Toshiba.

Going back to the era that popularized speed through the automobile
and train (employer-paid travel): these no longer addressed Paul Morand,
the automobile dandy, but a wider audience, through the democratiza-
tion of speed. Here again, the great posters were curiously associated
with the theme of transportation: the masterful poster for L'Étoile du
Nord [a train] and the other for *Transatlantique* [an ocean liner] were
exceptional examples of graphic art, almost Futuristic in style.

And then came stylization. The word has been forgotten. Stylization
at the time meant reducing an image to its simplest possible expression.
The posters were stylized. And that obviously influenced painting. It
was, I would say, a conventional mode of expression. The signposting
required in a city also seemed to be necessary in the image. The image
was no longer expressed in terms of an extraordinary realism, but instead
used its own method of identification. Graphic design began using sym-
bols. As young designers and painters, I remember we discussed a great
deal and we stylized! Our language was stylization. But for me, stylization and the use of signs were beginning to go hand in hand.

We then moved from a stable image to an unstable, rotating one, in
other words, where an image hid several others. And this led to sequences. The fixed, centered and traditional composition led to the animated
images of movie advertisements. For example, the image I painted for
Samson and Delilah, which represents Victor Mature pushing aside the

columns of the temple, also included photographs of the film below it. We could only consider the image by looking at the photographs of the film. We had to reinterpret the dynamics; it was not possible to simply take an image and enlarge it. The poster had to inspire some feeling: thus the choice of the falling temple for this movie. I therefore felt this change from a stable composition to an unstable one, right up to contemporary video clips, a change that has had an influence on the fixed image. There is always an interactive effect that occurs between a fixed image and an animated image, one always moving towards the other.

Something else interested me at the time, but for political and archaeological reasons: the Agit/Prop trains of the Russian revolution. The animated image, Vertov and so forth were also reflected in the painted trains. With names such as 'Long Live Lenin' or 'Red October', they carried the communist propaganda throughout the countryside, operating as an animated sequence that unfolded before the eyes of the peasants. Today we have advertising trucks driving through the streets and others that stop on highway overpasses so that they can be seen by more people. This is a continuation of the Agit/Prop. These elements lead directly to political publicity, to Dasibao and finally to graffiti artists, who also create a form of publicity. We are told that graffiti is a form of territorial marking, but I think we accept the American definition too readily. It is essentially an exhibition, that's why we can talk about it as an art, and not as terrorism.

We now come to publicity and poster art. There is a close link between the two. And here we have an incredible figure, a key personality: René Magritte. Magritte created advertisements. I found them: 'Mem' perfumes (that create the sound of 'm'aime', or 'love me'); some very beautiful posters for the Samuel furriers in Belgium; and following the First World War, publicity for the Chenard & Walker automobiles, signed 'René Magritte, 1918'. Magritte was inspired by the advertising and his work, in return, inspired future publicity efforts.[2]

CC: What about the question of ethics? A specific code of ethics for the graphic designer? One of our first exhibitions tried to define the terms of creative graphic design, which would oppose international marketing strategies.

PV: I am not a moralist, but I think this is a valid question. It is especially important now, where in the United States people are starting to talk about politically correct speech! Which seems to me absolutely monstrous! It is true, there is a risk of creating a politically correct look. There is thus an ocular training that began with religious prohibitions, which now has been extended to a manipulation of the eye, through the industrialization of vision. A sequence is a series of cuts and montages and is more than just the composition of the story. It also immediately involves the mentality of the individual who has been trained to see. We can see this clearly in contemporary movies with the violence of the 'cut' montages, with telescoping sequences, and so on. The eye has become somewhat accustomed to a violent montage, which to a certain extent seems to industrialize our vision. For me, painters and perspectivists contributed to a geometric vision, but in terms of the art and craft of vision. It has now become automated. In other words, vision is a kind of motor-driven response that moves through clips and synthesized images. There is virtually a mobilization of vision and therefore a way of training the spectator to see against his own will – and there is no need to insert any subliminal messages for this. This is not a mobilization for a specific message but for the intensity of a message, which can be compared to the excesses of alcoholism or drug abuse. There now exists a drug for the eyes: 'Cyberspaces', in which people 'shoot up' virtual images. We are told that it is less serious than hallucinogens, but I can't believe it.

With vision machines, it is possible, through the use of expert systems, to create a certain vision, a vision without regard for machines. Machine vision has therefore been developed through the automation of perception, by connecting a computer to a shape recognition camera. But at the same time, human vision has been somewhat twisted by these systems, which are systems of ocular training and rhythmic training. This training is accomplished through the use of a rhythm. The use of signs does not only involve images and lines; it also includes the intensity of the message speed, cuts and so forth. To what purpose? And what kind of training of humanity?

CC: In *Dialectique négative* Adorno wrote, 'Every step towards communication cheapens and falsifies the truth'.

PV: Simplification through signs is widespread. We started by saying that signposting is, in fact, the city, and as the city, is the power: signs are everywhere. They are in every position of power, be it religious, military or social power, in the sense of a communication through proximity. There is always a simplification of the content; communication occurs through simplification. An aesthetic in which meaning disappears also facilitates meaning, but it is a simplified one; there is always a loss.

DJ: Does this mean the disappearance of aesthetics?

PV: I don't think so, I hope not. More specifically, the aesthetics of disappearance is linked to visual phenomena. I believe that aesthetics began to disappear with the invention of photography, and of course, with instant photographs, when a cinematographic sequence could be made. The subject takes on a greater presence as it disappears. Movies add a considerable and hallucinatory presence to an image, because it is a fleeting medium. A stable image, one I would say that exists in its medium – paint or sculpture – in the persistence of the material, exists through its permanence, even the relative permanence of a painting or drawing. Yet with photography, followed by the framed sequence, the opposite is true: the permanence is cognitive and ocular; objects are retained in the memory or in a mental image, but do not remain elsewhere. They are made to live on in the mind. They are therefore cognitive.

DJ: Yet poster art is a craft. As long as there are walls, there will be posters.

PV: I'm not so sure. Walls are gradually being transformed into screens. There is a change in façades, which in the past were covered with sculptures. The first posters were the bas-reliefs, Roman or Egyptian sculptures, followed later by frescoes or mosaics, then advertising panels. Increasingly, screens have been incorporated into buildings, particularly in Japan, where they function as posters. Thus, just like in *Blade Runner*, a film that presents the city of the future quite well, we already have façades that talk and are animated: video façades.

CC: Now I would like to discuss the development of poster art in relation to new technologies. McLuhan predicted the disappearance of writing, which would be replaced by the audiovisual media. Yet we can see that writing has not disappeared, no more than the traditional media of poster art.

PV: The aesthetic of disappearance does not mean the disappearance of aesthetics. It is, rather, the dynamic that changes. We have to consider a new element here, which is the sense of touch. Up to now, we have had sound and visual, or audiovisual images, if you like. The new technologies that encompass teletactility, telepresence, mean that we can now touch things that aren't there. I am surprised to see to what extent tactile advertising is developing; in other words, objects that can be touched, that can be appropriated. I therefore think that there is a third dimension to advertising that is taking shape, a tactile preparation that goes hand in hand with the behavioral changes in relationships with others. This said, virtual images do not represent the death of the image. Every real image has a dual identity. We cannot compare a virtual image with a real image. Philosophically it must be compared to the existing image: the real is composed of the existing image and the virtual one. 'Real' is an overused word; we have forgotten it. We are told that the virtual stands in opposition to the real. Not so. The virtual is as real as the existing image, it simply does not 'appear' in the same way. I think that virtual images are in the process of winning out over real images. For example, a real image is a graphic output from a computer while a virtual image is produced on a screen. The virtual image is the image of dreams or the mental image. Thus I think that there is a shift in the supremacy, in the primacy of the real image, in favor of the virtual image. In the past, the opposite was true.

CC: Independent graphic artists give priority to autonomous work and reflection. Moreover, this involves the idea of a personal commitment and the development of a personal image. Do you see such a marked dichotomy or does it seem to you that these two elements are inter-linked?

PV: Personally I believe that one of the dangers we are facing today is auto-mation. The man/machine interface is replacing dialogue, business. All are in the process of losing the man/man dialogue in favor of the man/machine dialogue. I believe this is serious; the automatic vending machines and dispensers are prime examples. The vending machine does not need any publicity. It merely tells you to push here; you put in 10 francs there and you get a sack of peanuts. Advertising is designed to bring people to the market, to the shops. It attracts in the same way as a man or a woman attracts. It demands attention, it beckons – the sign/function as described by Roland Barthes – it flirts. The vending machine does not have to flirt. You press a button and are rewarded just like a laboratory rat: it either gets an electrical shock or a peanut. I believe that there is a loss in the human interface, in the sign/function, a loss to automatic vending machines, to answering machines.

Speaking of this, I have a joke from the 1950s, from the poster era I was speaking about earlier, which I believe is highly revealing. In the year 2000 – in the 1950s, the year 2000 represented something marvellous – the telephone rings in an apartment. Someone picks up the phone and hears on the other end, 'Hello, what's calling please'? Forty years later, this joke is still relevant.

In conclusion, we can determine four elements: the sign, the writing, the logo and the slogan. 'Slogan' means 'war cry'. Thus, the image has replaced the text, at least until the rapid image sequence replaces the image itself. A phenomenon that I call 'the aesthetic of disappearance', already exists in stable images, unstable then accelerated images, and in video advertisements, clips and even certain types of graphic techniques

(I'm thinking of soft-focus photographs which are used increasingly, about accelerated photographs in which we can see nothing). This is thus an important element. The logo and slogan are neither a kind of writing, nor a kind of cry, nor a type of sign. They are disappearing: this is the aesthetics of disappearance. Achievement has been severed from perception, which creates the power of the message's effect. I think that the key phrase, which is central to poster art, is the effect of the message. This brings me to a quote by Paul Valéry that I often use, because it is one of the greatest quotes in history, much greater than Godard's, who said: 'Just an image, is an image *juste*'. Valéry, on the other hand, said: 'An image is more than an image, and sometimes even more than the object that it represents'. This raises a more important question than does Godard's statement because it is so much more relevant. I would like to be able to ask Valéry: 'Yes, it's true that an image is often more than an image, more than the object it represents, but how far can we go? This is the crux of the issue. To what extent, Monsieur Valéry? To go so far as to disqualify the object – false advertising? To represent an unrealistic vision of the world and human relationships'? Because falsehood distorts reality, especially when it becomes a national industry as it does, for example, during a war. Churchill himself said: 'We will defend ourselves against the aggressor through a wall of lies ...'. This is the great question posed by poster art, publicity, propaganda and disinformation: it is easy to switch from one side to the other very quickly. From publicity to propaganda, in other words, to the propagation of a faith, and finally, to disinformation, which means manipulation. Poster design exists and has existed between these extremes. The problem of comparative or false advertising and the debates that have taken place confirm the famous quote *'faire croire'* ('make them believe') by the tyrant Napoleon who said, 'To govern is to make them believe'. To govern is to create propaganda, including the Propaganda Fide. To conclude, here is another quote by Napoleon, even though I was never that fond of the Emperor. He said: 'To command is to speak to the eyes'. Extraordinary! This is the world of poster design.

Notes

1. See *Guerre et cinéma* (*War and Cinema*), by Paul Virilio, Editions des cahiers du cinéma, enlarged edition 1991.
2. See *Magritte et la publicité*, by Georges Roque, Editions Flammarion, 1983.

9

THE DARK SPOT OF ART

Interview with Catherine David

CD: Your work explores the world of today, a world where telecommunications technology tends to abolish space and time. In this context of world-space, you advance the idea of a general delocalization. How would you define a delocalized art?

PV: It's clear that one of the great philosophical and political questions of the day is deconstruction, and deconstruction in a broad sense, not only that of Derrida. Myself, I would say that art may have anticipated this debate over deconstruction, long before architecture and long before the philosophical situation as it stands today.

I would like to recall that the word *delocalization* has the same root as the Latin verb *dislocare*, to dislocate; the two words have the same source. The question is then to what extent art can be dislocated, delocalized? And that leads to the question of virtual reality.

We have gone from spatial dislocation – in abstractionism as well as cubism – to the temporal dislocation that is now under way. This means virtualization in its very essence: the virtualization of actions *as they occur* and not just simply of *what was*, to recall Barthes's idea. This is not the virtualization of photography, of reproduction or of film; it's no longer only in a time lag, but in real time.

I would also say that relative speed has been the speed of art in general. All art has been a relative speeding-up, not only dance and music, but also painting. What is coming into play today is no longer relative velocity, but absolute velocity. We're running up against the time barrier. Virtuality is the electromagnetic speed that brings us to the limit of acceleration. It's a barrier in the sense of 'no crossing'. This is the whole question of live transmission, global time, near-instantaneous intercommunication. Is the time barrier not also a barrier for art? Doesn't art have to deal with this contingency, when it comes up short against the barrier of real time?

CD: How has art reached such a barrier? In what forms and under what conditions?

PV: In order to see what has happened between the inscription of art and its delocalization, we need to look back in time. Art was initially inscribed in bodies and in materials. With cave paintings and tattoos, art was traced in matter. The art of the inscription is what it was, in a material fixity. That was art's localization. Art and its localization were inseparable in the body of the marked man or in the body of the cave, and then later in frescoes, mosaics, etc. Thus there was a grounded localization of art since its origins; and then, in the course of time, delocalization began, with the easel painting that stepped free of the cave and the skin to become a displaceable, nomadic object. This was still just a relative delocalization, that is to say, not yet a loss of place, but a possibility of movement. Painting, for example, was still inscribed in the reliquary, the illustrated book, the canvas. The *Très Riches Heures du Duc de Berry* were delocalized in the sense that they could be taken away by the feudal lord, but they were still localized in the book. The delocalization we're dealing with today is nowhere. Art can be nowhere, it only exists in the emission and reception of a signal, only in feedback. The art of the virtual age is an art of feedback. And I'm not yet even talking about the Internet. So, moving from its initial inscription in a place, in a cave, pyramid, or castle, via museums, galleries, and travelling collections, and then through photographic reproduction – where the trip is of another nature – and the CD-Rom, which is still a material support, the art of today with its interactive techniques has now reached the level of instantaneous exchange between actor and spectator, the final delocalization.

Modern decomposition – divisionism, pointillism, cubism and abstractionism, which were all decompositions of figures – manifests another type of delocalization; these artistic movements are no longer to be read in human or animal figures, but in broken figures. This process of decomposition culminates in the fractal image and in computer graphics. We go from modern decomposition to fractalization, the digital image, and finally to absolute virtualization, that is to say, the emission-reception of images which are totally instrumental.

That's a brief summary of the process which has led to the dislocation or delocalization of art today.

Now, to understand what's at stake here, I'd like to briefly evoke what I call cybersexuality, the climax of virtualization, which is now being pushed, by the Japanese in particular, toward the separation of bodies, the most absolute divorce there is. You can make long-distance love from thousands of miles away, by means of sensors that transmit impulses. I never laugh about cybersexuality, I really don't find it funny ...

Now, if even sex becomes virtual, what will happen to art? Cybersexuality is the example of total dislocation or delocalization: there is no longer any specific place, just the emission and reception of sensations. It's clear that art will suffer the consequences. It seems to me now that land art was the last great figure of an art of inscription, before the total delocalization of art in virtual reality. It was inscribed on the scale of the earth, the largest territory possible. Is it the beginning of a possible reterritorialization of art, or is it the very last sign, the swan song of art's inscription on the terrain before its final disappearance into the virtual reality of instantaneous exchange?

CD: Let's pause for a moment over land art. It seems to me that it's one aspect of what was called the 'dematerialization of art' in the late sixties. The work took place in complex spaces – here and elsewhere – which Robert Smithson, but also Marcel Broodthaers, articulated in their exhibition structures. It was a way of expressing the fact that aesthetic experience takes shape in material and mental spaces which go beyond the singular object.

On the other hand, if you take a quick scan of the art scene today, what's interesting is to see that all these artistic moments or phases are still present. You still have painting, sculpture, installations, cinema, and so-called 'Internet works'. So there's quite a broad range ...

PV: Hasn't that always been the case? In the nineteenth century, impressionism coexisted with *art pompier*, with the very worst of art. What interests me is the leading edge ...

CD: There's just this one difference, that right now the most significant research is no longer necessarily connected to places of display, or to the traditional places for the experience of art. Could that be the problem today?

PV: That's exactly why land art is such an important phase. Contrary to other transient forms, land art lasts long enough to exist. Inscription came before exhibition: even if a man exhibited his tattoos, the tattooing was initially done to mark a body. In the same way, if you believe Leroi-Gourhan and other anthropologists, the cave is first of all a place of mystery and initiation. I'm wondering, then, if art didn't regress from the exhibition, the installation on a wall or in a gallery, to the inscriptions of land art, only finally to disappear, no longer inscribed anywhere but in the instantaneous exchange of sensations offered by virtual reality. What we have today would be a sidereal aesthetics, an aesthetics of disappearance, and no longer one of appearance. Can we hang on to the *Raft of the Medusa* represented by land art, like a kind of life-saver that would carry us toward a reinscription and reinstallation of art in the here and now, the *hic et nunc* that I insist on? Or is this life-saver the sign of a sinking ship, and will the victory fall to virtual reality as reciprocal electrocution, the instantaneousness of an art that leaves no trace?

CD: The works of land art which have best resisted are precisely those which were able to articulate different places and/or times: Smithson with *Spiral Jetty* and *The Monuments of Passaic*, or Walter de Maria with *Lightning Field*. In that last work, the lightning field is integrated by the artist. The work was conceived for a non-urban space, wild, magnetic, and so on, a place you can decide to go to … The access and the effect are deferred, mediated, controlled by the artist himself, particularly through a very rigorous use of photography, which in this case can in no way appear as a convenience or a concession.

PV: I'd like to remark that with *Lightning Field* it's also a case of electrocution! I feel like comparing this lightning field to the work of Stelarc, who is another man of electrocution. Body art doesn't interest me in the least, but Stelarc interests me. He is a lightning field; he is already the support of an electrocution, of a terrifying feedback, like the earth is for Walter de Maria. He returns to the body, a body that is being absorbed, destroyed by foreign cells. He wants to become a non-body, a post-human body, a 'beyond-body', to borrow the theme of an issue of *Kunstforum* in which I participated. You had a territorial body for land art, an animal body, male or female, for body art. There is a correlation between the lightning field with its electromagnetic activity and Stelarc's attempt to be the lightning field himself, through all his electric hook-ups.

CD: Don't you get the impression that it's a direct, almost archaic return to the body, a certain way of playing with living flesh, if I daresay … I'm wondering if he isn't replaying some of the actionists' strategies, or the strategy of Chris Burden when he had himself shot in the arm. These have never been precisely resituated in their context, the post-1945 context.

PV: Stelarc predates the attempt to replace man by machine, he is the contemporary of a crucifixion of the human body by technology. He is a pre-robotic man, the apostle of the machine that will come after him. In a certain way he is the end of his art. He wants to be the Saint John of the body's Apocalypse, the Saint John of Patmos who prophesies the Apocalypse. That's why I liken him to Antonin Artaud. Like Kafka, Artaud was a contemporary of the concentration camps. Stelarc is the contemporary of the terrifying things that are happening right now in Yugoslavia and elsewhere, which are not much discussed in art and which we should discuss. I'm still scandalized by a Venice Biennial that takes place a few cable's lengths from a civil war in Europe, and by the penury of references to that war in Venice. That war cuts right through us, and a man like Stelarc illustrates the fact that man has become useless, that the machine is replacing him. He plays out this loss of his own body; it's his Baroque side. He actually brags about letting his body be replaced by the machine. [*Outside, echoes of a demonstration by strikers and students.*] The people marching in Paris while we do this interview are people cast into the street by mass unemployment, because electronic automation and hyperproductivity replace man. Man as a producer, a soldier, a parent, a procreator, is outmoded.

But to return to Walter de Maria, those lightning fields were 'contemporary' with the atom bomb and the flash of Los Alamos. They aren't ordinary flashes of lightning. They come after the flashes of the bomb that exploded not far away ...

CD: Your interpretation is quite different from the traditional readings of Walter de Maria, which have locked him away between minimal and land art, or criticized the megalomaniacal, even authoritarian aspects of his work [B. Buchloh].

But I'd like to return to your regret over the lack of political involvement or strong testimony in contemporary art, apropos of Venice and Yugoslavia for example. Doesn't the fading or disappearance of what could be called the critical art of the seventies have to do with the growing domination of communications, with everything involving advertising, with television, or in short, with the forces that tend toward consensus and homogeneousness?

PV: Communication has been taken captive by the media system and the advertising system. The movement of advertising practices is interesting, because it has gone increasingly toward the sidereal and the subliminal, where there is nothing to be seen. Only imperceptible, unconscious sensations, but very effective ones.

The art market is an advertising market, and not only in the economic sense. It is clear that the critical function – and the function of art criticism – has in fact disappeared in the commercialization of signs. So when I refer to Artaud, for example, it is because Artaud was an art critic, he wasn't simply an artist: he criticized his time with his art. Like Kafka, he was a kind of prophet of artistic calamity, and at the same time, a prophet of political calamity. Through his confinement and his Judaism, Kafka anticipates the camps – and they'll all die there, even Milena, in Dachau. In his own way, Stelarc 'prophesies' through the very violence of his tribulation, through the dangerous pressure of technology on his body. Of course that's not a political commitment like Picasso's during the Cold War, with his doves and so on ... Nor does it have anything to do with Sartre's *engagement*.

So when I see Walter de Maria's lightning field, I can't help but think of Electromagnetic Impulses, EMP. I'm what's called a 'defensive intellectual', in the sense that I'm familiar with military affairs, and with generals! The time of *Lightning Field* – 1977 – corresponds to the period of tension between the power blocs. A debate was raised over the EMP effect, that is, the electromagnetic discharge provoked by nuclear explosions in the upper atmosphere: before attacking the other side, a bomb would be set off in the upper atmosphere to knock out all the communication systems, all the intercommunication between the chiefs of staff. In fact, this was why the Americans launched the Internet, which at the time was called Arpanet. In the event of atomic war it was supposed to function after EMP, allowing for communication despite the destruction of other networks. It's a matter of armouring the communication devices against this electromagnetic effect that blows all the fuses. Now we're really in the theme of the flash! And lo and behold, an artist, who may not know a thing about it, stages EMP. His field is more than just lightning flashes, it's a kind of atom bomb!

The delocalization I'm talking about proceeds from electromagnetism. The problems of proximity, of localization if you wish, have always been linked to energies. The first proximity was linked to animal energy, it meant walking or going on horseback. The animal is the energetic element of the past and it's no accident if people painted them in caves. Later the relations of proximity and localization are linked to mechanics, it's the railway, the automobile, we're still living in this one. But since the seventies we have entered an effect of electromagnetic proximity, through impulses, always that famous feedback between an emitter and a receiver.

Therefore I have the strong impression that this question of dislocation and delocalization in art is also linked to the energy that replaces the mechanical energy of Léger's *Ballet mécanique*, and of the experiments in concrete music which had such a formative influence on us. Because you need energy to delocalize, to lose your place.

CD: One also gets the feeling that excepting the minority of artists who are already working in virtual reality, the most visible, most spectacular development is the parasitic absorption of art by the aesthetics of communication, or better, of design, cultural, social, or political design.

Energy isn't really my specialty ... But if you take a quick look around the scene, doesn't it seem that the artistic postures or positions that can still hold their own are those that can mark distances, or as Godard would say, can still change speeds?

PV: That's exactly what's threatened ...

CD: Such works aren't caught up in events, in things, they avoid idiosyncrasy.

PV: Isn't dislocation precisely a resistance to this dissolution of art? Take the example of architecture: it too is threatened with dissolution by the new technologies. The various avenues of research into glass and steel are signs of a possible dissolution of the materiality of architecture. When architecture is threatened with dissolution, that is, with 'anything goes', what's brought into play is a kind of deconstruction: people invent forms that dislocate the geometrical orthodoxy of architectural space, of simple architectural figures. This is what you have with Libeskind, Zaha Hadid and Eisenmann.

Faced with the threat of a dissolution of art, could a form of dislocation be an attempt at resistance?

CD: How would you identify the artists of dislocation on the contemporary scene?

PV: They would be people working precisely with the fact that art no longer takes place, that it has become pure energy. Lots of artists have anticipated the loss of place, the non-place of art, they anticipate it in an energeticism that can include the most shocking of images, or the most rapid of images on the feedback level. Is this attempt at energeticism one of the last ways of standing up against dissolution? Like someone who feels his strength failing him and puts all his force into his last punch, precisely because he knows it's his last.

I see that in dance, in theatre, in video, in all the arts I still enjoy. I'm repelled by the plastic arts now, there's nothing left, for me it's over ...

CD: Great news!

PV: There's dance, there's theatre, and video installations in the broad sense. Theatre, for example, is playing with video. It no longer plays with film as it once tried to, with little success. I'll take the example of a very successful play by Heiner Müller which wasn't much talked about, *Bildbeschreibungen*, which appeared shortly after my book *Logistics of Perception: War and Cinema* [1984/1989], and which was influenced by it, as Heiner Müller readily admits. I have great admiration for Heiner Müller. Here is a theatre that really plays with the deferred time of video: you have a video receiver that functions as a rear-view mirror, letting the spectator see something other than what's to be seen on the stage. There's a direct vision of bodies on the stage, plus the retroactive time of video that plays something else. That's an experiment in the area of theatre; we could find many more. Let's take another example from dance. I like William Forsythe very much. The effort demanded from

Forsythe's dancers goes all the way to the breaking-point. It's a performance of the body. Forsythe is on the edge of dislocating his dancers.

As for video installations, they are dematerializing. The coherence and structure of Michael Snow's *La Région centrale* – an absolute masterpiece in my opinion, as Deleuze also said so well – made it *the* film of the here and now: you plant an object in the ground, make it turn, and on that basis you show a world. That was absolute localization. When you see installations now, they are dislocating themselves, delocalizing. They are efforts to break through, to lose place, to be nowhere. To be dislocated, delocalized – and the people out demonstrating in the streets don't realize this clearly enough – means being nowhere, not going somewhere else. In France people speak about delocalizing corporations and administrations. But being delocalized doesn't mean going to the suburbs or the provinces, it means no longer being anywhere! This year IBM delocalized its head office to go nowhere, next year IBM won't have any head office, the first delocalized corporation ...

I'm mixing levels, of course, and I'm doing it on purpose. I'm not an art critic, I'm a critic of new technologies.

So it seems to me, through these examples of dance and theatre, that in order to resist the dissolution of art, not to say the end of art and its total disappearance, people are risking the challenge of dislocation, of delocalization, of a transfer into energy. An art that would be nothing other than energetic.

CD: You haven't mentioned cinema at all.

PV: For me, cinema is over. For years I haven't been able to put up with cinema, first of all because I can no longer put up with the ritual of the movies. Cinema should have changed its theatres. It exists by virtue of a space called the movie theatre, and the movie theatre should be constantly revolutionized, like art. But obviously it's more expensive to make new movie theatres every two years than to make new films every two years ... Serge Daney and I often spoke of this: we need Godards of the movie theatre, otherwise Godard himself will disappear. Cinema takes place, it has its dark room, its camera obscura, and it needs to make that place evolve. Today the camera obscura is virtual space, it's the video-helmet, there's no more dark room. That's another delocalization ...

CD: Aren't the plastic arts somewhat like cinema in that they fundamentally need a place, even if it's only temporary?

PV: That brings us back to the same problem, the problem of the body. You no longer make a phone call from your home, in a place, but you phone out in the street, the telephone is on you, it's portable, cellular. Are we heading toward a cellular art, just as we have cellular telephones? A portable art, on you or even in you?

CD: How do you interpret the attitude of certain young artists today who claim to work on and in the social?

PV: Lucy Orta, for example, has done work along those lines. Work on the body, on clothes, on the portable. Her clothes are not for fashion but for survival, they are apocalyptic clothes in a certain way. She makes clothes for several people, five people who put on the same outfit: kinds of diving suits, places of junctural proximity ... She does it because there are more and more people out in the street. In fact she began at the Salvation Army where her first exhibitions took place. Her art is a kind of alarm signal: the symptomatic clothing of a drama, the drama of survival in the city under normal conditions.

CD: Would that be a critical contemporary art?

PV: Yes, in the sense of Kafka or Artaud. In the fundamental sense, not in the sense of political commitment.

I'd like to return to the last hold-outs against delocalization and dislocation. Since art has already left its spaces and begun floating through the worlds of advertising and the media, the last thing that resists is the body. Whatever artists like Stelarc may think, whatever dancers and theatre people may think, they are artists of *habeas corpus*, they bring their bodies. And yet they are on the front lines, the possibility of going beyond the body is posited through them. The dramatic thing in theatre, dance and body art in the sense we were just talking about, is that they prefigure a limit. They ask the question 'How far?' That's also an ethical question in the context of genetic engineering, in the problems of traffic in human beings as improvable raw materials, the body considered as raw material, the body of 'hominiculture', as some scientists say.

That's why I'm in love with bodies. I think that alongside 'SOS save our souls' we should invent an 'SOS save our bodies from electromagnetic electrocution'. Everybody ought to reread the great book of Villiers de l'Isle Adam, *Future Eve*, the source for the Maria of Fritz Lang's *Metropolis*, the electric woman. The book prefigures the overcoming of the body by wave bodies, bodies of emission and reception, and therefore cybersexuality, but also cybersociality and cyberculture in general ...

CD: How would you explain the paradoxical co-existence, among the youngest artists, of a certain kind of work on the body and a fascination for the Internet at the same time?

PV: It's very tempting to become an angel, but there's a thin line between being an angel and not being at all. Many young artists are tempted by dematerialization, it's the angel's leap. They don't want to die, they want to *be dead*, that is, to be deprived in a certain way of the bother of having a body, the bother of feeling tired, of being disturbed by the people around them. And telecommunicating is a way of zapping your communicatees, of privileging the farthest over your neighbour. 'Love the farthest as yourself', said Nietzsche: that means being able to zap him. On the contrary, loving your neighbour is more difficult, because there's no zapping; you have to deal directly with your neighbour, he smells bad or is demanding ...

There's a kind of myth of becoming an angel which is tempting. When you're older, you know that you will very soon be an angel ...

CD: If everything shifts, if even for a short time, you can no longer inscribe the meaning of it all, then what can you do?

PV: You shock the other, you electrocute him, you put him out of action. Terrorism isn't just a political phenomenon, it's also an artistic phenomenon. It exists in advertising, in the media, the reality show, the pornographic media. The last thing to do is to give the other a punch in the face to wake him up. It's the image of that blind, deaf, and dumb kid in the 1950s who was totally isolated from the world and who was knocked out of his isolation by a slap. The shock gave him his speech back.

You can see that in the suburbs right now, speech is replaced by violence. The punch is the beginning of communication: a punch brings you back into proximity when words are lacking. Art is at that point right now. The terrorist temptation of art has already settled in everywhere. But the exhibition *Fémininmasculin* should have been done as a punch in the 1950s, or in the Victorian age, today's it's just marketing.

Despite Auschwitz, it's true, everything has been done. One should never forget Adorno's idea, 'Can poetry still be written after Auschwitz?' After the end of abstract art, after all those people who were still people of culture, we have stuttered the horror revealed by Auschwitz and Hiroshima.

CD: And yet there was cinema, Rossellini ...

PV: It's true, at the same time there was Rossellini, *Rome Open City*, all that extraordinary documentary work ...

CD: In this context, what is the model for an exhibition?

PV: You have to fight for the here and now. Being here is now one of the great philosophical questions, but its also one of the great artistic questions. Telesexuality is the disappearance of being, it's a phenomenon of the diversion of the human species: making love with an angel, with the future Eve. The question of the here and now is an absolute question in all fields. It is absolute in democracy, in mores, in sociality.

In the same way, you have to ask the question of the presence of art. Is there a telepresence of art and to what point can art be telepresent without disappearing?

CD: This is the problem of the exhibition that must create or recreate a place for itself, even temporarily ...

PV: The installation interests me because it poses the problem of place and non-place. Let's take three examples in architecture: first, the non-place of the vestibule in the bourgeois home, a semi-public, semi-private space. The people entering are in a quasi-virtual space, because they enter without being greeted; that's the case for the postman, for example. The second place is the telephone booth, which is also a semi-private, semi-public space, there's no more body, there's only the voice, and even that ... And the third, which has just been brought into operation, is the virtual portal, what I refer to as the calling chamber. A room entered by the clone of your visitor, his spectre. Inside your data suit you see the clone, it sees you, you shake its hand, you smell its perfume. The only thing you can't do with it is drink a glass of Bordeaux, tele-tasting is not possible, not yet!

This example is the final delocalization, the meeting of spectres, of angels, the dislocation of the real encounter with the other.

Art participates in this situation. The here and now is equally put into question.

CD: The ultimate interest of an exhibition is to offer an alternative to the meeting of clones. You take the trouble to go, you travel to see things you would never see elsewhere, or at least not under the same conditions.

PV: What has actually happened to the real presence of art? Here's another image, Michel de Certeau gave me this one. When Galileo's telescope was invented, the Jesuits of the time raised a theological question: do we attend mass if we watch it through a telescope?

Today when Bill Gates calls up all the paintings of the Louvre onto the screens lining the walls of his bunker-architecture, he sets off the process of the telepresence of art. The question of reproduction has been asked with photography. Barthes said it all on that subject. It's a movement toward the spectralization of art, toward cloning!

Even the non-place evolves and progresses toward the immaterial. The non-place in the sense of Marc Augé, airports, telephone booths, freeway interchanges, is none the less a constructed non-place. While the telephone booth is still quite present, the modular structure heralds the spectre. The statue of the commander is all of us.

So, is there a phantom of art?

CD: The great contemporary artists, like Smithson, Broodthaers, and Dan Graham, have worked intensively with exhibition structures. With Broodthaers, for example, the work is conceived as an exhibition and the exhibition as a work. We're still far from telepresence.

PV: But they're threatened with dislocation! Let's take video, a medium that still had some materiality. Even if video was an art of the non-place, it still had an inscription, a materiality that virtual reality and computer graphics no longer have. So I come back to my question: what has happened to the presence of art? It's a philosophical question which is practically without an answer, and at the same time, it's the question being posed concretely right now.

CD: Nonetheless, it seems to me that there are two realities: possibility and actuality. I have the feeling that telesexuality, for example, is not widely available ... In the same way, only a minority of artists are working in virtual reality.

PV: Of course, but it's a tension. What's interesting is not the fact that it exists, but that it's being actively sought. The Gulf War was already a war by telecommand, long-distance. Now they're working on cyberwar, with insect-size sensors. Instead of reconnaissance aircraft or drones, you send out tiny sound-and-image sensors that survey space like bees. And at the same time, it's true, the war in Yugoslavia exists.

CD: In the same way that art still assumes a material presence.

For how long?

CD: An exhibition like *Documenta* tries to work in the here and now.[1] Therefore we have to enquire into the way of presenting works that still propose a real experience, an aesthetic, cognitive, sensible, even ethical experience.

PV: What should be shown is everything that fundamentally resists, not in a *conservative* way but a *provocative* way. I'm not a curator of ancient forms of art, I say that conservation becomes a provocative phenomenon. The conservation of the here and now, of presence and localization, is a provocative phenomenon. The Fauves of today are those who are working on the presence of art.

CD: That means inventing exhibition structures. It would be foolish and dangerous to try to outdo television. Some people consistently cite television as a possible model of exhibition. On the contrary, I believe it's urgent to set up barriers to zapping.

PV: Anyway, television is out of date. It's already in a state of breakdown! Multimedia will be the death of television, its absorption into virtual reality. Cinema is dead, as I already said, but cinema is what makes television resist. If there were no more cinema, television would be long gone. The two cadavers hold each other upright. I say that from within a love of cinema which I once had and can have no longer ...

In a period of occupation you don't speak of resistance, said Serge Daney. The occupation is by the media. We are occupied by tele-technologies and we must be part of the resistance. Today there are the collaborators and the resistance.

Me, I'm in the resistance. What we're actually doing here, with lots of questions, is exploring the dark spot of art today. That's resistance. It's not conservative resistance, but liberating resistance.

CD: How can an exhibition – which is more and more a place of cultural consumption 'without qualities' – be a space of resistance?

PV: At the time when François Burckardt was at the Pompidou Centre, after Lyotard's exhibition *Les Immatériaux*, Lyotard and I received two commissions. *Les Immatériaux* was one of the great exhibitions, a failure and a stroke of genius all at once, a successful failure, a contradiction. He got a commission on resistance, all forms of resistance, electric, social, military, etc. And I got a commission on acceleration. Two contradictory exhibitions, obviously. Everything I'm talking about happens within an acceleration that emancipates us from places, from the body, from ourselves, from others, and finally from democracy ...

CD: Can strategies be invented to resist acceleration, to maintain the distances, depths and heterogeneous elements that still exist in aesthetic production – strategies other than desperate attempts at restoration, like the one we saw in Venice this summer?

PV: Initially, at the time when the Pompidou Centre was still being planned, what was envisioned was to present not only exhibitions but also art in the making, studios and labs, a zoo of working artists. It's clear that it didn't come out that way, but that aspect was at the basis of Beaubourg. A place where creation would be exhibited while taking place, not a depot of works but a research centre. The Frisco exploratorium has the same kind of dimension in a certain way; you have the work of the day, the work is presented as a trajectory and not as an object. You're offered whatever has just arrived, like in a railway station. In this idea of Beaubourg, art was in the trajectory of art and not only in its arrival.

But that wasn't really a new idea, the romantic painters of the nineteenth century had artistic duels at their openings, they finished the canvas in front of the visitors. When Turner added the steam to the locomotive emerging from the fog and figured speed for the first time in a painting, he was anticipating art as a trajectory by trying to finish the painting in front of people. Something was played out there which continues in the idea of Beaubourg. Not consuming the finished product, but being at the level of the act, of the theatricalization of the act. It's the idea of an art that wouldn't be deferred but would exist in real time, live. Behind this temptation, something is being declared about the time of art, I don't know what. It's the same interest in improvisation, in jazz, an interest in art being made.

CD: Nonetheless I have the impression that behind this desire for real time there are other, less admissible preoccupations, the search for the spectacular, the exhibitionism of the medium ... Everything is art, all the time, everybody is an artist – absolute relativism!

PV: It's true that if everyone is an artist there's no more art, and that's what's happening. That's the reason why I say that for me, the plastic arts are finished, it's over, *alles fertig*. I'm not joking!

CD: You're saying that to someone in charge of a major exhibition! ...

PV: ... which is called *'alles fertig'*, it's all over? No, let's get serious again! The presence of art, and therefore its localization, is threatened. And yet that's exactly where the solution to the threat lies, in the question of the temporality of art today. We have attained the limit of velocity, the capacity for ubiquity, for instantaneousness and immediacy. The fact of having reached the wall of the speed of light makes us the contemporaries of ubiquity. Art is in the phase of globalization.

I don't have the answer, but it is in this question that the answer lies, and it's up to the artists to answer. Some video artists have done it, Gary Hill, Michael Snow, Bill Viola; theatre does it, choreographers do it, plastic artists don't do it enough.

CD: But what's happening in theatre, contrary to the plastic arts, is of the order of representation, and representation implies distance. An aesthetics with no step back is just advertising. How would you discuss this question of distance?

PV: It's the problem of the interval. The interval of space, of time, and the third interval, according to physicists, the interval of light, the zero sign. This third interval is what brings ubiquity into play. It's what allows you to be the contemporary of an event on the other side of the world.

CD: Without an interval you're in 'the same', you cannot be a witness. To be a witness is to have seen, from not far away. Can art still bear witness? I don't want to subscribe to all the sociological recipes that are being served up just now. But the dimension of witnessing is important.

PV: We always come back to the dark spot of the presence of art today ... The possibility of a disappearance of art was evoked in the nineteenth century by Rodin, Cézanne and many others, who thought at that time that art could disappear. They weren't pretending. Nor did they say it was apocalyptic. Art can disappear. In a certain way Auschwitz was a disappearance of art, an event so far outside history that it is a kind of proof that the worst can happen. I am of the generation that can envisage the disappearance of art. All the questions that we're asking here turn around this possible disappearance. As long as people censor the possible disappearance of art there will be no art. To think about the here and now, the temporality and presence of art, is to oppose its disappearance, to refuse being a collaborator.

Now, art plays with this possible disappearance, finds it amusing, because it doesn't take it seriously. Lots of artists are already profiting from the death of art, they're not like Artaud who announced the possibility of the end, they're already in the after-death and they're profiting. They're inheriting from the cadaver.

I think our time is as unheard-of as the period before the Renaissance. Before the incredible explosion of the Renaissance there was the tragedy. Today we're entering the tragedy. A world is coming to an end. Careful – it's not the end of *the* world, I can't stand all the apocalyptic ravings people indulge in today. But I'm sure it's the end of *a* world. Once you recognize this situation – and what a daunting situation it is, to topple over into an unheard-of and ungraspable world – then you also have to recognize that it's fantastically exciting!

Translated by Brian Holmes.

Note

1. On the Documenta exhibition see: Herausgeber documenta Gmbtt (1996) (ed.) *documenta documents 1*. Kassel: Cantz Verlag.

10

LANDSCAPE OF EVENTS SEEN AT SPEED

Interview with Pierre Sterckx

PS: You always give your interviews on the covered *terrasse* of La Coupole on Boulevard Montparnasse. Could this be taken as one of your favorite sites, a place where you can watch the movement of the street from a 'limit position' behind glass?

PV: Yes, that suits me very well. I am 'littoralist', a man of the interface. I like places that are under the influence of frontiers. This is probably because my father was an Italian immigrant (and a clandestine one to boot). For me the sea represents the interface between three elements; earth, water and air. That is where I feel most fully myself, and it is also a graphic space, a line. As a young man I used to paint, but I was more a draftsman than a colorist. For me, drawing is painting's virtue. I have always kept this idea of drawing as a trajectory.

Drawn or written, a line is always a trajectory, not only from one point to another but from one world to another. The littoral, which is a site at the frontier of the solid and the fluid, is clearly a line from which you observe from within a bunker, not only coming danger or freedom (the Landings), but also the state of nature. All my work consists in studying, from a fixed point, a territory, that which traverses in – speed, to be exact.

PS: Can you tell me about this landscape, which you present as a site of events in your latest book?

PV: The title of my book [*Un paysage d'événements*, 1996] refers to an timeless landscape which belongs to teleological vision of Deus, that is to say, a vision that freezes history, from its beginning to its end. You could say that it is like Marey's chrono-sculpture, using chronophotographic images of moments of the flight of a seagull. My interest in trajectory, in trajection and trajectiles, underpins this conception of landscape. I have tried to depict it in terms of the historical events of the last twelve years. A landscape is a horizon. The one I describe in my book forms a trans-historical horizon which interests me because it translates the ascendancy of event-based history over global history. Before now, events as such were considered secondary compared, say, to historical materialism.

PS: Is this a new kind of panoptics? A global vision obtained through detail?

PV: Yes, because according to this divine vision which is also a human vision, it is the event that constructs the world. History is becoming fractalized and losing its generality. It is now built with details, not unlike the writing technique of the Nouveau Roman. In Butor and in Robbe-Grillet, one tends to perceive everything through the detail. Similarly, the famous 'end of history' everyone was talking about is not so much an end as a backwards movement. What came up against the wall of real time was history as generality, which disappeared with the Soviet Union and Marxism. In the resulting shock we are back with the history of events and local happenings. Suddenly, they are the landscape, because there are no overarching trends. My book is a flashback composed of bizarre events.

Speed is absolute power

PS: How do the themes of *Un paysage d'événements* – such as terrorist attacks in the US, serial killers, the commemoration of the Normandy Landings – fit into your general concerns, the main one of which is speed?

PV: The event landscape of the last twelve years strikes me as extremely important. The end of the century is approaching not in the form of an explosion but as an unapproachable territory. And this is directly related to speed, which I consider not as movement from one point to another, or the acceleration of a vectorial movement, but as an element. Now, an element needs to be cultivated and organized, and even to be urbanized, in the sense of being made urbane, given a culture. How are we to inhabit the element of absolute speed? We are going to have to live in the world of real time, which means that we first reconnoiter, for we know only the world of real space. We must realize that we are dealing here with a negativity devoid of references. It has nothing to do with the earlier negativities of relative speed, as illustrated by the *Blitzkrieg* with its bombers and Panzer tanks, or by road accidents, which are a kind of civil cold war. The accident gestating within the acquisition of absolute speed is a total accident. Not a local accident but accident as element.

PS: But if acceleration has become impossible and (economically at least) it is impracticable to stop, all we have left is deceleration. How can we regress without being reactionary?

PV: Whenever you come to a wall, you bounce back. Before we can develop an intelligent idea of future societies, we need to note the current backwards movement. I am not talking about decadence like that of the Roman Empire. We are regressing because we have reached the limit of acceleration. If the time of societies is accelerating, so is the reality of time. We are now experiencing this dual acceleration, which is why, if we want to understand history, we must do more than pore over the traces and books of formulae, but also study wave functions, instantaneous emission-reception systems, CD-Roms and information superhighways. We need a political economy of time, just as there is a political economy of wealth. If time is money, speed means absolute power. The power of a computer is its speed. One could consider the speed of a locomotive as progress, but this new speed, which is an element, must be sanctioned as a form of violence, otherwise there can be no city.

The loss of space

PS: Like all the great inventions, surely, the virtual is capable of both the best and the worst.

PV: We will have to find a way of housing virtual space in real space. The virtual is the antithesis not of the real but of the actual. The new technologies are not the devil, but to use them properly we need to understand and counter their negativity. An airplane is not an ideal. Santos Dumont, the great pioneer of aviation, was so horrified to see his dragonflies massacring each other when he saw a dogfight during the 1914–18 War that he went back to Brazil and killed himself. At this very moment, on the Internet you can find all you need to make the kind of bomb that went off in Atlanta, so we cannot say that it automatically opens the doors to a democracy of knowledge: it is also a network of highways, like those built by the Nazis to further their military conquests.

PS: I imagine you are sometimes accused of being a pessimist?

PV: Let's put it this way, I am not an optimist in the medium term, but in the long term. I think that, up to the 1980s/90s, the twentieth century was the product of the nineteenth. There has been no twentieth century, only a prolongation of the nineteenth. If, as Camus said, our epoch is 'pitiless', that is because it reproduces but does not innovate. We have repeated and created nothing, apart, that is, from great disasters.

PS: The author of *Crash*, J.G. Ballard, has declared that our century has been one of 'unlimited possibilities'.

PV: As for the twenty-first century, there is a big question mark hanging over it. Perhaps it will answer that question, because the 'unlimited possibilities' are all there, whether in biology, communications or the conquest of space, both cosmic and terrestrial. One of the great problems of the near future will be the dramatic shrinking of space on earth, of life-size reality. The effect of being enclosed which Foucault noted in the eighteenth century will in fact characterize the twenty-first. What will human space be like in a world reduced to nothing by supersonic transport and instantaneous communications? Space as emptiness will be unlimited and space as fullness drastically limited. There will be a new interface between the solid and the fluid, except that now the terrestrial littoral is vertical!

PS: Before being a critic of modernity, you are an urbanist and architect. What are your thoughts about ecology?

PV: Ecology is an old passion of mine. I published Félix Guattari's remarkable book, *Les Trois Ecologies*. To put the issue in context, let's say that there are no gains without losses. The monks and copyists of the Middle Ages were the losers in the leap forward that was printing. We have inherited all these losses, so much so that we even wonder if they don't outweigh the gains. When we invented the elevator we lost the staircase. There are no Palladian stairways today, only emergency exits. My fear is that we may end up with an 'emergency humanity'. In a sense, cyberspace is our colony, just like the colonies that saturated industrial societies needed in order to extend their life span. This question of the loss of space has to do with an ecology of distances. There is also an ecology of substances, centring on material problems. Personally, I am trying to promote an ecology of qualities, an ecology that is both material and spiritual.

The angle of divergence

PS: Could you explain what you mean by 'angle of divergence'?

PV: Angles have always fascinated me. I worked on them once as an architect with Claude Parent. Divergence is a way of approaching an angle.
Bikers, for example, ride at an angle when negotiating a turn at speed,
using the power of their bikes. Whenever a technology accelerates, we
would be wrong to adopt it, to treat it like an idol and worship its performance: we need to look elsewhere, take an angle. This was the case in
painting when the Impressionists adopted a different angle with regard
to photography.
　　Up to now, speeds were always relative, to do mainly with transport.
Today, however, we are coming to the revolution of transmission, i.e.,
absolute speed, that of the limits of speed, the wall of time. The question
of speed as element needs to be articulated differently now. We can no
longer think in terms of aerodynamics and trajectories.

PS: By taking the right angle of divergence, we would I suppose avoid being
crushed against the wall of speed, rather as, in the physics of Lucretius,
certain atoms avoid the drop and accede to life, to form.

PV: Exactly, the point is to prevent things from getting caught on a single
point. This aesthetic of purification and transparency is summed up in
Mies van der Rohe's famous 'less is more'. But to what extent is this
true? The invention of printing led to an acceleration of reading, the
transition from oral reading to a silent activity. In a way, this marks the
beginning of an aesthetics of disappearance – that of the sound of the
reader's voice. With the advent of the photogram, from Niepce to the
Lumières, we witness an upheaval in the order of appearance. Before
then, there was an aesthetic of appearance comprising the emergence of
lines or volumes on a support that itself remained present. Matter *persists*. In cinema, however, the persistence becomes perceptual and cognitive. In a film, things exist only in terms of what follows. The price of
their animation is disappearance and their support ceases to exist. The
only art to anticipate this was music, in which the disappearance of
sounds is the condition of melody. What is so serious today is that, with
this extreme acceleration which affects transmission as well as transport, virtuality as well as reality, the aesthetics of disappearance is
becoming a generalized reality.

PS: What about the role of electricity in all this? Is it not the element *par
excellence*? There is a Richard Brautigan character who tells a woman
that she is 'as beautiful as electricity'.

PV: If water was central to ancient history, and fire built the world, then electricity (which is now totally banalized – it is *current*) is the point where all the new technologies plug in. It is as if lightning, which our ancestors held to be divine, had become a tool. Electricity created a new light, not only direct lighting but also the indirect light, as video. Electricity functions as energy and power, but also as light and spirituality.

PS: One thinks of the famous passage in the Book of Exodus: 'the Angel of the Lord appeared unto him in a flame of fire out of the midst of a bush; and he looked, and, behold, the bush burned with fire, and the bush was not consumed'.

PV: What attracts Moses is permanence, not light. In fact, one cannot understand the new technologies if one has no religious culture, in the broad sense, because these technologies raise the kind of questions that are dealt with in religious thought. I myself am a believer. I was converted as an adult.

PS: You said recently that you were – or wanted to become – an art critic for the new technologies. In today's atmosphere of decadence and disillusionment, isn't there a risk of criticism replacing creativity?

PV: I am displacing the question of art criticism towards technology. Progress is one thing nobody sees as an object for criticism. Yet technology is the vector of progress and I would say that there can be no art without criticism. An art lover is at the same time an art critic, since a taste for art implies a certain quality of judgment. As a lover of new technology art, I totally contest the objective status accorded to the technosciences. I acknowledge the existence of exact, experimental sciences, but technology has no claim to the grandeur of those sciences. For me, a technological object is first and foremost an art object: a Concorde is no different than a Cézanne painting. Until we widen this culture of technological art and its concomitant art criticism, we will not have democracy but idolatry, submission to 'divine' technologies. Those who claim to have killed the God of Transcendence have become the zealots of the God of Technology. Criticism, as I envisage it, is the freedom to love. One is free when one is able to criticize technology. There are few critics in the sphere of technology precisely because technology is not really loved: it is too dominant for that.

Loss of the body

PS: This brings us to the question of your role at the next *Documenta*.[1]

PV: One of the great themes for art to explore, I think, is that of dislocation. The word *dislocare* is the root of both dislocate and delocalize. Now, while art has undergone numerous dislocations since cubism, I am not sure it is ready to take on the phenomena of today's delocalization. Looking at the historical context, this is not just a problem of deterritorialization, but a problem of the loss of traces and of the capacity for inscription not only in a territory but in any stable support. Today, the new technologies, digitization, pixels and so on, have brought art to an unprecedented loss of place, and an equally serious fractalization. Hence, for some years now, the interest in place in land art, or in the beyond-place of music. The art form of the new generations is not visual art but music. As for land art, was it not the clinical symptom of this will to reinscribe art in a territory? Given that the primitive cave is now the entire planet – from an extra-horizontal point of view.

Art began with the cave and the tattooed body. Then there was the fresco and the mosaic, which are still inscribed in architecture. Then we have the portable work, the missal or easel painting, which is housed in a gallery such as the Uffizi, itself a passageway, a kind of *dromos*. This delocalization has increased and has played a not inconsiderable role in modern art and its dislocation of the fixed image, from perspective and then photography to today's virtual space, CD-Roms and clones – those specters which are not a double, the copy of an original, but active figures that refer to who knows what, and which are much more than specters.

PS: Do you mean that the visual arts are in a situation of absolute (not relative) dislocation in the same way as the world of communication is in a state of absolute speed? One could conclude that this was the end of painting, or that it had become impossible, or at least improbable.

PV: I lost interest in painting well before Pop! Even when I look at Bacon, I'm still not convinced. What interests me are the drawings of Rodin. This has nothing to do with the reputation for eroticism that is too often foisted onto them. These drawings are traces which engendered Matisse and Giacometti. They inaugurate things which have not been developed. He puts down the line without even looking at the shape he is tracing. One day I shall write something about them. In his drawings, Rodin dances. We come back here to the language of the body.

PS: So your interest in art tends to focus on the body?

PV: The art that most interests me nowadays is dance and the video installation, the work of Nam June Paik, Bill Viola, Gary Hill, Vasulka and Michael Snow (*La Région centrale* is an absolute masterpiece). They are working with the great questions of the age: the body and its virtualization.

Video installations raise the problem of space and time with singular acuity. Future actors will be called 'vactors', a mixture of action and virtuality.

PS: Paul Valéry said that 'The artist brings with him his body.' In the context of the dislocation and virtualization that you describe, does not this remark sound like a cry of despair?

PV: The two arts that raised the question of resistance by the body were dance and theatre. I spoke to dancers, to actors, to the playwright Heiner Müller. I asked 'What are you going to do with the virtual body, with cloning, etc.?' No answer. William Forsythe replied that a sofa is already a virtual body, but that's a witticism, not an answer. It is true that theatre people and dancers are using video and cinema more and more. The loss of the body is not just the loss of the earth. If we can imagine the replication of the planet in cyberspace, can we also conceive of this repetition of the individual body as a disqualified body? This would be a new gemination which would make the specific body disappear, wrenching it away from art, where its appearance was crucial. The implications are so far-reaching I cannot answer. It is nihilistic. I would even say that Nazi nihilism in a sense introduced this question. The death camps were an attempt to bring on this disappearance. I think this feeling of perfecting disappearance is there among the dangers of the virtual. We would be confronted with a kind of negationism, a virtual one denying the reality of bodies, of the earth, of the mind.

PS: One cannot consider the vitality of an art form without looking at its collective meaning. Paul Klee was worried that he lacked the strength of the land and the people. This says something about the relation between an experimental or, let us say, 'extreme' art, and a popular, 'everyday' art.

PV: As regards extremes, we have just reached their limits by means of speed. There is no point in being afraid of accidents, in turning away. On the contrary, we need to look for the great rifts. Be connoisseurs – as I am – of serious accidents. I dream of a museum of accidents. Perhaps at the end of the century. The men I admire are those who look into the abyss. Not many do; it's too problematic, you never come away from it unscarred. Some get burnt, like my friend, the poet Mohammed Kiridine. It was true of Van Gogh, it's true of Müller today. I think we're getting to have more and more need of such men to sense the great accidents that are on the way, to pick up on the positive pieces left among the ruins. 'Where danger grows there also grows that which saves,' wrote Rilke. Salvation is to be found in the place of greatest danger, and the diviners we mentioned a moment ago are heroes of the limits, of the terrifying, the monstrous.

The artist as diviner

PS: What about art in everyday life, do you believe it can have a complementary, decorative and playful role?

PV: In our society, everyday art is totally dominated by advertising. It is in grave danger of contamination by everything that has to do with the media. In the old days, when it was known here as '*la réclame*', advertising simply promoted a product, which was a normal function in an industrialized society. But then came '*la publicité*', which refers to the action of the publicist, the person who makes public what is private. However, the effect of generalization here goes beyond the action of the eighteenth century publicist, who published encyclopaedic knowledge. We are now coming to the stage of communication, which is a form of propaganda and contamination, of tyranny. Advertising has lost its original identity, it has become the information revolution. That is why I do not contest the technology involved in the Internet but the propaganda around it. Art cannot be part of that.

For me, artists of all kinds – plasticians, dancers, etc. – are organs of perception of a society or species. I think some people are like sensors: just as we use organs such as the eyes, the hands and the ears as sensors, so, in the human race, there are men and women who apprehend. Take the example of Kafka. He is a diviner, especially in his letters. Apparently, he writes only for himself, he is a loner, but in fact he does it for others. The sensor is a profoundly social being, through the perspicacity of his perception. I believe that this function is extremely important for a society.

We must also defend all forms of trace or inscription, be they literary, gestural or musical. Let us save phenomena by resisting: writing against the screen, for example. All this is bound up with the continuation of language and, I think, with the supranational language that will replace English. What superior kind of Babel will that be?

PS: I remember you saying that you were a jazz lover. Doesn't the dynamic and backbeat of swing make it exemplary of the aesthetics of speed?

PV: I am a jazz fan first of all because, for me, it was the music of the Liberation. During the War, the music that I heard was military music, plus the sound of boots. Swing freed me from that. Moreover, jazz has a special structure, a melodic scheme, a kind of phrasing, and so on. In my youth I tried to become a drummer. My idol was Zutty Singleton. Then came Parker, Miles and Coltrane. What I love is the clarity of this music. It is concrete music with a purpose, unlike another form of concrete music, which I loathe. Jazz is the pleasure of playing together, as in chamber music, the opposite of rave parties and the confused hysteria they generate. The destruction of jazz by rock was a very significant moment of deconstruction.

The process of subjectivization in jazz is based on alterity. And to have alterity, you need two bodies. Hence the jam session. In rock, though, the link with alterity is broken. People have ended up dancing on their own. It has been said they were displaying themselves to others, but it's not true. They were looking at themselves from within. Something was shattered here, there was a loss of trajection which I think is tragic.

PS: Listening to you speak I cannot help seeing the persona and physique of Michael Jackson. Would he not make a good conclusion to this survey of the aesthetics of disappearance?

PV: Michael Jackson goes all the way to the dissolution of the body. He is the antithesis of Ella Fitzgerald, or of opera singers, whose body, though not obese, is an emanation – its size being the result of music, vibration. Michael Jackson is skinny and wears a suit of optical fibres that react to his voice. It's the same with his whitening skin. You could say that he is never satisfied with his lightness, his whiteness, that what he wants is not even light but to disappear in transparency. He is a victim of the rock war, and of Negritude. All of which shows that rock is not about individuation.

PS: What do you think of these words of Bergson's: 'What is the point of time? Time is what prevents everything from being present all at once. It delays, or rather, it is delay'?

PV: – that space is what prevents everything from being all together, all piled up. That might be a truism, but that's what's good about it.

Translated by C. Penwarden.

© 1996 *Art Press* and Paul Virilio. Interview with Pierre Sterckx, in *Art Press* 217, 1996. © 1996 translation by C. Penwarden.

Note

1. On the *Documenta* exhibition see: Herausberger documenta Gmbtt (1996) (ed.) *documenta documents 1.* Kassel: Cantz Verlag.

11

NOT WORDS BUT VISIONS!

Interview with Nicholas Zurbrugg

NZ: In *L'Inertie polaire* [1990], you describe the 'accidents' of contemporary technoculture as a kind of secular 'miracle'. What exactly did you mean by this?

PV: I argue that every time a new technological breakthrough occurs – a new kind of ship or plane for example – there's a new kind of accident. The *Titanic* was a kind of accident, bringing about a new kind of disaster at sea. In other words, I think that every technological innovation is accompanied by a kind of particular negative form or accident. People talk of natural accidents or disasters such as earthquakes or floods, but these aren't really accidents in my sense of the word. What interests me are the technological dimensions of the accident – the derailed train, the crash, Chernobyl, the *Titanic* and so on. The twentieth century interests me above all as the century of accidents. For me, it's the century of technological and scientific revolution. It's not so much the century of Auschwitz and Hiroshima as the century of the *Titanic* and Chernobyl. So one can't really begin to understand the twentieth century unless one understands the dimensions of its accidental revelations. Accidents are a revelation of science and technology's original sin. Science and technology are flawed – in the same way that we are.

NZ: While you suggest that accidents have a miraculous quality as revelations, you also argue that new technologies are a negative force leading to terminal inertia or frenzied hyperactivity. Couldn't one argue instead that researchers who are exploring new technologies are in a sense hyperactive in more positive ways, successfully mastering new technologies?

PV: When I use the term 'polar inertia' I'm referring to absolute speed. I argue that this kind of inertia is the consequence of energy and the consequence of speed. I refer for example to the inertia of the pilot, sitting in his jet, watching his screens. So for me, telecommunications lead to a sort of paralysis. And this is seldom discussed. People say it's marvellous to travel at the speed of jets, it's marvellous to fly so rapidly between Sydney and Paris, but all this comes at the cost of inertia, at the cost of paralysis!

NZ: Isn't this a rather monodimensional response to the potential of contemporary technology?

PV: No! I believe in both possibilities – I believe in both of them. That's why my research focuses both on speed and on inertia! And on the positive potential of the *Titanic* – that fabulous ocean liner! – and the catastrophe of the iceberg! They're the two sides of the same thing!

NZ: Isn't the biggest problem here one's choice of examples? If one looks at these things in terms of military, industrial or commercial contexts, one can easily conclude that all these technologies lead to stagnation. But sometimes you also discuss more positive forms of substantial energy that you associate with electroacoustic media.

PV: That's the speed of liberation! That's the theme of my book *Open Sky – La Vitesse de libération* [1995]. The speed of liberation is the energy that lets you escape from the laws of gravity! I always work on both aspects. Always! Many people only seem to notice the pessimistic dimension of my writing. They don't realize that it's the global dimensions of the twentieth century that interest me – both the absolute speed and power of the twentieth century's telecommunications, nuclear energy and so on, and at the same time the absolute catastrophe of this same energy! We're living with both of these things!

And I'm the child of this century of ambivalent science and technology! This is my century! It's not the century of the crusades! It's not the century of the Renaissance! It's the century of techno-scientific power! And techno-scientific power, like political power, or like religious power, is at once both a blessing and a calamity!

NZ: This leads to a major question, doesn't it? How can one negotiate these two forces? If one looks at things in general, then one's diagnosis will always be pessimistic. But as I was reading *L'Inertie polaire* and *Open Sky* I continually kept thinking of the ways in which the recent performances of the Australian artist Stelarc exemplify ways of orchestrating Internet activity in highly energetic performances that seem the very reverse of the kind of inertia that you associate with cyberculture.

PV: I think of Stelarc as being the Antonin Artaud of technology – that's what I find so interesting in his work. He's completely committed to his research. He's not playing with technology – his work has the same authenticity as that of Artaud. But I fear that things may go as badly for him as for Artaud, and that he will end up the victim of his machines. But that's the nature of his artistic research, that's the nature of his research.

He's an artist whose work has religious dimensions without really being aware of it! That's to say, he's searching for a kind of transfiguration. He thinks that technological forces will allow him to transfigure himself – to become something other than what he is. An angel, an archangel, a mutant, a cyborg or whatever. So there's a sort of devotion in his work to the machine god – to a *deus ex machina* – and Stelarc is its prophet.

But for me, man is the last of God's miracles. Or put another way, man is not the centre of the world, but the end of the world. Man is its end! Hence, my rejection of all eugenic theories based upon the argument that man is only a prototype awaiting improvement. And Stelarc's research is quintessentially eugenicist in the sense that he's trying to improve his condition. His is a kind of body-building, a kind of body-art! And I'm fundamentally opposed to eugenics! I believe that man is finished!

But there's nothing sad about what I'm saying! When I say things have reached their end, I don't mean their end in the sense of the end of the world, but rather, that we can only ever experience the 'end' of things. I think Baudrillard says the same thing. We've never experienced anything other than the end of things because we're mortal. That's the basis of philosophy.

We exist because we are mortal; therefore, we exist because we are the end of things. It's in relation to death that we exist. It's in relation to the end of life – as it were – that we are men and women – that we are powerful, that we are poets – marvellous poets such as Beckett! It's therefore an immense end. Life itself is this end – man is the end of the world – it's not Hiroshima that's the end of the world, it's you and it's me. The end of things is our lives. It's because we're mortal that we're conscious.

None of this is sad at all; none of this is at all apocalyptic! What's apocalyptic, is to say that man is the centre of the world! That's ridiculous! Ridiculous! Anthropomorphism is an aberration! At a conference on the apocalypse last year, I said that I was absolutely disinterested in ideas about the apocalypse and the end of the world. What interests me is my end – not the end of the world. I lived through the bombing of Nantes in the Second World War and I saw the apocalypse at the age of 8!

NZ: Aren't there intellectual apocalypses every twenty years? For example, cubism seemed incomprehensible when it first appeared, and now just seems another addition to the early twentieth-century vocabulary. Isn't our greatest problem that of understanding and using new technologies?

PV: Quite so. Are we still free in the face of science and technology? Personally, I think that the next political struggle – taking the concept of political struggle in its broadest terms – will be the struggle against techno-science, against the reign of techno-science, against cloning, robotics and so on. But this kind of struggle doesn't imply a return to a previous situation. It means the attempt to fight against technology itself – not in order to destroy it, but in order to transfigure it.

NZ: That's much more interesting.

PV: Obviously. I've never been an 'ecologist' as it were, proposing a return to a lost paradise. Not at all. All my books advocate this kind of combat.

NZ: So for you, 'combat' with technology implies 'contact' with technology, or the attempt to collaborate with technology?

PV: I prefer to think of it in terms of the wonderful biblical image of Jacob wrestling with the angel. Abraham, Isaac and Jacob were the inventors or discoverers of monotheism – of Yahweh, the biblical God. And Jacob met his God in the person of an angel and he wrestled with this angel for a whole night and at the end of the night he said to the angel, 'Bless me, because I have fought all night'.

What does this symbolize? It means that Jacob did not want to sleep before God. He wanted to respect him as a man. He wanted to remain a man before God. That was the greatness of Israel. God told him, 'Thy name shall be called no longer Jacob, but Israel', because he fought rather than just sleeping as though he was before an idol.

Technology places us in the same situation. We have to fight against it rather than sleeping before it. And me, I don't sleep at all before technology. I adore it! I adore technology!

NZ: Where Stelarc's ideas differ most obviously from yours, I suppose, is in their consistent rejection of metaphysical rhetoric. For Stelarc, any real attempt to struggle with – or against – technology implies the need to abandon old rhetorical terms in order to enter new dimensions of practice and theory. For Stelarc, new actions require new kinds of definition.

PV: Isn't that rather a fashion-driven vision? That makes me think of fashion – of the latest spring collections, the summer collections, the winter collections. What does it mean to say that past ideas are no longer relevant? Old ideas are no longer valid, and one has new ideas! What does this mean?

NZ: Perhaps these kind of 'new' ideas can best be defined by differentiating the positive potential of new kinds of technological art from the more repressive or negative impact of dominant commercial technological practices? In other words, I'm not really convinced when *L'Inertie polaire* discusses such disparate audiovisual technologies as pornographic video cabins and the installations of video artists as examples of the same kind of paralysing 'Dataland'. You don't really seem to discuss the way in which art offers exceptions to the general rules of commercial media.

PV: That wasn't my concern here. My main concern here was the general impact of technologies – of technological vehicles.

NZ: But doesn't that leave one with the problem of defining the significance of art in the context of these developments?

PV: Naturally, other things remain to be said. For the moment, as I suggest in *Cybermonde: la politique du pire* [1996], which is about to be translated by Semiotext(e) in New York [1999], the most exciting thing is that every time that a new technology appears, art diverges from it. Art develops at a tangent from the technology, changes it, and does something else. That's, for example, what happened with impressionism, pointillism, cubism and so on, when photography appeared. When the camera appeared art took another direction and went elsewhere.

NZ: With the exception of Italian Futurism?

PV: Exactly. Which also became Fascist! Don't forget that, because I still have a score to settle with Italian Futurism. Like them, my approach is Futurist, but whereas their work is positive, mine is negative. And I completely reject the Fascist impulse that I perceive in their work. For me it's quite clear. Those who are optimistic about technology are very closely allied to Fascism. He who is critical of technology is not Fascist. If one is a critic one doesn't ever accept things at face value and one doesn't ever just sleep in front of new technologies. A real artist never just sleeps in front of new technologies, but deforms them and transforms them.

NZ: But at the same time the artist embraces new technologies.

PV: Yes, but of course, in a struggle, like Jacob with the angel. Whereas today, art is far more uncertain in its responses to technology. And I can't see many signs of this kind of divergence or struggle in contemporary art save in dance, which I adore, and theatre, which I adore – Heiner Müller, for example! Apart from dance, from theatre and one or two video-installation artists, I can't see any real traces of critical divergence or of any attempt to do something else, in some other way. I can't see it.

Like Baudrillard, I'm conscious of a crisis in contemporary art and even of something like the end of contemporary art. But not an end in the sense of there no longer being any art, but in the sense of witnessing the end of a certain kind of art, or what Beckett would call the 'endgame' of art – in every sense of the word. One feels that for the moment, art is dead – for the moment. Just as it has been dead in the past! There have always been periods when art broke down, and then it began again!

NZ: Perhaps it's art criticism that has broken down?

PV: Oh yes – yes, even more so!

NZ: In other words, perhaps we're facing the dilemma of blind anthropologists incapable of identifying significant practices?

PV: Yes, I also agree with that. The two things go together. For me, an artist is a critic – one can't be a creator unless one's a critic. So the two are in a state of crisis – that's true. But such crises always reflect a certain moment in time. History never completely comes to a standstill.

NZ: Looking on the bright side of things, what kind of video installations do you find most interesting at the present moment?

PV: For me, Michael Snow's *La Région centrale* is a masterpiece equivalent to the work of Beckett or Kafka – a masterpiece of video installation.

There are other works too – many other works. I'm interested in all video installation artists to a greater or lesser degree. The Vasulkas, Paik – although I don't really like Paik's work very much – Gary Hill, Bill Viola, but above all Michael Snow. For me, *La Région centrale* is a work like Kafka's *Metamorphosis* – it's an exceptional piece of video-writing, a masterpiece, a masterpiece. So for me three things are interesting – theatre, dance and video installation. But I'm less sensitive to things like Paik's work. It's like painting, where you can't like everything. One's limited – and that's it! I prefer Vermeer and the old paintings, I like Bach and Bob Dylan, but not everything!

NZ: Proust speaks of the way in which Vermeer's *View of Delft* isolates 'a little yellow patch of wall', and curiously, in one of Baudrillard's photographs of stone steps in Rome there's the same sort of detail – a little patch of sunlit stone. So at this point, perhaps, new technologies such as photography re-explore the same sort of perceptions that one admires in earlier paintings?

PV: But at this point one enters into the realm of emotional responses. I'm so involved in the world of painting and the world of art that I don't speak about it much in my books because I live it! I'm a painter who writes, you know! Surely, you feel that my books are very visual – they're very, very visual books! They're not words, they're visions! I'm painting, you know! If I can't see it I can't write about it. I have to be able to see it. I also take photographs. I took photographs for ten years, although they were nothing like those of Jean – they were the architectural photographs in *Bunker Archeology*. But they're related to art – to the art of architecture!

NZ: Are there any other parallels between your writing and your photographs?

PV: There is an architecture – a theoretical architecture. My writings have an architecture though I wouldn't say that they offer a theory in the strict sense of the term. I have a very architectural vision of thought. Before being associated with structuralism, the word structure was imported from architecture, where it was associated with constructions like the Eiffel Tower, indeed Eiffel and the whole tradition of iron architecture were both closely associated with the origins of the architectural college that I directed for thirty years. More generally, this architecture reflects a Saint-Simonian geostratic vision according to which railways would create a kind of global village interconnected by the Suez and the

Panama canals – a vision in other words which is very close to my vision of the impact of technology upon the face of the world, and of the impact of architecture upon thought. In other words, my discussions are the thoughts of an architect.

NZ: It's very speculative thought, isn't it? Every two or three pages you seem to invent new kinds of terminology.

PV: I'm obliged to, I'm obliged to. Over and over again, I've argued that in addition to the political economy of wealth, there has to be a political economy of speed. The physiocrats who provided the basic studies of political economy worked in the tradition of Hume, they were men of perceptions, men of precepts. And when I discuss an economy of speed I'm doing the same sort of work, with the difference that my research examines the comparable power of speed and its influence on morals, on politics, strategies and so on.

My epoch is the epoch of the *Blitzkrieg*! I'm a physiocrat of speed and not of wealth. So I'm working in the context of very old traditions and absolutely open situations. At present, we still don't really know what a political economy of speed really means. It's research which still awaits subsequent realization.

NZ: At the same time, your work also sometimes seems to offer a more or less mystical celebration of relativity.

PV: Well of course, I'm a Christian. It's true that for me relativity isn't simply a theory – it's a way of life. For me, every life is relative, insofar as it is mortal.

NZ: But it's a positive relativism? It's not a perspective leading you to abandon values?

PV: No, no, not at all.

NZ: Nevertheless, isn't there a certain sense of conflict between your general forms of analysis examining the worst collective aspects of mass culture, and your more affirmative analysis of individual examples?

PV: Perhaps. But I'm primarily looking at breakdowns. My generation is obliged to acknowledge breakdowns and examine accidents. I'm a consequence of the accidents of political sociology. We believed in the grand narratives! My father was a Marxist and I was more of an anarchist, but we believed that the grand narratives offered salvation. But all of that is finished!

Bourdieu – whom I like a great deal – is still trying to resuscitate all that, and doesn't seem to have understood the implications of the breakdown of Marxism, the breakdown of socialism and the breakdown of communism.

Once again, this doesn't mean that one should vote for the National Front, but rather that considerable work remains to be done in terms of the accident of communism's implosion – of communism's death. There's no point in pretending that its corpse is still alive! Let's work instead at something else, in terms of the relationship between the individual and collectivity, which is always at the heart of history – always!

NZ: Interestingly, Baudrillard's recent writings suggest that if life in general is disappointing, its exceptions are more inspiring. Isn't there a danger that your readers and Baudrillard's readers may respond over-literally to the general arguments in your books, without recognizing their accompanying qualifications and irony?

PV: Of course! Jean's work is often misunderstood and like my work, it's often dismissed in terms of scandalous charges! Neither Baudrillard nor I are accepted here – we're not good Cartesians. It's no coincidence that our writings have been much more successful in Anglo-Saxon countries and in other countries with non-Cartesian mentalities. Relatively speaking, we're isolated here – we're not accepted. There's no tolerance here for irony, for wordplay, for argument that takes things to the limit and to excess.

In this regard, I share Clausewitz's impulse to examine war in terms of the logic of extremes. As Clausewitz suggests, when one studies war, one finds that the logic of warfare is inseparable from the logic of extremes. One can't examine war without examining extremes, without considering the very worst scenario.

And I always consider the worst. I'm forced to consider the worst! But in France this kind of thought is unacceptable. This kind of expression is virtually forbidden. And Baudrillard received exactly the same treatment when he spoke of simulation.

NZ: Do you think things will eventually improve?

PV: Certainly, but not for a long time, and at present I'm not sure what's in store. My fear is that things will become even more violent. Our violence was essentially symbolic and theoretical. It wasn't bloody, it wasn't revolutionary in the sense of the massacre – it took place in the realm of ideas and of the imagination. I'm afraid that the next phase of revolution will be very violent and that it will not be very intelligent.

NZ: Where do you see this coming from?

PV: From poverty. From inactivity. From the inertia of unemployment. Unemployment is also a form of polar inertia, and the crisis of unemployment carries the germ of civil war. If we can't restore mass activity, intelligent activity – but at least, activity – we're going to see a general state of global civil war. You only have to look at American cities. Even the most developed countries are constantly on the brink of civil war, not to mention the suburbs of Paris, London or elsewhere. That's the problem.

NZ: Where does this leave you, as a writer? Do you think that artists or intellectuals have any capacity to change or influence this condition?

PV: I don't think that artists and intellectuals have any influence any more. I think it's all finished for the moment. When one thinks of the influence of a Gide, of a Merleau-Ponty, of a Husserl or of a Heidegger, and one looks at the situation today, there's nothing.

The Sorbonne is dead. French universities are dead. There are no more thinkers at the Sorbonne. It's over. And that's not just my opinion – when French universities were evaluated, the Sorbonne was found to be one of the worst. There are no longer any great thinkers there. When I was young, it was fabulous! The courses were so extraordinary that it was like going to the opera! Even the lecturers you hissed were still extraordinary! But now it's just awful. It's just awful.

Translated by Nicholas Zurbrugg.

Note

This is the first time this interview has been published.

PART FIVE

ON THE STRATEGIES OF DECEPTION

12

THE KOSOVO W@R DID TAKE PLACE

Interview with John Armitage

1 *Stratégie de la déception*: **a position statement by Paul Virilio**

> Under the Mirabeau bridge flows the Seine
> And our loves
> Should I remember them
> The days are passing, I remain
>
> (Extract from 'The Mirabeau Bridge' by
> Guillaume Apollinaire, recited by Paul
> Virilio at the beginning of his statement
> and adopted by him as his position toward
> the Internet)

Dear friends, since my new book, *Stratégie de la déception*, has only just been published, and you have not yet been able to read it, I thought it would be of interest to you if I first of all outlined the book's main points before we proceed to the interview.[1]

This book is first and foremost the outcome of my refusal of what I call 'strategically correct thinking'. By this term I mean not only to reject the catastrophic modalities of the intervention against Slobodan Milošević's Serbia but also to reject absolutely the idea of fusing military and humanitarian affairs. In this respect, I am against the invention of 'secular holy wars', and especially in the name of a so-called 'duty to intervene'. However, I do share with my friend Bernard Kouchner – and who is now the United Nations' (UN) proconsul in Kosovo – the idea of a 'right to intervene', as long as such rights are exercised through the auspices of the UN. I am, therefore, against establishing a duty to intervene *per se*. To my mind, the idea of a duty to intervene amounts to a return to 'the state of nature', a return to the veritable 'war of all against all'. This, then, is the background to the thinking contained in my new book and constitutes an introduction of sorts.

Now, if someone were to ask me what my perspective is on the Kosovo War I would answer the question in the following manner: *the Kosovo War was a fool's war*. It was a fool's war first of all because, to put it in the words of a British friend of mine, it was the first time that a 'fly' like Kosovo could boast that it effectively occupied the fly paper!

However, for the United States (US), the Kosovo War was a successful war. This is because the US not only engineered the strategic failure of NATO but also successfully challenged the legitimacy of the UN. But for us Europeans, the Kosovo War resolved nothing at all. For instance, the chief outcome of the Kosovo War in Europe is not merely an *increase* in the number of displaced people, inclusive of Serbs and gypsies, but also an increase in the number of privately run militia groups and Mafia-type gangs. Nevertheless, for the US, the most significant results of the Kosovo War are, first, the successful development and deployment of the 'Revolution in Military Affairs' (RMA) and second the re-launching of the military–industrial complex, or, as it should be re-titled today, the military–*scientific* complex. The term RMA, of course, refers to the new military theories of information, communication and technology associated with the techno-scientific development of 'cyberwar'. But what is important for us in Europe to note about the role of the US in the Kosovo War is that it *conducted an experiment on Europe in the same manner that it did on Japan at the end of the Second World War.* For the US, therefore, Kosovo was used as an experimental test site for the further development of the RMA. And, for me, such experiments are of great significance. For example, about ten years ago, I went to Japan and met with a number of provincial governors. However, while I was there, I took the opportunity to speak to them about nearby Hiroshima and the dropping of the atomic bomb at the end of the Second World War. And one of the governors said to me: 'We Japanese are originally a military nation, a nation of warriors and farmers. We do not blame the Americans for having won the Second World War, or for having killed soldiers and even civilians. That is acceptable. What we reproach them for is the fact that, at Hiroshima and Nagasaki, they conducted an experiment on us.' I will never forget this sentence! For neither the Japanese nor we Europeans are laboratory animals!

But, you may ask, what was the nature of the US RMA experiment and why were the Americans so keen to use Kosovo as a test site? My interpretation is that such an experiment was necessary because the US is presently seeking to establish what I call the 'second deterrence'. Let me remind you that the 'first deterrence' was nuclear deterrence, an 'absolute deterrence' founded on the energy of atomic particles. The first deterrence was introduced in the period between 1945 and 1950. Thus, the period of the first deterrence predates the era of 'mutual deterrence' between the East and the West. All the same, what is significant about the era of the first deterrence is that the US was the sole possessor of nuclear capability. Today, therefore, we are presently entering a period that resembles the period of the first deterrence. There is, though, one crucial difference: the era of the second deterrence is based on cyberwar. And, as I have said many times before, the development of cyberwar is one of the chief results of the detonation of what I call 'the information bomb'. The information bomb is a bomb that is similar to the atomic bomb but only to the extent that it is a device based on energy. However, whereas the atom bomb was triggered by the energy of the atom, the information bomb is triggered by the energy of information and communications technologies. As I noted some time ago: 'if *interactivity* is to information what *radioactivity* is to energy, then we are confronted with the fearsome emergence of the "Accident to end all accidents", an accident which is no longer *local* and precisely situated, but *global* and generalized.'[2]

Let me be clear: the information bomb is a new type of weapons system. And this is a very important point for me, because, as I have argued in numerous books, historically, progress has depended upon the speed of three very different types of weapons systems.[3] The first of these weapons systems is the system of 'obstruction weapons' (fortifications and so on). One cannot, for instance, understand the nature of the Great Wall of China or any modern urban centre without reference to obstruction weapons. This is because no fortress or city has ever managed to survive without fortifications. The second of these weapons systems is the system of 'destructive weapons' (cannon balls, atomic bombs and so on). Destructive weapons destroy the fortifications. Moreover, destructive weapons have reigned supreme from the Middle Ages to the twentieth century. Equally importantly, the continued development of destructive weapons is the chief reason why we invented the whole idea of deterrence or what I call 'pure war'.[4] The third of these weapons systems is the information bomb, the system that is currently being put into place. It is a weapons system founded on information and communications technologies, inclusive of the Internet.

As a result, we can say that the first point to make about the Kosovo War is that it was a cyberwar. It was a cyberwar that took place in the 'orbital spaces' inhabited by information and communications technologies. There is, therefore, a major distinction to be made between the war that took place in the Persian Gulf in 1991 and the war that took place in Kosovo in 1999. For, unlike the classic air and land war that was the Persian Gulf War, the Kosovo War took place in orbital space.[5] For example, in the intervening period between the Persian Gulf War and the Kosovo War, Cruise missiles were transformed by the politicians into '*Crusade* missiles'! But, of course, we have to ask ourselves what kind of crusade it was? What are its results? The results are plain for all to see. For instance, we can see that, for all the humanitarian rhetoric of the politicians and the high technology deployed by the military, the Kosovo adventure has resulted in victory only for the privatized warriors and the paramilitary outfits of the warring sides. That is, for the Mafia and for the Serbian gangs.[6] This can only be described as a catastrophe. For example, when the Allies liberated France in 1944–5 – and I for one am really thankful to them for liberating my country – it would have been considered a disaster if state power had simply fallen into the hands of the Resistance! There would have been civil war and, in all likelihood, France would have been turned into a so-called 'People's Republic', as happened in Eastern Europe. For another important and contemporary example, one needs only to look at the role played by the militias, paramilitary and special police intelligence troops in East Timor, troops that were trained by the US at the beginning of the Suharto period in 1965.

These points, then, are the launch pad for my refusal of the strategically correct form of thinking that was adopted by NATO towards the crisis in Kosovo. By the way, my refusal earned me a lot of criticism in France because some people seemed to think that my refusal meant that I was pro-Milošević. I am anti-Milošević. But my anti-Milošević stance was not the sole basis of my refusal. Indeed, I refused strategically correct thinking for one very good reason: *one does not bomb a civil war from the air. Period.* For me, the bombing of Kosovo amounted to *an air war waged against civilians.* For instance, it is interesting to note that, and unlike the civilians, during the war, the official military personnel on both sides were treated as if they were a protected species. This is what I call an *'ecological putsch'*!

But let's return to the important question of why the Kosovo War was, principally, an air war. In my view, the most significant aspect of the Kosovo War in this respect was the idea that air superiority is the present-day equivalent of nineteenth-century naval superiority. The idea of air superiority conjures up the spectre of 'Global Air Power' (GAP). Thus, if we look at what took place during the war in Kosovo, we can easily see that it was not a war that took place on the horizontal level, as was the case with all wars that have taken place since the time of Napoleon. It was a war that took place in the air, in orbital space. For example, at one stage, there were over fifty reconnaissance, radar and eavesdropping satellites orbiting above Kosovo, not to mention the Global Positioning Systems, the 'Blackbird' spy planes flying at very high altitudes, the manned reconnaissance flights at 15,000 feet, and, under that ceiling, the unmanned drones. Unmanned drones are, of course, nothing but flying cameras. However, such important developments illustrate exactly what I noted almost twenty years ago in *War and Cinema*.[7] For, in that book, I suggested that unmanned drones were to cyberwar what intercontinental ballistic missiles were to nuclear war. Unmanned drones are weapons systems concerned with the collection and communication of information, whereas ballistic missiles are weapons of destruction. Thus one can assert that the Kosovo War was indeed a cyberwar. The idea was that, as automation takes command of the barracks, one could dispense with troops, just as when automation takes command of the factory, the idea is that one can dispense with the proletariat. Of course, the results are the same: both soldiers and workers are made redundant. One could also say much the same about the fully automated and unmanned NASA space expeditionary rockets such as Voyager. Such rockets are the Cruise missiles of the space programme.

In my analysis, therefore, the results of the Kosovo War are twofold. For Europe, the result is that the war has not only solved nothing but it has also increased the numbers of displaced civilians. For the US, however, the result of the war is it allowed for the successful further development of the RMA and the military–scientific complex. But in order to conduct a cyberwar two other essential components are required if the experiment is to be a success. The first component is the idea of 'Global Information Dominance' (GID). The General in charge of GID at the Pentagon is Andrew Marshall. Marshall is the driving force behind the notion of the second deterrence and the

Director of the Office of Net Assessment. In other words, he is in charge of the development of cyberwar. The basic idea of GID is to *revolutionize information and communication technologies in all possible realms*. The second component of cyberwar is one that I have already mentioned and that is GAP. The development of GAP has been entrusted to the US Air Force and to the US Space Command. However, what is crucial to note about both these components of cyberwar is that they are totally 'deterritorialized' and, to a large extent, 'virtualized'. Here, of course, we meet face to face with the historical traditions of Anglo-Saxon military culture. It is a culture based on naval power and the absence of attachment to physical territory.

Deterritorialization is a modern term for what the British admirals of old used to call 'the strategy of the fleet in being'.[8] But, where in the old days the theatre of operations resided in the Atlantic or the Pacific Ocean, today it resides in the air, in orbital space. *This is an extraordinary strategic and political revolution*! We can say, therefore, that the destructive weapons, gunboat politics and diplomacy of yesteryear have now been extended, through the application of information and communications technologies, into the air. For example, let us look at the kind of pressure that was exercised by Commodore Perry's destroyers in 1853 against Japan. Perry was trying to force Japan to 'open up', to engage in trade. Is it not the same logic that is being put to work again today? But, this time, in the air? Aren't those automated Cruise missile air strikes against Sudan, Afghanistan, Iraq and now Kosovo a form of long-range naval gunnery? Of course, such automated air strikes are not in the hands of the militias and the paramilitary groups warring in Kosovo but in the hands of the US state in the form of the highly secretive National Imagery Mapping Agency (NIMA). Thus, while the NIMA supplies the US with its 'Big Eyes', the National Security Agency (NSA) supplies it with its 'Big Ears'! Consequently, the development of the RMA revolution also implies a revolution in the secret services and in intelligence gathering on an unprecedented scale. This is also why the current debate over cryptography is so significant.

Today, then, the US is embarking on a line of research that involves the construction and deployment of spy satellites with a view to setting in train an optical form of surveillance and control based in the air. For example, surveillance used to take place orally, or in writing. But, nowadays, the surveillance of civilians only takes place optically. For me, therefore, seeing *is* surveillance. When we used to talk about optics, for instance, we used to refer to Galileo's eyepiece, to the telescope, and to the optical discovery of the universe. Now, through its militarization, *optics has become an airborne vision machine*.[9] This is a theme of major interest to me, since recent developments in optics also imply developments in aesthetics. For example, when people say to me that ours is the epoch of the civilization of the image, I say no! It is the epoch of the militarization of airborne optics. Gaston Bachelard once said that 'every image is poised for enlargement' and, to my mind, this is exactly what is happening to optics today. What we are faced with, then, is the globalization of the image, the terminal enlargement of the image. And this is what I call the orbital utopia of the *Global Eye!* However, and although the Global Eye *is* a utopia, it is a utopia that is a constituent part of ongoing military research into unmanned drones and cyberwar.

Before we proceed to the interview, let me conclude by emphasizing the following points about the Kosovo War. First, while the US can view the war as a success, Europe must see it as a failure for it and, in particular, for the institutions of the European Union (EU). For the US, the Kosovo War was a success because it encouraged the development of the RMA. The war provided a test site for experimentation, and paved the way for emergence of what I have called the second deterrence. It is, therefore, my firm belief that the US is currently seeking to revert to the position it held after the triggering of atomic bombs at Hiroshima and Nagasaki in the 1940s, when the US was the sole nuclear power. And here I repeat what I suggested at the beginning of my position statement. The first deterrence, nuclear deterrence, is presently being superseded by the second deterrence: a type of deterrence based on the information bomb and the new weaponry of information and communications technologies. Thus, in the very near future, and I stress this important point, *it will no longer be war that is the continuation of politics by other means, it will be the integral accident that is the continuation of politics by other means*.

The automation of warfare has, then, come a long way since the Persian Gulf War. Needless to say, none of these developments will help the plight of the refugees in Kosovo or stop the actions of the militias operating there. However, the automation of warfare will allow for the continuation not only of war in the air but also of the further development of the RMA, GID and GAP. It is for these reasons that, in my new book, I focus for example on the use of the 'graphite bomb' to shut off the Serbian electricity supply as well as the cutting off of the service provision to Serbia of the EuTelSat television satellite by the EU. And, let me remind you that the latter action was carried out against the explicit wishes of the UN. To my mind, therefore, the integral accident, the automation of warfare and the RMA are all part of the shift towards the second deterrence and the explosion of the information bomb. For me, these developments are revolutionary because, today, the age of the locally situated bomb such as the atomic bomb has passed. The atomic bomb provoked a *specific* accident. But the information bomb gives rise to the integral and *globally constituted accident*. The globally constituted accident can be compared to what people who work at the stock exchange call 'systemic risk'. And, of course, we have already seen some instances of systemic risk in recent times in the current Asian financial crisis. But what sparked off the Asian financial crisis? Automated trading programs!

Here, then, we meet again the problems I noted earlier with regard to interactivity. Moreover, it is clear that the era of the information bomb, the era of aerial warfare, the era of the RMA and global surveillance is also the era of *the integral accident*. Cyberwar has nothing to do with the destruction brought about by bombs and grenades and so on. It is specifically linked to the information systems of life itself. It is in this sense that, as I have said many times before, interactivity is the equivalent of radioactivity. For interactivity effects a kind of disintegration, a kind of *rupture*. For me, the Asian financial crisis of 1998 and the war in Kosovo in 1999 are the prelude to the integral accident of the year 2000. Now, my friends, to the interview!

2   'The Kosovo W@r Did Take Place': interview with John Armitage

From geopolitics to psychopolitics

JA: Professor Virilio, I would like to start by charting your theoretical and architectural interest in questions concerning the two concepts of military space and the organization of territory. For example, even your earliest research – into the 'Atlantic Wall' in the 1950s and 1960s – was founded on these two concepts. Moreover, your most recently published study, *Stratégie de la déception*, is a study of military space and the organization of territory within the context of the recent Kosovo War. However, before we discuss *Stratégie de la déception* and the war in Kosovo in some detail, could you explain what you mean by military space and the organization of territory and why these concepts are so important for an understanding of your work?

PV: These concepts are important quite simply because I am an urbanist. And, may I remind your readers yet again; I am not a philosopher. Thus the whole of my work is focused on geopolitics and geostrategy. However, a second aspect of my work is movement. This, of course, I pursue through my research on speed and my study of the organization of the revolution of the means of transportation. For me, then, territory and movement are linked. For instance, territory is controlled by the movements of horsemen, of tanks, of planes, and so on. Thus my research on dromology, on the logic and impact of speed, necessarily implies the study of the organization of territory. Whoever controls the territory possesses it. Possession of territory is not primarily about laws and contracts, but first and foremost a matter of movement and circulation. Hence I am always concerned with ideas of territory and movement. Indeed, my first book after *Bunker Archeology* (1994) was entitled *L'Insécurité du territoire* (1976).[10]

JA: To what extent does your intellectual and artistic work on the architecture of war, and architecture more generally, inform your thinking in *Stratégie de la déception*? Is it the case that, in common with other so-called 'postmodern' wars, such as the Persian Gulf War in 1991, the architecture of war, along with architecture itself, is 'disappearing'? How did you approach the question of the architecture of war and its disappearance in *Stratégie de la déception*?[11]

PV: Well, let me put it this way, I have always been interested in the architecture of war, as can be seen in *Bunker Archeology*. However, at the time that I did the research for that book, I was very young. My aim was to understand the notion of 'Total War'. As I have said many times before, I was among the first people to experience the German Occupation of France during the Second World War. I was 7–13 years old during the war and did not really internalize its significance. More specifically, under the Occupation, we in Nantes were denied access to the coast of the Atlantic Ocean. It was therefore not until after the war was over that I saw the sea for the first time, in the vicinity of St Nazaire. It was there that I discovered the bunkers. But what I also discovered was that, during the war, the whole of Europe had become a fortress. And thus I saw to what extent an immense territory, a whole continent, had effectively been reorganized into one city, and just like the cities of old. From that moment on, I became more interested in urban matters, in logistics, in the organization of transport, in maintenance and supplies.

But what is so astonishing about the war in Kosovo for me is that it was a war that totally bypassed territorial space. It was a war that took place almost entirely in the air. There were hardly any Allied armed personnel on the ground. There was, for example, no real state of siege and practically no blockade. However, may I remind you that France and Germany were opposed to a maritime blockade of the Adriatic Sea without a mandate from the UN. So, what we witnessed in Kosovo was an extraordinary war, a war waged solely with bombs from the air. What happened in Kosovo was the exact reversal of what happened in 'Fortress Europe' in 1943–5. Let me explain. Air Marshall 'Bomber' Harris used to say that 'Fortress Europe' was a fortress without a roof, since the Allies had air supremacy. Now, if we look at the Kosovo War, what do we see? We see a fortress without walls – but with a roof! Isn't that disappearance extraordinary?!

JA: The results of the *Architecture Principe* group in the early 1960s were a review, a theory of the 'oblique function', and the construction of a modern 'bunker church' in Nevers.[12] And, as you have already indicated, your architecture has always been a highly *politicized* architecture. What kinds of links, if any, were there between the work of *Architecture Principe* on the oblique function, the bunker church, politics and the conduct of the war in Kosovo?

PV: Many things could be said about *Architecture Principe* and the oblique function. But much of it belongs to another age. However, I could say a few things about the bunker church in Nevers and the war in Kosovo. First of all, one must remember that the church was dedicated to St Bernadette of Lourdes. Naturally, had it been dedicated to St Francis of

Assisi, it would have been a different church. It would have been a transparent church, a church for the birds! Second, it is important to remind you that, in 1858, St Bernadette saw the Virgin Mary in the grotto at Lourdes. Nevertheless, at the time that the bunker church was built, in 1966, it was in the middle of the Cold War, in the middle of the balance of nuclear terror. And, of course, the emblematic building *par excellence* was the atomic shelter. My church is meant to be an architectural equivalent of all that. At the time I said that, in the present day, a church could only refer to the eventuality of total destruction. Hence the bunker church is not modelled after its German namesake. Instead, it is modelled after – and is a pointer to – the atomic shelter. In other words, the atomic threat to a particular territory had become a threat to the whole of the earth. Thus it is a political architecture. I am a Christian. But I am also *totally* committed to the political issues and struggles of the times I am living in!

Yet not everyone shares my politics or my particular Christian vision. For example, when the bunker church was consecrated by the local bishop, the priest, who was conducting the ceremony, was walking around the building and performing the sign of the Cross. Now, the public, myself included, was inside the church. Consequently, we did not know what was going on outside because we were patiently waiting for the mass of consecration to begin. However, a few years ago, the priest told me that while the bishop was outside consecrating the church, he was constantly muttering to himself the following words: 'What a ghastly thing! Amen! What a ghastly thing! Amen!' At this point, my friend the priest turned towards the bishop and said: 'Monsignor, this is not an exorcism! It is a consecration!' [*Laughs*]

Still, for me, the bunker is the archetypal symbol of deterrence. The nuclear shelter and the underground corridors, for instance, are part of the urban infrastructure in a country like Switzerland. There are nuclear shelters stocked with food in all Swiss cities. We have lived with them for forty years! But now, all this has been forgotten. But not by me!

As to the conduct of the war in Kosovo, it is really difficult to formulate an answer to the question of how to concretize it. This is not simply because it was an 'occult' war but also because it was a small and yet very important one. I would say that the whole ex-Yugoslavia conflict, a conflict that has been going on for almost ten years now, is principally about militias and paramilitary outfits. Above all, what we have witnessed is the reappearance of the 'war entrepreneur', that is, of the 'privatization of war'.[13] It is a kind of return to fifteenth-century warfare, a return to the era of the warlord. In this regard, the Kosovo War represents a regressive development in terms of international warfare. If you compare the situation in Kosovo to the beaches of D-day or the big battles like the one that took place at Stalingrad, it is clear that what we are seeing is the end of national or international wars and warriors and the return to private wars and warriors.

JA: Would it be correct to say that *Stratégie de la déception*, like the bulk of your other writings, is principally informed by a phenomenological philosophical approach to the Kosovo War? What, for you, are the advantages and disadvantages of such an approach to questions of strategy and deception?

PV: War, even before it sets about organizing the battlefield, is primarily about organizing the field of perception. In that respect, I am fully a phenomenologist. But I am also, and in the deepest sense, a strategist. For the strategist *sees* the full extent of the battle, even before he dispatches his tacticians and soldiers into it. And it is from there that not only *Stratégie de la déception* but also *War and Cinema* emerged. So, in that sense, yes, I am an 'old warrior' in phenomenology.

JA: In *Stratégie de la déception*, in what ways, if any, did you find the work of Einstein helpful in explaining the military space of Kosovo and the temporal organization of Balkan territory?

PV: I did not find the work of Einstein helpful at all! In fact, the first page of my new book opens with a quotation from Vauvenargues and it is a quotation that happens to answer your question very well. It reads as follows: '*La raison nous trompe plus souvent que la nature*' (Reason misleads us more often than nature). For me, then, it was the reasoning employed by the NATO war-chiefs that was completely mislead by the nature of the terrain in Kosovo. The Kosovo War was a war that saw a movement away from 'geostrategy' and a movement towards 'chronostrategy', the strategy of speed. For example, when the US Secretary of State Madeleine Albright launched the US's Cruise missiles, she thought the Kosovo War would be over in three days. It lasted three months! And therein lies the catastrophe. Had it indeed lasted for three days, it would have been a success. But three months is an abject failure from a chronostrategic point of view.

JA: Recently, I was thinking about the exhibition of your photographs organized prior to the publication of *Bunker Archeology* in 1975 at the Museum of Decorative Arts in Paris. I was wondering if you were asked to organize an exhibition on the architecture of the war in Kosovo today what sort of things you might put in it?

PV: Aerial views! Satellite photos! Pictures taken by drones! I would very much like to make an overview of all these different views from above!

JA: Throughout the Kosovo conflict, via the mass media, we were constantly bombarded with the now familiar language of postmodern warfare. For example, 'Rock 'n' roll' was, apparently, the code name for the beginning of NATO air strikes on Serbian military forces. Is the relationship between the mass media, language and warfare an important relationship for you and your work in *Stratégie de la déception*?

PV: Well, let me begin with a story about the code name used for the Allied landing in Normandy, a codename used to alert the Resistance movement in France. It was a verse taken from a poem of Verlaine's and which went as follows: '*Les sanglots longs des violons de l'automne/ Brisent mon coeur d'une langueur monotone*' (The long sighs of autumn's violins/break my heart with monotonous languor). The first part of this verse was the forewarning, while the second part was the signal for the actual landing operations. Now, how can you compare this key phrase from fifty years ago with the phrase 'Rock 'n' roll' today? Make up your own mind. However, let us be clear: the Kosovo War was a war of the 'politically correct'. Indeed, one cannot understand that war without an understanding of what I call 'NGO-Speak'. For example, an illustration of NGO-Speak is the way in which the NGOs inflated terms such as genocide. It was nothing less than outrageous propaganda in the name of humanitarianism. It was a crusade. And the use of the language of the crusade in such situations is something that I, as a Christian, *cannot stand*! The abuse of the vocabulary of the crusades is well drawn if one compares the war against the Serbs with the war against the Nazis. In the war against the Nazis there was no talk of crusades. Why? *Because it was not needed*! But back then, things were much clearer for everyone: everyone knew they were being oppressed.

JA: In addition to the language of postmodern warfare and the politically correct during the conflict in Kosovo, media institutions such as the BBC and CNN also subjected those of us outside Serbia to the imagery of postmodern warfare. Is the role of media imagery during the Kosovo conflict a key element of your thinking in *Stratégie de la déception*?

PV: No, on the contrary. In fact, I believe that, during the Kosovo War, as opposed to the Persian Gulf War, it was the discussions that took place in the press, in the realm of the spoken word, and on the radio, that were more important than TV imagery. This is because there was an element of surprise in the Gulf War that, through live coverage, I would say, stunned the audience. However, with respect to the Kosovo War, people were already accustomed to this sort of imagery. So, what was needed was more emphasis on the message, a reinforcement of content as it were, and this is where newspapers and magazines played a key role alongside radio broadcasts. In this sense, it was not television imagery but radio broadcasts that were the most important element in the Kosovo War. Having said that, it is also true to say that we were fed a lot of repetitive images of the conflict in Kosovo. For instance, we were fed a lot of images of refugees. But, in the end, this strategy simply did not work. Why? Because it looked like a TV show, a kind of 'telethon war' but featuring the wounded, the sick and the handicapped.

JA: Although it is well known that you are unsympathetic to psychoanalytic interpretations of human behaviour, I wondered whether the Kosovo War writings of psychoanalytically influenced and radical cultural theorists such as Slavoj Žižek had had any impact on your analyses of the war? Žižek, for example, noted how the media tended to elevate Milošević into the 'embodiment of evil' while presenting President Clinton as the instrument of a 'higher law': almost of God Himself. How do you respond to such interpretations?[14]

PV: Well, first of all, I do not have a psychoanalytic background or training. It is not my world. Hence, I do not have very much to say in this respect. Yet it is clear that given the region of the world where the Kosovo War took place the psychoanalytic dimension is of crucial importance. However, I recently met Claudio Magris, a great writer. And I was very impressed by his intelligent explanation of that region. I believe that one would need to ask a writer, not necessarily someone with a psychoanalytic background, but a writer, to portray the Kosovo War. I believe that a person like Magris could do it very well.[15] But, then again, Peter Handke did it. However, in my opinion, he did it very badly. I disagree with Handke, of course, because he took a pro-Serbia stand. How could I agree with that?[16] As for Žižek, I do know of him by name but I have not read him.

From economic warfare to ethnic cleansing

JA: A number of cultural and social theorists on the left sought to explain the Kosovo conflict largely in economic terms – in terms of the needs of US imperialism in Europe and elsewhere. Edward Said, Professor of Comparative Literature at Columbia and long-time Palestinian activist, for example, spoke of the US's naked 'display of military might', while others talked of the US's need for strategic and economic advantage in relation to Europe in the era of economic globalization. Is the economic dimension of the war in Kosovo an important one for your analysis in *Stratégie de la déception*?[17]

PV: What Said refers to as a naked display of military might, I have called *an experiment*. But, yes, of course, an economic analysis of the war is important. However, I do not touch upon this aspect of the Kosovo War in my new book because I was writing it during the war itself. Additionally, I had enough material to handle! And I was much more taken by the new air and information gathering strategies. Thus, I did not delve very deep into the economic dimensions of the war. But, yes, I do believe that the economic aspects of the Kosovo War are very important. For instance, one cannot dissociate cyberwarfare from economic warfare. They are indissociable. But, please remember that my new book is not a magnum opus! It is just a small book! [*Laughs*]

JA: Do you think that responsibility for the war in Kosovo can be said to lie with particular individuals such as Slobodan Milošević or with the British Prime Minister, Tony Blair? Or was the war the outcome of other, perhaps deeper, structural factors such as the development of the mass media?

PV: I do not think that one should only focus on individuals. Indeed, one should consider much deeper factors like the media. Look at what took place at the Rambouillet conference. What Rambouillet made clear was that, today, diplomacy – and particularly the diplomats – have lost their power to the media, to the Internet, and to the 'live' coverage of events. The problem is that things are moving so fast today that all serious issues are now debated and decided in the context of an emergency. And, on the international plane, issues are only discussed if they already represent an emergency. However, diplomacy needs time and lots of talking. It is a spoken intelligence, a specific kind of discourse. But it is a discourse that does not suit the epoch of multimedia networks.

JA: While the mass media played an important role during the Kosovo conflict, it soon became evident that the Internet was also perceived to be playing its part in the war. Radio B92, via OpenNet, for example, continued broadcasting through Real Audio streaming long after the Serbian authorities removed its signal. Despite the fact that you are a vehement critic of the Internet, don't you think that, in cases like the above, the Internet can be perceived as a technology of liberation?[18]

PV: As I have said before, for me, the Internet, as Aesop might put it, is at the same time the worst and the best of all things. That being said, the Kosovo War was indeed the first Internet war. That makes it interesting in its own right. However, I must say that I am surprised that, so far, no proper evaluation of the role of the Internet in the Kosovo War appears to have been forthcoming. After all, the Internet is normally a technology that seems to be able to manage its own public relations. I would be really interested in such an evaluation since I do not have enough information about the part played by the Internet in the Kosovo War myself. To me, this is a very important issue because the Kosovo War was truly the inspiration for the inauguration of democracy on the Internet. Of course, I have been aware of the Internet for years now. For example, I invited Nicholas Negroponte here to the Ecole Spéciale d'Architecture over twenty years ago. That was when he was working with the 'Architecture Machine Group'.[19] So, it would be wrong to suggest that I am against the technological environment of the Internet. My position, as I indicated in my position statement prior to this interview, is that I want to be objective about it in order that I can maintain a distance from it, something that, so far, the majority of French people have totally failed to do. Thus what annoys me about the Internet is, first, the hype surrounding its deployment and second, the denial of critique, particularly surrounding its military development.

JA: Conversely, what role do you think the Internet and cyberspace played in the strategies of deception developed and deployed by the NATO military command and control structure?

PV: It is clear that, from a military perspective, the Internet can play the same role as radio jamming. Let us take an example: during the Second World War, one could not listen to Allied radio stations without experiencing a disturbing and ear-splitting noise. It was not a very sophisticated form of jamming. However, in my opinion, nowadays, it is on the Internet where jamming takes place. But the Internet does not jam in the same way that radio does. This is because, today, jamming takes the form of information confusion and the Internet is the premier site of such confusion. As I point out in *Stratégie de la déception*, censorship is no longer concerned with the addition or the subtraction of information but with *the multiplication of information* on a given subject. In this way, the multiplication of information jams any sensible interpretation. As the architect Mies van der Rohe said, 'Less is more'. However, in our case, we could say that more is less! That sums up the risks of the Internet.

JA: Even so, it seems to me that, in the context of the Kosovo War, both the anti-militarists like Radio B92 and the pro-militarists in NATO were using the same technology: the Internet. Today, then, it appears that both opposing a war and prosecuting one involves the use of the same technology. How do you interpret this situation? Is there no longer any other way of challenging the social implications of the cultural logic of late militarism and its role in the culture of 'hypermodernism'?[20]

PV: I believe that we have entered the era of cyberwarfare. As a result, any opposition to militarism must no longer take the form of an opposition to the armed forces and their weaponry, as in the old days of pacifism. This is because, today, opposition to war is also opposition to the cybernetic perversion of information. And this, of course, is what cyberwarfare is all about. For instance, some twenty years ago, I was not simply an active participant in the non-violent anti-war movement but also writing my book on *War and Cinema*. Moreover, I was at that time already criticizing the 'logistics of perception' and the misuse of film with a view to producing cyberwar. However, my friends in the anti-war movement told me that such claims made no sense and that my position was not militant enough. I replied that while it was true that one can march through the streets with placards demanding that we 'Ban the Bomb' or 'Rid the World of Poison Gas' one cannot easily march through the streets shouting 'Down with flight simulators!', 'Down with cameras!', or 'Down with the Internet!' On the other hand, this example does show that, as early as the 1980s, such questions were starting to appear. It also illustrates the perversity of the military revolution.

JA: Doesn't the perversion of information, its links with the Internet and movie cameras, raise *new* social and cultural questions *other* than those associated with the military revolution? For example, doesn't the corruption of sexual information and its connections with the Internet in the shape of 'live' Webcams of women's bedrooms (e.g. 'Jennycam') and so on present new and critical questions about Foucault's conception of social control and the metaphor of the 'Panopticon'?[21] It seems to me that, far from being uneasy about insidious forms of visual policing and surveillance, many people today appear to become anxious if they are *not* subject to the piercing gaze of the technologized Other. Moreover, such people are even willing to invest in the Internet precisely in order that they can control their own – in this case sexual – behaviour for the enjoyment of the technologized Other. What are your views on this phenomenon?

PV: I completely agree. But, here too, exhibitionism and voyeurism are two faces of the same phenomenon. Indeed, for me, this is one of today's great questions. For what we are seeing here is *the desire to become a film oneself*. Nowadays, no one wants to become a real man or woman, a hero, or even a star. *They want to become a film!* This goes way beyond what Andy Warhol was alluding to when he said that, in the future, we would all be famous for fifteen minutes. For example, for the Romans, the goal of life was to become a statue, to become like Caesar. Now, however, for us, the increasingly hyped aim of life is the celebration of the human being but mediated through film. But wanting to become a film means not only wanting to show oneself to others but also wanting to *confirm one's own existence*. Such a desire on the part of women or men is, like Webcams themselves, tragic. You see there is something of a loss there. That said, these are some of the very big questions I would like to write about eventually.

JA: For me, one of the most interesting and alarming developments in the Kosovo conflict was the fact that Milošević and the other Serbian state elites appeared to take great pride in destroying Serbia's own economic and social infrastructure. Moreover, this reminded me very much of your discussion of the Nazi state and its power during the Second World War in *L'Insécurité du territoire*. For, in the essay entitled 'The Suicidal State', you write of how Hitler's Total War and decolonization policies eventually led to the erection of 'the suicidal state'.[22] Do you think that it would be legitimate to make a comparison between the strategy of the Serbian Sate and that of the Nazi State?

PV: Well, first of all, comparison is not reason. Or, as a friend of mine said, 'to compare is not to prove'. Milošević is not Hitler. So much is clear. But it is true that Milošević has suicidal tendencies. But what is true for Milošević and for Serbia is also true for a number of others and their countries. Look at Cambodia or any number of other countries, particularly in the Islamic world. Look at Iraq, Afghanistan and Iran. The suicidal state has a promising future! But let us be clear. Today, the phenomenon of the suicidal state is linked to the crisis of the nation-state, a crisis that is linked to globalization, and to the current parlous state of many modern governments. And it is clear that, in this context, Milošević has a suicidal tendency. But the same can be said of Algeria, if not of its President, Bouteflika. However, it was Hitler who inaugurated the suicidal state. And, of course, after Hitler came the invention and the explosion of the atom bomb, an invention that only reinforced the suicidal tendency through the *truly* suicidal policy of Mutually Assured Destruction (MAD). In this sense, we are all Hitler's children.

JA: In *Speed and Politics: An Essay on Dromology* (1986), you write of the military and political revolution in transportation and information transmission. Indeed, for you, the speed of the military–industrial complex is the driving force of cultural and social development, or, as you put it, 'history progresses at the speed of its weapons systems'. In what ways do you think that speed politics played a role in the military and political conflict in Kosovo? For instance, was the speed of transportation and information transmission the most important factor in the war? Or, more generally, for you, is the military–industrial complex still the motor of history?[23]

PV: I believe that the military–industrial complex is more important than ever. This is because the war in Kosovo gave fresh impetus not to the military–industrial complex but to the military–*scientific* complex. You can see this in China. You can also see it in Russia with its development of stealth planes and other very sophisticated military machines. I am of course thinking aloud here about new planes such as the Sukhois. There is very little discussion about such developments but, for me, I am constantly astonished by the current developments within, for example, the Russian air force. And, despite the economic disaster that is Russia, there are still air shows taking place in the country. For these reasons, then, I believe that the politics of intervention and the Kosovo War have also prompted a fresh resumption of the arms race worldwide. However, this situation has arisen because the sovereignty of the nation-state is no longer accepted. This is also why we are witnessing states rushing forward in order to safeguard themselves against an intervention similar to the one that took place in Kosovo. This is one of the most disturbing, if indirect, aspects of the war in Kosovo and one that I discuss at length in my new book. Of course, one of the most disturbing features is the fact that while we have had roughly a ten-year pause in the arms race where a lot of good work was carried out, this period has now come to an end. For what we are seeing at the present time are new developments in the production of anti-missile weaponry, drones and so on. Thus, some of the most dramatic consequences of the Kosovo War are linked to the resumption of the arms race and the suicidal political and economic policies of countries like India and Pakistan where literally tons of money is currently being spent on atomic weaponry. This is abhorrent!

JA: In *Popular Defense and Ecological Struggles* (1990), you argue that the 'principle aim of any truly popular resistance is thus to oppose the establishment of a social situation based solely on the illegality of armed force, which reduces a population to the status of a movable slave, a commodity'. To what extent to do you think that such an aim characterized the popular resistance of the Kosovo Albanians in opposing Milošević's efforts to reduce them to the status of movable slaves, of commodities?[24]

PV: First, I believe that there is an ethnic and religious dimension to the conflicts in the Balkans that vastly complicates the issues of democratic resistance and military power. But it is nevertheless self-evident that countering Milošević was a necessity, within the Serbian State, within the ex-Yugoslavia Federation and outside it, at the level of the EU, and on the part of the US. For me, though, it was the *political methods and military techniques* that were used that were disastrous and, in the end, counter-productive in terms of popular resistance. For example, such methods greatly accelerated ethnic cleansing. Moreover, they led to a situation similar to that which currently exists in Iraq, another situation where not only has nothing has been solved but also where the fly is proud to occupy the fly paper!

From the disintegration of the nation-state to the second deterrence

JA: It is now some twenty years since you and Alain Joxe founded the Inter-disciplinary Centre for Research into Peace and Strategic Studies (CIRPES) at the House of the Human Sciences. Looking back, how, if at all, has the research you undertook into peace and strategic studies in the late 1970s informed your work in the late 1990s in works such as *Stratégie de la déception*?

PV: Alain Joxe took a stand in favour of the NATO intervention. We remain friends but differ on this issue since I was against the intervention of NATO. However, the work we did at CIRPES anticipated many situa-tions. It even played a part in shaping French cabinet ministers' opinions, such as Alain Joxe's brother, Pierre Joxe, and Jean-Pierre Chevenement. But the one thing that we did not anticipate – our mistake if I might put it that way – was the break up not only of the Soviet Union but also of the other surrounding states. This is a very important point because, today, there is the very real threat of the disintegration of *all* nation-states. We did not see that coming. Nor did we anticipate the regression towards a situation where the Mafia or the paramilitaries of privatized warfare would begin to dominate the world political scene.

JA: Before we turn to consider the aesthetic aspects of the 'disappearance' of military space and the organization of territory in Kosovo, I would like to ask why it was that in the late 1970s and early 1980s you first began to consider the technological aspects of these phenomena? What was it that prompted you to focus on the technological aspects at that time?

PV: Because it was from that time onwards that *real time superseded real space!* Today, almost all current technologies put the speed of light to work. And, as you know, here we are not only talking about information at a distance but also operation at a distance, or, the possibility to act instantaneously, from afar. For example, the RMA *begins* with the application of the speed of light. This means that history is now rushing headlong into the wall of time. As I have said many times before, *the speed of light does not merely transform the world. It becomes the world. Globalization is the speed of light. And it is nothing else!* Globalization cannot take shape without the speed of light. In this way, history now inscribes itself in real time, in the 'live', in the realm of interactivity. Consequently, history no longer resides in the extension of territory. Look at the US, look at Russia. Both of these countries are immense geographical territories. But, nowadays, immense territories amount to nothing! Today, everything is about speed and real time. We are no longer concerned with real space. Hence not only the crisis of geopolitics and geostrategy but also the shift towards the emergence and dominance of *chronostrategy*. As I have been arguing for a long time now, there is a real need not simply for a political economy of wealth but also for a political economy of speed.

JA: But what about the cultural dimensions of chronostrategy? For instance, although modernist artists such as Marinetti suggested to us that 'war is the highest form of modern art', Benjamin warned us against the 'aestheticization' of war. Additionally, in *The Aesthetics of Disappearance* (1991), you make several references to the relationship between war and aesthetics.[25] To what extent do you think that the Kosovo War can or should be perceived in cultural or aesthetic terms?

PV: First of all, if I have spoken of a link between war and aesthetics, it is because there is something I am very interested in and that is what Sun Tzu calls 'the art of war'. This is because, for me, *war consists of the organization of the field of perception*. But war is also, as the Japanese call it, 'the art of embellishing death'. And, in this sense, the relationship between war and aesthetics is a matter of very serious concern. Conversely, one could say that religion – in the broadest sense of the word – is 'the art of embellishing life'. Thus, anything that strives to aestheticize death is profoundly tragic. But, nowadays, *the tragedy of war is mediated through technology*. It is no longer mediated through a human being with moral responsibilities. It is mediated through the destructive power of the atomic bomb, as in Stanley Kubrick's film *Dr Strangelove*.[26]

   Now, if we turn to the war in Kosovo, what do we find? We find the manipulation of the audience's emotions by the mass media. Today, the media handle information as if it was a religious artefact. In this way, the media is more concerned with what we *feel* about the refugees and so on rather than what we *think* about them. Indeed, the truth, the reality of

the Kosovo War, was actually hidden behind all the 'humanitarian'
faces. This is a very different situation from the one faced by General
Patton and the American army when they first encountered the concentration camps at the end of the Second World War. Then, it was a total
and absolute surprise to find out that what was inside the concentration
camps was a sea of skeletons. What is clear to me, therefore, is that
while the tragedy of war grinds on, the contemporary aesthetics of the
tragedy seem not only confused but, in some way, suspicious.

JA: Almost inevitably, reviewers will compare *Stratégie de la déception* with
      your earlier works and, in particular, *War and Cinema*. Indeed, the very
      first chapter of the latter book is called 'Military force is based upon
      deception'. Could you summarize the most important developments
      that, for you, have taken place in the relationship between war, cinema
      and deception since you wrote *War and Cinema*?

PV: For me, Sun Tzu's statement that military force is based upon deception
      is an extraordinary statement. But let us start with the title of *War and
      Cinema*. The important part of the title is not *War and Cinema*. It is the
      subtitle, *The Logistics of Perception*. As I said back in 1984, the idea of
      logistics is not only about oil, about ammunitions and supplies but also
      about *images*. Troops must be fed with ammunition and so on but also
      with information, with images, with visual intelligence. Without these
      elements troops cannot perform their duties properly. This is what is
      meant by the logistics of perception.
          Now, if we consider my latest book, *Stratégie de la déception*, what we
      need to focus on are the other aspects of the same phenomenon. For the
      strategies of deception are concerned with deceiving an opponent
      through the logistics of perception. But these strategies are not merely
      aimed at the Serbs or the Iraqis but also at all those who might support
      Milošević or Saddam Hussein. Moreover, such strategies are also aimed
      at deceiving the general public through radio, television and so on.
          In this way, it seems to me that, since 1984, my book on the logistics of
      perception has been proved totally correct. For instance, almost every
      conflict since then has involved the logistics of perception, including the
      war in Lebanon, where Israel made use of cheap drones in order to
      track Yasser Arafat with the aim of killing him. If we look at the Gulf
      War, the same is also true. Indeed, my work on the logistics of percep-
      tion and the Gulf War was so accurate that I was even asked to discuss it
      with high-ranking French military officers. They asked me: 'How is it
      that you wrote that book in 1984 and now it's happening for real?' My
      answer was: 'The problem is not mine but yours: you have not been
      doing your job properly!' [*Laughs*]

But let us link all this to something that is not discussed very often. I am referring here to the impact of the launch of the television news service CNN in 1984 or thereabouts. However, what I want to draw your attention to is CNN's so-called 'Newshounds'. Newshounds are people with mini-video cameras, people who are continually taking pictures in the street and sending the tapes in to CNN. These Newshounds are a sort of pack of wolves, continually on the look out for quarry, *but quarry in the form of images*. For example, it was this pack of wolves that sparked off the Rodney King affair a few years ago in Los Angeles. Let us consider the situation: a person videos Rodney King being beaten up by the cops. That person then sends in the footage to the TV station. Within hours riots flare up in the city! There is, then, a link between the logistics of perception, the wars in Lebanon and the Gulf as well as with CNN and the Pentagon. But what interests me here is that what starts out as a story of a black man being beaten up in the street, a story that, unfortunately, happens all the time, everywhere, escalates into something that is little short of a war in Los Angeles!

JA: Your discussion of Newshounds reminds me of an interesting story about the media written by the veteran Polish reporter Ryszard Kapuscinski. In the piece, Kapuscinski describes how, during a trip to Mexico, he unexpectedly found himself in the middle of a riot. However, as luck would have it, he met a cameraman whom he knew and who happened to be shooting video footage of the riot. But when Kapuscinski asked his friend: 'What's happening here, John?', his friend merely replied: 'I don't have the faintest idea. I just get the shots. I send them to the channel, and they do what they want with them.' For me, this is a very interesting statement because it highlights how the notion of the logistics of perception is no longer restricted to the military sphere but is, in fact, now part of the civilian arena. In this example, the cameraman is supplying images to the front line, but the front line is no longer the war room but the newsroom![27]

PV: This is exactly what I mean! And, as in your example, one finds that the logistics of perception are not only military and civilian but also linked to general policing. The logistics of perception can, for example, be linked to the phenomenon of private detectives, to tele-surveillance, and to the phenomenon of 'watching-at-a-distance'. The logistics of perception are thus highly political. This is because they bring in their wake the phenomenon of total surveillance. Watching-at-a-distance also brings with it a sort of multiplier effect. For instance, if we consider the Rodney King affair, there was no sense of proportionality between the content of the videotape and the ensuing riots in Los Angeles! The same sort of thing happened with the O.J. Simpson court case. But what is

188 THE KOSOVO W@R DID TAKE PLACE

important to remember is that, after the entire world saw Simpson being followed in his car on TV, what followed was a totally bogus TV court case. Here, again, we not only saw the multiplier effect at work but an effect that *completely distorts the nature of the court case and the entire judicial system!* The Simpson trial was a parody of justice! And the same thing currently applies to the absurd court case surrounding the death of Princess Diana. Today, therefore, *all* cities are overexposed. London was overexposed at the time of Diana's funeral. New York was overexposed at the time of Clinton's confessions concerning Monica Lewinsky. All this belongs to what I call 'the overexposed city'.[28]

JA: I would like to return to Sun Tzu if I may? I'm curious as to whether you believe we can still look to Sun Tzu's *The Art of War* for an understanding of wars such as the one that took place in Kosovo? Or, is it the case that so-called postmodern wars are simply too far removed from Sun Tzu's ancient world?

PV: No. For me, it is Clausewitz who is outdated, not Sun Tzu. Today, it is *the accident and not wars that are the continuation of politics by other means!* This is a post-Clausewitzian concept. This is due to the fact that Sun Tzu has a much more fluid approach to the question of war. It is also a very interesting approach and reflects the profound Chinese way of thinking more generally. For example, the Chinese often describe power in terms of water. And water cannot be stopped from flowing. Thus the Chinese do not compare war with fire since fire can be stopped. But what has happened to war today? In the old days, there were two armies at war. One army lost the war and the other won. There were rules. *Victory or defeat was a given.* Each was definitive. *But, nowadays, there is never a victory.* Everyone loses. There is no definitive result. And this is why Sun Tzu's writings are still relevant. He wrote about warring kingdoms. In today's terms, therefore, he was already writing about the privatization of warfare, about wars that are constantly changing their shape like water does as it traverses the territory. For Sun Tzu, then, as for me, war is concerned with a form of movement that can be compared to water. War is no longer about confrontation. However, one could say that, during the war in Kosovo, the form of the movement should not be compared to water and its waves but to electromagnetic waves! Indeed, the Kosovo War was an electromagnetic flood! In this sense, the war of the airwaves in Kosovo had a maritime quality to it. As I have written before in *Speed and Politics*, this is very similar to the strategy of 'the fleet in being'. But, in this case, the fleet in being is moored in the waters of immateriality, in the airwaves. In addition, this fleet cannot only carry images and sounds but also engage in 'tele-action', in action-at-a-distance. Thus, in essence, the Kosovo War took place in Hertzian space, in the electromagnetic ether. In this sense, the Kosovo War was a postmodern war. For example, what we saw in Kosovo was the return of gunboat diplomacy and the return of the fleet in being. But the fleet took to the air in the form of Cruise missiles. And, although I know that Alain Joxe would not agree with me, this is why, for me, we are in a post-Clausewitzian era. For me, therefore, Clausewitz should be taken to the Cenotaph! [*Laughs*]

JA: But what about those masters of the fleet in being, the jet pilots? For example, in his book *Mythologies* (1993), the semiologist Roland Barthes speaks of 'The jet-man' as the 'elimination of speed', as a man who inhabits a technological condition that, in contemporary societies, is verging on the sacred. And, of course, the US Air Force jet pilots were a constant feature of the Kosovo War as far as the media were concerned. What aspects, if any, of the role of the jet pilots in the Kosovo conflict were important for you?[29]

PV: Well, there is no doubt that, today, the professionals in the armed services are given the attributes of the Gods. They are the Gods of ubiquity, instantaneity and immediacy. But, as far as the jet pilots are concerned, to me, they are the survivors of a bygone age. The jet-man is the 'last man'. He is the last man before automaton takes command. For, right now, very sophisticated forms of automated piloting systems are replacing flying crews in the US Air Force and elsewhere. And these automated systems are not simply made up of observation drones but also of fighter and bomber drones that are the equivalent of the Typhoons, Mustangs, P51s, and Lightnings of the Second World War. For me, therefore, the fighter pilot is the last man. He was indeed the hero who led the war in Kosovo but he did so without risk to his own life. For a hero, this is not a very comfortable position to be in. For instance, when Peter Townsend became a national hero in England with his Spitfire, he had taken great risks and had helped the Royal Air Force save England from the Nazis. However, to me, the jet pilots of the Kosovo War are survivors of an age that has already passed. As in the NASA space programmes, it is now too expensive to send astronauts to Mars, so one launches the Voyager probe, or the Mars Pathfinder.

JA: To what extent do you think that the jet pilots contribute to their own elimination? I ask this question because, during the Kosovo conflict, I was watching a British ex-Air Marshal talk on TV one evening and he spoke about how the speed of the jet's technological systems contributed to the infamous and tragic incident where the jet pilots mistook a convoy of tractors and trailers for a row of tanks. It was an incident that killed many innocent civilians. However, what interested me was that the ex-Air Marshal went on to say that this incident was the result of what is known as 'taxi ranking' among jet pilots. Broadly, taxi ranking means that when one pilot sees what he thinks is a row of tanks and calls back to base to report his sighting, all the other jet pilots are immediately sent into the air. But, when they arrive on the scene, they do not check the first pilot's sighting or question whether what they are about to fire at is actually a row of tanks. As far as they are concerned, it *is* a row of tanks and they fire without hesitation. Consequently, one error by a jet pilot travelling at speed is multiplied into a catastrophe. What is your opinion?

PV: Indeed! In fact, I remember that when I was a small boy during the Second World War, I was bathing with friends near a river. And moored on the river nearby was an abandoned boat, a war launch. Suddenly, we were startled by an American Thunderbolt flying overhead. It was about to strafe the war launch. But, before it did so, the pilot *saw* that we were bathing there, and he made a turn. We saw him and he waved back at us because he could see that we were happy it was an American plane. He went off without firing a round of ammunition. You see, unlike today, where the planes fly very high, the Thunderbolt flew very low and we could actually *see* the pilot in the cockpit as he waved at us as we stood on the banks of the river.

JA: Do you think, given tragic incidents such as the mistaken attack on a civilian convoy, that it is conceivable to characterize the Kosovo War not as the deliberate outcome of 'rational' political and military forces but as one more 'accident' on the road to nowhere, on the road to the end of modernity?

PV: [*Laughs*] Well, first of all, I do not believe that the war in Kosovo was an accident! Indeed, I think it has helped the Americans to develop the notion of the accident through the use of graphite bombs, through the cutting off of the EuTelSat signal, and through the so-called 'accident' of the bombing of the Chinese embassy. So, for me, the war in Kosovo was one in which the Americans took part, but they did so in a rational manner. But that was not the case with the participation of the Europeans. This is because, militarily speaking, the European Union was not, at that juncture, in charge of its own destiny. The Americans imposed the strategy that was applied in the war in Kosovo on the EU. For the Americans, then, the strategy was a success. But *for us*, for us Europeans, and for NATO, the strategy was a failure. Now, I readily concede that many people believe that while the UN lost the war in Kosovo, NATO won it.

But, for me, NATO *also* lost. Naturally, when I suggest this to people, just as I suggest it in *Stratégie de la déception*, I am arguing that the US is currently seeking global domination through the establishment of what I call the second deterrence. And this second deterrence is a form of deterrence that cannot be shared with the EU or anyone else. This, then, is *my* interpretation and it is an interpretation that I am adamant about. But let me make it absolutely clear: I am not anti-American. In fact, I often prefer Americans to the French! Indeed, my position is that, while, on the one hand, I love Americans, I am wary of America. On the other hand, while I *love* France, I am very suspicious of the French!

From sightless vision to secular crusades and beyond

JA: In *The Vision Machine* (1994) you were concerned with highlighting the role of the military in the 'contemporary crisis in perceptive faith' and the 'automation of perception' more broadly. Has the Kosovo War led you to modify your claims about the role of the military in the contemporary production and destruction of automated perception via Cruise missiles, so-called 'smart bombs' and so on?[30]

PV: On the contrary. The development and deployment of drones and Cruise missiles involves the continuing development of the vision machine. Research on Cruise missiles is intrinsically linked to the development of vision machines. The aim, of course, is not only to give vision to a machine but, as in the case of the Cruise missiles that were aimed at Leningrad and Moscow, also to enable a machine to deploy radar readings and pre-programmed maps as it follows its course towards its target. Cruise missiles necessarily fly low, in order to check on the details of the terrain they are flying over. They are equipped with a memory that gives them bearings on the terrain. However, when the missiles arrive at their destination, they need more subtle vision, in order to choose right or left. This, then, is the reason why vision was given to Cruise missiles. But in one sense, such missiles are really only flying cameras, whose results are interpreted by a computer. This, therefore, is what I call 'sightless vision', vision without looking. The research on vision machines was mainly conducted at the Stanford Research Institute in the US. So, we can say that the events that took place in the Kosovo War were a total confirmation of the thesis of *The Vision Machine*.

JA: Turning to vision machines of a different variety, to what extent do you think that watching the Kosovo War on TV reduced us all to a state of 'polar inertia', to the status of Howard Hughes, the imprisoned and impotent state of what you call 'technological monks'?[31]

PV:　There can be no doubt about this. It even held true for the soldiers involved in the Kosovo War. For the soldiers stayed mostly in their barracks! In this way, polar inertia has truly become a *mass phenomenon*. And not only for the TV audiences watching the war at home but also for the army that watches the battle from the barracks. Today, *the army only occupies the territory once the war is over.* Clearly, there is a kind of inertia here. Moreover, I would like to say that the sort of polar inertia we witnessed in the Kosovo War, the polar inertia involving 'automated war' and 'war-at-a-distance' is also terribly weak in the face of terrorism. For instance, in such situations, any individual who decides to place or throw a bomb can simply walk away. He or she *has the freedom to move*. This also applies to militant political groups and their actions. Look at the Intifadah in Jerusalem. One cannot understand that phenomenon, a phenomenon where people, often very young boys, are successfully harassing one of the best armies in the world, without appreciating their freedom to move!

JA:　Jean Baudrillard infamously argued that '*The Gulf War Did Not Take Place*' (1995). Could it be argued that the Kosovo War did not take place?[32]

PV:　Although Jean Baudrillard is a friend of mine, I do not agree with him on that one! For me, the significance of the war in Kosovo was that it was a war that moved into space. For instance, the Persian Gulf War was a miniature world war. It took place in a small geographical area. In this sense it was a local war. But it was one that made use of all the power normally reserved for global war. However, the Kosovo War took place in orbital space. In other words, war now takes place in 'aero-electromagnetic space'. It is equivalent to the birth of a new type of flotilla, a home fleet, of a new type of naval power, but in orbital space!

JA:　But what, in this instance, constitutes the flotilla, the fleet, or the new type of naval power? The Cruise missiles?

PV:　The flotilla is made up of the robots, the drones, the missiles, the planes and the satellites. For these machines are the new cruisers, the new dreadnoughts and the new gunboats. Let us take an example. How did France or Britain proceed to conquer their former colonies? They took their fleet and their whole naval power to the shores of a country like Morocco and then began shooting, thereby conveying the message to the local inhabitants to leave the area or else! At that point, one lands one's troops and sets up a colonial trading outpost while simultaneously building roads in order to gain access to slaves, minerals and so forth. What I am describing here is the classic colonial outpost. But, today, one conquers a colony by taking one's fleet to the airspace of a region such as Kosovo. And success is achieved through the application of the techniques of cyberwar, through the techniques of global air war. Colonialism today is therefore no longer a French or a British affair. It is a new kind of colonialism. It is the media colonialism of modernity, a colonialism that does not involve the taking of slaves but does involve *the law of the air taking over from the law of the land!*

JA: How do these developments relate to Global Positioning Systems (GPS)? For example, in *The Art of the Motor* (1995), you were very interested in the relationship between globalization, physical space and the phenomenon of virtual spaces, positioning, or, 'delocalization'. In what ways, if any, do you think that militarized GPS played a 'delocalizing' role in the war in Kosovo?[33]

PV: GPS not only played a large and delocalizing role in the war in Kosovo but is increasingly playing a role in social life. For instance, it was the GPS that directed the planes, the missiles and the bombs to localized targets in Kosovo. But may I remind you that the bombs that were dropped by the B-2 plane on the Chinese embassy – or at least that is what we were told – were GPS bombs. And the B-2 flew in from the United States. However, GPS are everywhere. They are in cars. They were even in the half-tracks that, initially at least, were going to make the ground invasion in Kosovo possible. Yet, for all the sophistication of GPS, there still remain numerous problems with their use. The most obvious problem in this context is the problem of landmines. For example, when the French troops went into Kosovo they were told that they were going to enter in half-tracks, over the open fields. But their leaders had forgotten about the landmines. And this was a major problem because, these days, landmines are no longer localized. They are launched via tubes and distributed haphazardly over the territory. As a result, one cannot remove them after the war because one cannot find them! And yet the ability to detect such landmines, especially in a global war of movement, is absolutely crucial. Thus, for the US, GPS are a form of sovereignty! It is hardly surprising, then, that the EU has proposed its own GPS in order to be able to localize and to compete with the American GPS. As I have said before, sovereignty no longer resides in the territory itself, but in the control of the territory. And localization is an inherent part of that territorial control. As I pointed out in *The Art of the Motor* and elsewhere, from now on we need *two* watches: a wristwatch to tell us what time it is and a GPS watch to tell us what space it is!

JA: Given your analysis of technology and the general accident in recent works such as *Open Sky* (1997), *La Bombe informatique* (1998) and *Politics of the Very Worst* (1999), I would like to focus on the prospective counter-measures to such developments. Are there, in your view, any obvious strategies of resistance that can be deployed against the relentless advance of automation?[34]

PV: Resistance is *always* possible! But we must engage in resistance first of all by developing the idea of a technological culture. However, at the present time, this idea is grossly underdeveloped. For example, we have developed an artistic and a literary culture. Nevertheless, the ideals of technological culture remain underdeveloped and therefore outside of popular culture and the practical ideals of democracy. This is also why society as a whole has no control over technological developments. And this is one of the gravest threats to democracy in the near future. It is, then, imperative to develop a democratic technological culture. Even among the elite, in government circles, technological culture is somewhat deficient. I could give examples of cabinet ministers, including defence ministers, who have no technological culture at all. In other words, what I am suggesting is that the hype generated by the publicity around the Internet and so on is not counter-balanced by a political intelligence that is based on a technological culture. For instance, in 1999, Bill Gates not only published a new book on work at the speed of thought but also detailed how Microsoft's 'Falconview' software would enable the destruction of bridges in Kosovo. Thus it is no longer a Caesar or a Napoleon who decides on the fate of any particular war but a piece of software! In short, the political intelligence of war and the political intelligence of society no longer penetrate the techno-scientific world. Or, let us put it this way, techno-scientific intelligence is presently insufficiently spread among society at large to enable us to *interpret* the sorts of techno-scientific advances that are taking shape today.

JA: Finally, now that *Stratégie de la déception* has been published, could you indicate what future projects you might consider working on and why they might be of interest to you?

PV: Well, I could say something about what I feel I did not expand on enough in the book and that is the new dimensions of 'humanitarian' warfare. There is, for example, a lot of research required on the technical and the social dimensions of this new type of so-called 'just war'. And this is something where I think the International Court on War Crimes in the Balkans needs to be more involved. This is because the invention of the 'secular holy war', the invention of the 'secular crusade' are, to my mind, inventions of major importance. Such inventions are landmarks in Western history. In this respect, we have a lot of work to do on the nature and complexity of militarized 'humanitarian' intervention. This work is, of course, both political and legal in nature. However, in my opinion, without it, we are heading for a frightful regression. It will be a regression towards the state of nature, that is, towards the permanent state of war of all against all. And, as far as I can see if such developments are allowed to come to pass, there will be no end to it. In the name of the right to intervene, we will end up waging war against each other all the time. Therefore, there will be a regression from the formally regulated state of war. For what is starting to take place in Kosovo and elsewhere is that the achievements of regulated warfare are being threatened with extinction. For example, President Clinton stated that the war in Kosovo was not a war but a 'police operation' against 'rogue states'. This is very serious indeed and not simply because it opens the door to all kinds of aberrations. It is very serious because it means that while the Kosovo War *did* take place, it was never declared!

Translated by Patrice Riemens.

Notes

'The Kosovo War Did Take Place' was conducted by John Armitage on 13 September 1999 at the Ecole Spéciale d'Architecture in Paris. An edited version of this interview, 'The Kosovo War Took Place in Orbital Space: Paul Virilio in Conversation with John Armitage', appeared in the electronic journal *CTheory*, (www.ctheory.com) on 18 October 2000. The interview could not have taken place without the continued interest, goodwill and generosity of Paul Virilio and Patrice Riemens. I would like to record my sincere thanks to them both. I would also like to formally thank Verena Andermatt Conley and Cathryn Vasseleu for their valuable comments on an earlier draft of this interview.

1. See P. Virilio (1999) *Stratégie de la déception* (Paris: Galilée). Since this interview was conducted, this book has been translated and published in English as P. Virilio (2000) *Strategy of Deception*, trans. C. Turner (London: Verso).
2. The most important references relating to Virilio's concept of the information bomb are the following: P. Virilio and F. Kittler (1999) 'The Information Bomb: A Conversation', trans. P. Riemens (edited and introduced by J. Armitage). The latter can be found in this volume and in J. Armitage (ed.) (1999) *Machinic Modulations: New Cultural Theory and Technopolitics*. Special Issue. *Angelaki* 4 (2) (September): 81–90; P. Virilio (1998) *La Bombe informatique* (Paris: Galilée). For a review of *La Bombe informatique*, see, for example, J. Armitage (2000) 'The Theorist of Speed', *New Left Review*, No. 2 (March/April), Second Series: 145–7. The English translation of *La Bombe informatique* has recently been published as P. Virilio (2000) *The Information Bomb*, trans. C. Turner (London: Verso). In particular, see Chapter 14, p. 134 of the English translation, where this quotation is taken from.
3. Virilio elaborates his ideas on history, progress and the speed of weapons systems mainly in his *Speed and Politics: An Essay on Dromology* (1986 [1977]), trans. M. Polizzotti (New York: Semiotext (e)). In particular, see Part 3, Chapter 1, 'Unable Bodies', pp. 61–74.
4. See P. Virilio and S. Lotringer (1997 [1983]) *Pure War*, trans. M. Polizzotti, revised edition (New York: Semiotext (e)).
5. Virilio's views on the Persian Gulf War are to be found in his *L'Écran du désert: chroniques de guerre* (1991) (Paris: Galilée). This book has recently been translated and published in English

as P. Virilio (2001) *Desert Screen: War at the Speed of Light*, trans. M. Degener (London: The Athlone Press). For an alternative perspective but one that also views the Persian Gulf War not as the first 'postmodern war' but as the last modern war see: M. Ignatieff (2000) *Virtual War: Kosovo and Beyond* (London: Chatto and Windus). Virilio and Ignatieff differ in their analyses of the Persian Gulf War and the Kosovo War. However, they do inadvertently agree that it is probably incorrect to view the Persian Gulf War as the first postmodern war. The latter view is normally attributed (usually by others) to Jean Baudrillard's (1995 [1991]) *The Gulf War Did Not Take Place*, trans. P. Patton (Sydney: Power Institute).

6. On the continued rise of private armies in the post-Cold War era, see, for example, K. Silverstein (2000) *Private Warriors* (London: Verso).

7. See P. Virilio (1989 [1984]) *War and Cinema: The Logistics of Perception* (London: Verso).

8. Virilio discusses his thoughts on 'the fleet in being' in *Speed and Politics: An Essay on Dromology* (see Note 3). In particular, see Part 2, Chapter 1, 'From Space Right to State Right', pp. 37–49.

9. For Virilio's detailed essay on vision machines see: P. Virilio (1994 [1988]) *The Vision Machine*, trans. J. Rose (London, Bloomington and Indianapolis: British Film Institute and Indiana University Press).

10. See P. Virilio (1994 [1975]) *Bunker Archeology*, trans. G. Collins (Princeton: Princeton Architectural Press); and P. Virilio (1976) *L'Insécurité du territoire* (Paris: Stock).

11. Virilio's concept of 'the aesthetics of disappearance' first appears in *Bunker Archeology* (see Note 10). See also P. Virilio (1991 [1980]) *The Aesthetics of Disappearance*, trans. P. Beitchman (New York: Semiotext (e)).

12. On *Architecture Principe* see, for example, P. Virilio and C. Parent (eds) (1996) *Architecture Principe, 1966 et 1996* (Besançon: L'Imprimeur).

13. See P. Virilio (1986) 'The privatisation of war', trans. M. Imrie, *New Statesman*, 112 (10 October): 19.

14. See S. Žižek (1999) 'Against the double blackmail', *New Left Review*, 234 (March/April): 76–82.

15. Claudio Magris is an Italian essayist, Professor of German Literature at the University of Trieste, and a regular contributor to European newspapers and magazines. Born in Trieste in 1939, Magris's writings explore the idea of European culture from the standpoint of a literary historian and social critic. Increasingly influential in European intellectual circles, Magris's latest book to be published in English is *Microcosms* (2000), trans. I. Halliday (London: The Harvill Press).

16. Peter Handke (1942–) is an Austrian writer, translator, film author and director. However, and although Handke has long been associated with the European literary *avant-garde*, he recently caused much controversy in Europe through his efforts to re-conceptualize the West's view of Milošević's Serbia. Handke's views on Serbia are contained in his book entitled *Journey to the Rivers: Justice for Serbia* (1997), trans. S. Abbott (London: Viking). Like Virilio, numerous other radical cultural theorists and European intellectuals have denounced Handke's book.

17. See E. Said (1999) 'Protecting the Kosovars?', *New Left Review*, 234 (March/April): 73–5.

18. Generally, Virilio presents himself as a 'critic of the art of technology' rather than as a particular critic of the Internet. However, in recent books and book-length interviews he has written and spoken of the potential for destruction inherent in the Internet. See, for example, P. Virilio and S. Lotringer (1997 [1983]) *Pure War*, trans. M. Polizzotti and B. O'Keeffe (New York: Semiotext (e)); P. Virilio (1997 [1995]) *Open Sky*, trans. J. Rose (London: Verso); P. Virilio and P. Petit (1999 [1996]) *Politics of the Very Worst*, trans. M. Cavaliere (New York: Semiotext (e)); and P. Virilio (2000 [1998]) *The Information Bomb*, trans. C. Turner (London: Verso).

19. Nicholas Negroponte is well known for his work on the Internet at MIT. He is a regular contributor to *Wired* magazine and the author of *Being Digital* (1995) (London: Hodder and Stoughton).

20. Hypermodernism is a theoretical term I have used to describe Virilio's cultural conception of the social implications of militarization. See, for example, my other interview in this collection and J. Armitage (ed.) (2000) *Paul Virilio: From Modernism to Hypermodernism and Beyond* (London: Sage Publications in association with *Theory, Culture and Society*).

21. Michel Foucault's description and analysis of the Panopticon can be found in his *Discipline and Punish: The Birth of the Prison* (1977), trans. A. Sheridan. (Harmondsworth: Penguin).

22. On *L'Insécurité du territoire* see Note 10. Virilio's essay on 'The Suicidal State' can be found in J. Der Derian (ed.) (1998) *The Virilio Reader*, trans. J. Der Derian, M. Degener and L. Osepchuk (Oxford: Blackwell), pp. 29–45.

23. Virilio's idea that 'history progresses at the speed of its weapons systems' can be found in *Speed and Politics: An Essay on Dromology* (see Note 3). In particular, see Part 3, Chapter 1, 'Unable Bodies', pp. 61–74.

24. See P. Virilio (1990 [1978]) *Popular Defense and Ecological Struggles*, trans. M. Polizzotti (New York: Semiotext (e)). In particular, see Part 2, 'Revolutionary Resistance', pp. 41–106.

25. On Marinetti and the Futurist tradition in modern art see C. Tisdall and A. Bozzolla (1977) *Futurism* (London: Thames and Hudson). Walter Benjamin's discussion on the aesthetics of war can be found in his essay 'The work of art in the age of mechanical reproduction' in his *Illuminations* (1968) (New York: Schocken Books), pp. 217–52. On Virilio's *The Aesthetics of Disappearance* see Note 11.

26. See Sun Tzu (1993 [ancient Chinese text]) *The Art of War* (Ware: Wordsworth Editions).

27. See R. Kapuscinski (1999) 'New censorship, subtle manipulation', *Le monde diplomatique* (English electronic edition), September.

28. See P. Virilio (1991 [1984]) 'The overexposed city', trans. D. Moshenberg, in *The Lost Dimension* (New York: Semiotext (e)), pp. 9–28.

29. See R. Barthes (1993 [1957]) 'The jet-man', trans. A. Lavers, in *Mythologies* (London: Vintage), pp. 71–3.

30. For a discussion of these issues see Virilio's *The Vision Machine* (see Note 9).

31. See P. Virilio (1999 [1980]) *Polar Inertia*, trans. P. Camiller (London: Sage Publications in association with *Theory, Culture and Society*); *The Aesthetics of Disappearance* (see Note 11); P. Virilio (1999 [1996]) *Politics of the Very Worst*, trans. M. Cavaliere (New York: Semiotext (e)).

32. See Note 5.

33. See P. Virilio (1995 [1993]) *The Art of the Motor*, trans. J. Rose (Minneapolis: University of Minnesota Press).

34. See P. Virilio (1997 [1995]) *Open Sky*, trans. J. Rose (London: Verso); *La Bombe informatique* (see Note 2); and *Politics of the Very Worst* (see Note 28).

SUGGESTED FURTHER READING

Aidar, M. (1997) 'IDEAL CAR', *Speed* (Electronic journal), 1 (4): 1–4.

Armitage, J. (1996) 'The Vision Thing', *Radical Philosophy*, 77: 45–6. (Book review of *The Vision Machine*.)

Armitage, J. (1997) 'Accelerated Aesthetics: Paul Virilio's *The Vision Machine*', in C. Blake and L. Blake (eds), *Intellectuals and Global Culture*, Special Issue of *Angelaki*, 2 (3): 199–209.

Armitage, J. (1999a) 'Paul Virilio', in E. Cashmore and C. Rojek (eds), *Dictionary of Cultural Theorists*. London: Arnold. pp. 464–5.

Armitage, J. (1999b) 'Resisting the Neoliberal Discourse of Technology: The Politics of Cyberculture in the Age of the Virtual Class', *CTheory* (Electronic journal), 22 (1–2) Article 68: 1–10.

Armitage, J. (ed.) (1999c) *Theory, Culture and Society*, Special Issue on Paul Virilio. 16 (5–6).

Armitage, J. (1999d) 'Paul Virilio: An Introduction', in J. Armitage (ed.), *Theory, Culture and Society*, Special Issue on Paul Virilio. 16 (5–6): 1–24.

Armitage, J. (1999e) 'From Modernism to Hypermodernism and Beyond: An Interview with Paul Virilio' in J. Armitage (ed.) *Theory, Culture and Society*, Special Issue on Paul Virilio. 16 (5–6): 25–56.

Armitage, J. (1999f) 'Paul Virilio: A Select Bibliography', in J. Armitage (ed.), *Theory, Culture and Society*, Special Issue on Paul Virilio. 16 (5–6): 229–40.

Armitage, J. (1999g) 'Into the War Zone', *International Studies Review*, 1 (3): 135–9. (Book review of J. Der Derian's *The Virilio Reader*.)

Armitage, J. (ed.) (2000a) *Paul Virilio: From Modernism to Hypermodernism and Beyond*, London: Sage. (Book version of *Theory, Culture and Society*, Special Issue on Paul Virilio. 16 (5–6))

Armitage, J. (2000b) 'The Theorist of Speed', in *New Left Review*, Number 2, Second Series, March–April (146–8). (Book review of *La Bombe informatique*.)

Armitage, J. (2000c) 'Beyond Postmodernism? Paul Virilio's Hypermodern Cultural Theory', *3rd International Crossroads in Cultural Studies*, Conference Paper, Birmingham, UK, 25 June. pp. 1–20.

Armitage, J. (2000d) 'The Uncertainty Principle: Paul Virilio's *The Information Bomb*', in *M/C: A Journal of Media and Culture* (Electronic journal). Theme issue on 'Speed', 3 (3) July. (Review article on *The Information Bomb*.)

Armitage, J. (2000e) 'Beyond Postmodernism? Paul Virilio's Hypermodern Cultural Theory', in *CTheory* (Electronic journal), Autumn.

Armitage, J. (2000f) 'The Kosovo W@r Took Place in Orbital Space: Paul Virilio in Conversation with John Armitage' in *CTheory* (Electronic journal) October 18.

Armitage, J. (2001a) 'Paul Virilio', in A. Elliott and B.S. Turner (eds), *Contemporary Profiles in Social Theory*. London: Sage.

Armitage, J. (2001b) 'The Military is the Message', in J. Armitage and J. Roberts (eds), *Living with Cyberspace: Technology and Society in the 21st Century*. London: The Athlone Press.

Armitage, J. and Graham, P. (2001c) 'Dromoeconomics: Towards a Political Economy of Speed', in J. Armitage (ed.), Theme issue on 'Economies of Excess', *Parallax*, 18 (January).

Ascherson, N. (1997) 'Nowhere to Retreat in a World without Absence or Darkness' *The Independent on Sunday*, 23 November 1997. (Book review of *Open Sky*.)

Auber, O. (1997) 'Esquisse d'une position théorique pour un art de la vitesse', *Speed* (Electronic journal), 1 (4): 1–10.

Brigham, L. (1992) 'Motion and Destruction', *American Book Review*, 14 (2): 10. (Book review of *The Aesthetics of Disappearance*.)

Brigham, L. (1997) 'Transpolitical Technocracy and the Hope of Language', *Speed* (Electronic journal), 1 (4): 1–6.

Conley, V.A. (1997) *Ecopolitics: The Environment in Poststructuralist Thought.* London: Routledge. (Contains chapter section on Virilio.)

Conley, V.A. (1999) 'The Passenger: Paul Virilio and Feminism', in J. Armitage (ed.), *Theory, Culture and Society*, Special Issue on Paul Virilio. 16 (5–6): 201–14.

Conrad, P. (1989) 'Screen Spectaculars', *Times Literary Supplement*, 1–7 September: 939. (Book review of *War and Cinema*.)

Crawford, T.H. (1999) 'Conducting Technologies: Virilio's and Latour's Philosophies of the Present State', in J. Armitage (ed.), *Machinic Modulations: New Cultural Theory and Technopolitics*, Special Issue of *Angelaki*, 4 (2): 171–82.

Crogan, P. (1996a) 'Paul Virilio and the Aporia of Speed'. Unpublished PhD thesis, Sydney, Power Department of Fine Arts.

Crogan, P. (1996b) 'Paul Virilio and the Aporia of Speed', *Virtual Cultures*, Conference Paper, Sydney, 13 July. pp. 1–5.

Crogan, P. (1997) 'Metaphoric Vehicles', *Speed* (Electronic journal), 1 (4): 1–6.

Crogan, P. (1999a) 'Theory of State: Deleuze, Guattari and Virilio on the State, Technology, and Speed', in J. Armitage (ed.), *Machinic Modulations: New Cultural Theory and Technopolitics*, Special Issue of *Angelaki*, 4 (2): 137–48.

Crogan, P. (1999b) 'The Tendency, the Accident and the Untimely: Paul Virilio's Engagement with the Future', in J. Armitage (ed.), *Theory, Culture and Society*, Special Issue on Paul Virilio. 16 (5–6): 161–76.

Cronin, M.A. (1999) 'Seeing through Transparency: Performativity, Vision and Intent', *Cultural Values*, 3 (1): 54–72.

Couples, C. (1996) 'Virilio, the Cyborg, and Me'. Archived at: http://ebbs.english.vt.edu/exper/couples/personal/academia/reviews/art.of.motor.html. (Book review of *The Art of the Motor*.)

Coyle, R. (1992) 'Sound and Speed in Convocation: An Analysis of *The Listening Room* Radio Programs on Paul Virilio', *Continuum*, 6 (1): 118–38.

Cubitt, S. (1999a) 'Unnatural Reality', *Film-Philosophy* (Electronic journal), Salon review. (Book review of *The Vision Machine*.)

Cubitt, S. (1999b) 'Virilio and New Media', in J. Armitage (ed.) *Theory, Culture and Society*, Special Issue on Paul Virilio. 16 (5–6): 127–42.

Der Derian, J. (1992) *Antidiplomacy: Spies, Terror, Speed, and War.* Oxford: Blackwell. (Contains chapters discussing Virilio's work.)

Der Derian, J. (1998) 'Virtually Wagging the Dog', *Theory and Event* (Electronic journal), 2 (1): 1–7. (Book review of *The Art of the Motor*.)

Der Derian, J. (ed.) (1998) *The Virilio Reader.* Oxford: Blackwell. (Contains a reprint of Der Derian's interview with Virilio in *Wired*. Contains 'A Select Bibliography of Works by Paul Virilio'. This bibliography also includes some Spanish, Italian and German Virilio references.)

Der Derian, J. (1999) 'The Conceptual Cosmology of Paul Virilio', in J. Armitage (ed.), *Theory, Culture and Society*, Special Issue on Paul Virilio. 16 (5–6): 215–28.

Deleuze, G. and Guattari, F. (1986) *Nomadology: The War Machine*, trans. B. Massumi. New York: Semiotext (e). (Contains a critical discussion of Virilio's work. This book is also one of the 'plateaus' in Deleuze and Guattari's *A Thousand Plateaus*.)

Deleuze, G. and Guattari, F. (1987) 'Nomadology: The War Machine', in their *A Thousand Plateaus: Capitalism and Schizophrenia*, trans. B. Massumi. Minneapolis: University of Minnesota Press.

Drake, M. (1997) 'The Question of Military Technology: Apocalyptics or Politics?', *Speed* (Electronic journal), 1 (4): 1–13.

Douglas, I.R. (1997a) 'Ecology to the New Pollution', *Theory and Event* (Electronic journal), 2 (2): 1–5. (Book review of *Open Sky*.)

Douglas, I.R. (1997b) 'The Calm Before the Storm: Virilio's Debt to Foucault, and Some Notes on Contemporary Global Capital', *Speed* (Electronic journal), 1 (4): 1–18.

Gane, M. (1999) 'Paul Virilio's Bunker Theorizing', in J. Armitage (ed.), *Theory, Culture and Society*, Special Issue on Paul Virilio. 16 (5–6): 85–102.

Gilfedder, D. (1994) 'VIRILIO: The Cars that Ate Paris', *Transition*, 43: 36–43.

Hake, S. (1989) 'War and Cinema', *Film Criticism*, 14 (1): 40–2. (Book review of *War and Cinema*.)

Hanke, R. (1999) 'Virilio's Plea for Time: From Global Village to World City', in *Media, Culture and Technology* (Electronic journal), Issue 2: 1–6. Archived at: http://www.kk.kau.se/mct.

Johnson, P. (ed.) (1996) *The Function of the Oblique: The Architecture of Claude Parent and Paul Virilio*, trans. P. Johnson. London: Architectural Association. (Contains Virilio's early architectural writings, drawings and photographs. Also included is an interview with Parent.)

Kellner, D. (1998) 'Virilio on Vision Machines', *Film-Philosophy* (Electronic journal), Salon review: 1–10. (Book review of *Open Sky*.)

Kellner, D. (1999) 'Virilio, War and Technology: Some Critical Reflections', in J. Armitage (ed.), *Theory, Culture and Society*, Special Issue on Paul Virilio. 16 (5–6): 103–26.

Kerrigan, J. (1997) 'When Eyesight is Fully Industrialised', *London Review of Books*, 16 October: 14–15. (Book review of *Open Sky*.)

Koppes, C.R. (1991) 'War and Cinema', *Technology and Culture*, 32 (2): 447–8. (Book review of *War and Cinema*.)

Kroker, A. (1992) *The Possessed Individual: Technology and Postmodernity*. Basingstoke: Macmillan. (Contains a chapter critically discussing Virilio's works.)

Leach, N. (1999) 'Virilio and Architecture', in J. Armitage (ed.), *Theory, Culture and Society*, Special Issue on Paul Virilio. 16 (5–6): 71–84.

Leslie, E. (2000) 'Aching for the Crash', in *Radical Philosophy*, 99: 55–6. (Review of J. Der Derian's *The Virilio Reader*.)

Manovich, L. (1997) 'Film/Telecommunication, Benjamin/Virilio', *Speed* (Electronic journal), 1 (4): 1–5.

McQuire, S. (1999) 'Blinded by the (Speed of) Light', in J. Armitage (ed.), *Theory, Culture and Society*, Special Issue on Paul Virilio. 16 (5–6): 143–60.

Messmer, M.W. (1989) 'War and Cinema', *The Minnesota Review*, 34 (3): 175–81. (Book review of *War and Cinema*.)

Oki, K. (1997) 'Decisions at the Speed of Electronic Circuitry', *Speed* (Electronic journal), 1 (4): 1–4.

Sokal, A. and Bricmont, J. (1998) *Intellectual Impostures: Postmodern Philosopher's Abuse of Science*. London: Profile Books. (Contains a critique of Virilio.)

Waite, G. (1996) *Nietzsche's Corps/e: Aesthetics, Politics, Prophecy, or, the Spectacular Technoculture of Everyday Life*. Durham, NC and London: Duke University Press. (Contains discussions of Virilio's thought.)

Wark, M. (1988) 'On Technological Time: Virilio's Overexposed City', *Arena*, 83: 82–100.

Wark, M. (1990) 'The Logistics of Perception', *Meanjin*, 49 (1): 95–101. (Review article on *War and Cinema*.)

Weissberg, J.-L. (1996) 'Ralentir la communication', *Terminal*, 63: 1–10.

Wilbur, S. (1994/7) 'Paul Virilio: Speed, Cinema, and the End of the Political State', *Speed* (Electronic journal), 1 (4): 1–10. (Originally posted on the Net in 1994. Reprinted in *Speed*.)

Zurbrugg, N. (1995) '"Apocalyptic!" "Negative!" "Pessimistic!": Baudrillard, Virilio, and Technoculture', in S. Koop (ed.), *Post: Photography: Post Photography*. pp. 72–90. Fitzroy: Centre for Contemporary Photography.

Zurbrugg, N. (1999) 'Virilio, Stelarc and "Terminal" Technoculture', in J. Armitage (ed.), *Theory, Culture and Society*, Special Issue on Paul Virilio. 16 (5–6): 177–200.

SELECT BIBLIOGRAPHY OF THE WORKS OF PAUL VIRILIO

Compiled and introduced by John Armitage

Introduction

This select bibliography of the cultural and theoretical works of Paul Virilio in French and English has been complied from all the references to Virilio's published works that I have been able to find in books, articles, periodicals and newspapers.[1] However, my efforts have benefited greatly from the research skills and generosity of Virilian scholars and others from around the world.[2] Prior to beginning, some brief notes are in order.

   The first section simply lists the main published works of Paul Virilio in French. I have also included in this section one or two second editions of Virilio's main published works where new material (for example, a new Preface or Afterword) has been added. The second section records all of Virilio's articles, collaborations, working papers, discussions and edited works in French. In some instances, I was unable to verify page numbers and this, rather than inattention to bibliographical detail, explains the occasional absence of page numbers not only in this section but also in all the other sections. Some references in the second section have an asterisk (*) attached. The asterisk simply signals that, in this case, Virilio is not the sole author of the piece but has collaborated in some way, usually through the writing of a working paper, or, more generally, through a published roundtable discussion or the editorial process. Section three catalogues all of Virilio's interviews first published in French. Where I was able to ascertain the name of the interviewer, I have included it. The absence of an interviewer's name indicates only that I was unable to confirm it at the time of writing.

   The fourth section lists all of the English translations of Virilio's main published works. Translators are noted where credited or known throughout the English sections. Section five is an inventory of all of Virilio's articles that have been translated into English. Section six itemizes all Virilio's interviews published in English. Interviewers are named where credited or known. I have also noted where an interview published in English is a translation from the French original and where an interview in English has been reprinted elsewhere.

   My hope is that I have provided the most complete bibliography of Virilio's works available in French and English. No doubt there are a great many

Virilian texts contained in obscure journals or still swirling around the Internet that I have not been able to find or access. Indeed, some Virilio publications are so marginal that I often get the impression that once he has finished writing a piece he simply hands it to the first person he meets. Consequently, I would be most interested to receive the details of any omissions from this bibliography at the Division of Government and Politics, University of Northumbria, Newcastle upon Tyne, NE1 8ST, UK. Happy reading.

1 Main published works of Paul Virilio in French

(1975) *Bunker archéologie*. Paris: Centre Georges Pompidou, Centre de Création Industrielle.

(1976) *L'Insécurité du territoire*. Paris: Stock.

(1977) *Vitesse et politique. Essai de dromologie*. Paris: Galilée.

(1978) *Défense populaire et luttes écologiques*. Paris: Galilée.

(1978) *La Dromoscopie ou la lumière de la vitesse*. Paris: Minuit.

(1980) *Esthétique de la disparition*. Paris: Balland.

(1984) *L'Espace critique*. Paris: Christian Bourgois.

(1984) *Guerre et cinéma 1. Logistique de la perception*. Paris: l'Étoile.

(1984) *L'Horizon négatif: essai de dromoscopie*. Paris: Galilée.

(1988) *La Machine de vision*. Paris: Galilée.

(1989) *Esthétique de la disparition* (2nd edn, contains a new Preface.) Paris: Galilée.

(1990) *L'Inertie polaire*. Paris: Christian Bourgois.

(1991) *L'Écran du désert: chroniques de guerre*. Paris: Galilée.

(1991) *Bunker archéologie*. (2nd edn, contains a new Afterword, '1945/1990'.) Paris: Demi-Cercle.

(1991) *Guerre et cinéma 1. Logistique de la perception*. (2nd edn, contains a new Preface.) Paris: Galilée.

(1993) *L'Insécurité du territoire* (2nd edn, contains a new Afterword, 'Postface: De l'extrême limite à l'extrême proximité'.) Paris: Galilée.

(1993) *L'Art du moteur*. Paris: Galilée.

(1995) *La Vitesse de libération*. Paris: Galilée.

(1996) *Un paysage d'événements*. Paris: Galilée.

(1998) *La Bombe informatique*. Paris: Galilée.

(1999) *Stratégie de la déception*. Paris: Galilée.

2 Articles, collaborations, working papers, discussions, and edited works of Paul Virilio in French

(1967) 'Bunker archéologie', *Architecture Principe*, 7 (March).

(1971) 'Architecture of the Open Systems', *Architecture, Formes et Fonctions*, pp. 155–64.

(1974) 'Le Littoral vertical', *Critique*, 30 (320): 48–53.

(1975) 'La Guerre pure', *Critique*, 31 (341): 1090–103.

(1975) 'La délation de masse ... ou la contre-subversion', in Paul Virilio and Georges Perec (eds), *Le Pourrissement des sociétés*. Paris: Union Générale d'Éditions, collection 10/18. pp. 13–57.*

(1976) 'Le Soldat inconnu', *Les Temps Modernes*, 32 (360): 2334–53.

(1977) 'Métempsychose du passager', *Traverses*, 8: 11–19.

(1978) *Architecture d'ingénieurs XIXᵉ–XXᵉ siècles*. Paris: Centre de Création Industrielle.*

(1978) 'La Dromoscopies ou la lumière de la vitesse', *Critique*, 34 (370): 324–37.

(1980) *Le Nouvel Ordre gendarmique*. Paris: Seuil.*

(1980) 'Tabas, la stratégie de l'accident', *Libération*, May, p. 7.

(1981) 'La Ville idéale', *Quinzaine Litteraire*, 353: 39.

(1981) 'Les Folles de la Place de Mai', *Traverses*, 21–2: 9–18.

(1982) 'Le Compte à rebours a commencé', *Quinzaine Litteraire*, 376: 5–6.

(1982) 'Perec, ami paisible', *Quinzaine Litteraire*, 368: 4.

(1982) 'L'Accident originel', *Confrontation*, 7 (Spring): 5–10.

(1983) *La Crise des dimensions: la représentation de l'espace et la notion de dimension*. Paris: l'UDRA–ESA (Unité de recherche appliqué – École Spéciale d'Architecture).*

(1983) *Portes de la ville*. Paris: Centre de Création Industrielle.*

(1984) 'Une ville surexposée', *Change International*, 1: 19–22.

(1984) 'Le Cinéma, ce n'est pas je vois, c'est je vole', *Cahiers du Cinéma*, 357: 30–3.

(1984) 'L'État nucléaire', *Change International*, 2: 9–23.*

(1984) 'Un habitat exorbitant', *Corps Écrit*, 9: 25–7.

(1985) 'Guerre des étoiles: la propagande–fiction', *Cahiers du Cinéma*, 378: xv.

(1985) 'Le Devoir de dépeupler', *Traverses*, 33/4: 154–60.

(1985) 'Un jour, le jour viendra ou le jour ne viendra pas', *Traverses*, 35: 5–11.

(1986) *Reinhard Mucha*. Paris: Musée National d'Art Moderne.*

(1986) 'Le Cinéma instrumental', *Cahiers du Cinéma*, 385: xiv.

(1986) 'L'Engin exterminateur', *Cahiers du Cinéma*, 388: 29–30.

(1986) 'L'Opération de la cataracte', *Cahiers du Cinéma*, 386: 35–9.

(1986) (With J.-P. Fargier) 'The Cinema of Speed', *Revue d'Esthétique*, 10: 37–43.

(1986) 'Video Technology and the Perception of the Image', *Revue d'Esthétique*, 10: 33–5.

(1986) 'Image virtuelle', *Revue d'Esthétique*, 10.

(1986) 'Le Cinéma instrumental: "L'imaginaire numerique" à Saint-Etienne', *Cahiers du Cinéma*, 385: 14.

(1987) *Jean Nouvel*. Paris: Institut Françaises d'Architecture.*

(1987) 'Permis de détruire', *Cahiers du Cinéma*, 401: 29–30.

(1987) 'Le Rest du temps', *Corps Écrit*, 24: 11–15.

(1987) 'Un cockpit en ville', *Traverses*, 41: 69.

(1988) 'De dromoscopie', *Museum journal*, 33 (5/6): 310–16.

(1988) 'L'Image virtuelle mentale et instrumentale', *Traverses*, 44 (5): 35–9.

(1988) 'La Lumière indirecte', *Communications*, 48: 45–52.

(1989) *De l'instabilité*. Paris: Centre National des Arts Plastiques. Novembre–Decembre. Paris: Centre National des Arts Plastiques.*

(1989) 'Le Phénomène Rybczinski', *Cahiers du Cinéma*, 415: 64.

(1989) 'Le Mer à vior', *Cahiers du Cinéma*, 424: 17.

(1990) 'L'Horizon au carré', *Libération*, 29 September.

(1990) 'L'Inertie dromotique', *Techniques et Architecture*, 390: 119–21, 181.

(1990) 'La Nouvelle Domesticité', *ARQ: Architecture/Québec*, 57: 29–30.

(1990) 'Marcel Odenbach: Die Einen Den Anderen, 1987', in R. Bellour (ed.), *Passages de l'image*. Paris: Éditions du Centre Pompidou.

(1991) 'L'Insécurité des territoires', in *ART LAB Concept Book*. Tokyo: ART LAB.

(1991) 'Quarante ans d'histoire', *Cahiers du Cinéma*, 443 (4): 62.

(1991) *L'Odyssée du virtuel*. Paris: Dossiers de l'Audiovisuel. INA Numéro 40, Novembre–Decembre. Sous la direction d'A.-M. Dugent et J.-M. Peyron.

(1991) 'La Guerre des dupes', *L'Événement du Jeudi*, pp. 36–7.

(1991) (with P. Goulet and J. Nouvel) 'Aesthetic des versch windens', *Arch Plus*, 108: 32–40.

(1992) 'Une guerre non conventionnelle', *Transversales*, 14: 4–6.

(1994) *Yann Kersalé/L'Instant Lúmiére*. Paris: Hamzan.*

(1994) *Atom Egoyan*. Paris: Distributed Art Publications.*

(1995) 'Alerte dans le cyberspace', *Le Monde Diplomatique*, 28 August: 1.

(1995) 'Mémoire de l'ait: une politique du relief', in U. Pfammater (ed.), *Cuno Brullman*. Basel: Birkhäuser. pp. 7–8.

(1996) 'L'Horizon du trait', in M. Jacques and A. Lavalou (eds), *Christian de Portzamparc*. Basel: Birkhäuser. pp. 74–7.

(1996) '"Dangers, périls et menaces"', Manière de voir: Internet: L'extase et l'effroi', *Le Monde Diplomatique*, October: 54–6.

(1996) (with C. Parent) *Architecture principe, 1966 et 1996*. Besançon: L'Imprimeur.

(1996) 'Le Musée du soleil', *InterCommunication*, 15 (Winter): 25–8.

(1997) 'Un monde surexposé', *Le Monde Diplomatique*, August: 20.

(1998) 'Le Règne de la délation optique', *Le Monde Diplomatique*, August: 20.

3 Interviews with Paul Virilio first published in French

(1981) 'Vidéo, vitesse, technologie: la troisième fenêtre', *Cahiers du Cinéma*, 322: 35–40. (Interview with the editors of *Cahiers du Cinéma*.)

(1984) 'Entretien avec Paul Virilio', *Empreintes*, 6: 28–31. (Interview with D. Dobbels and B. Remy.)

(1986) 'Vers l'espace des interfaces: entretien avec Paul Virilio', *Technique et Architecture*, 364: 130–3. (Interview with A. Pelissier.)

(1987) 'Paul Virilio', 8 May. (Interview on the French cultural channel, *La Sept*.) (Interviewer unknown.)

(1990) *Architecture Interieure-Crée*, 239: 108–14 (Interviewer unknown.)

(1993) 'La Défaite des faits', *L'Autre Journal*, 4: 12–17. (Interview with K. Bros and M. Weitzman.)

(1993) 'Interview avec Paul Virilio', *Archithese*, 23 (2): 54–6. (Interview with M. Brausch.)

(1994) 'Nous allons vers des Tchernobyls informatiques', *Revue Terminal: Une réflexion sur le concept de technoscience* 62. (Interview with G. Lacroix.)

(1994) 'La Ville, espace mutant: entretien avec Paul Virilio', *Architecture Interieure Crée*, 261: 104–7. (Interview with M. Brausch.)

(1995) 'Bientôt, seuls ceux qui seront dans la virtualité s'aimeront', *Supplément multimedia du journal Le Monde*, 30 Septembre. (Interviewer unknown.)

(1995) 'La Guerre de l'information', *Telecom Observer* 11 Octobre. (Interview with F. Burman on Swiss Radio International.)

(1995) 'L'Utopie du cybermonde', *France Culture*. (Radio interview with J. de Rosnay.)

(1995) 'Devant la liquidation du monde', *Black Notes*. (Interview with A. Kyrou and J.Y. Barbichon.)

(1995) 'Vitesse, guerre et vidéo', *Le Magazine Litteraire* 337 (Novembre): 96–103. (Interview with F. Ewald.)

(1996) 'L'Urbanité virtuelle, l'être au monde au temps réel', *Fluctuation fugitive: revue d'architecture*. (Interview with A. Sina.)

(1996) *Cybermonde, la politique du pire*. Paris: Textuel. (Book-length interview with P. Petit.)

(1996) 'Cybermonde, la politique du pire', *Libération*, 10 May. (Interviewer unknown.)

(1996) 'Les Formes virtuelles', *Les Sciences de la Forme Aujourd'hui*, Points Sciences (October.) (Interview with É. Noël.)

(1996) 'Caution against the Cyberworld', *Connaissance des Arts*, 532 (Octobre.) (Interview with P. Jodidio.)

(1996) 'Quaud il n'y a plus temps à partager, il n'y a plus de democratie possible', *Les Grands Entretiens du Monde*, 3: 37–9. (Interview with J.-M. Frodon.)

(1996) 'Paysage d'événements sur fond de vitesse', *Art Press*, 217: 19–26. (Interview with P. Sterckx.)

(1996) 'Virilio, cybéresistant', *Libération*, 10 May. (Interviewer unknown.)

(1996) 'Entrer en cyberésistance', *La Rafalé*, 19 May. (Interviewer unknown.)

(1996) 'Le Bombardement de Nantes', *Cahiers du Cinéma*, 503. (Interviewer unknown.)

(1996) 'Les Grands Entretiens du monde', Chapter 1 in *Dossiers et documents du monde*, June: Part 3. (Interviewer unknown.)

(1996) 'Un monde sans espace', *Le Nouvel Observateur*, Novembre. (Interview with P. Gari.)

(1997) 'La Révolution de l'information est une révolution de la dénonciation', *L'Événement du Jeudi*, 656 (May–June): 60. (Interview with B. Ponlet.)

(1997) *Voyage d'hiver*. Marseille: Parenthèses (Book of interviews with M. Brausch.)

4 English translations of the main published works of Paul Virilio

(1986) *Speed and Politics: An Essay on Dromology*, trans. M. Polizzotti. New York: Semiotext (e).

(1986) *Negative Horizon*, trans. M. Polizzotti. New York: Semiotext (e).

(1989) *War and Cinema: The Logistics of Perception*, trans. P. Camiller. London and New York: Verso.

(1990) *Popular Defense and Ecological Struggles*, trans. M. Polizzotti. New York: Semiotext (e).

(1991) *The Lost Dimension*, trans. D. Moshenberg. New York: Semiotext (e).

(1991) *The Aesthetics of Disappearance*, trans. P. Beitchman. New York: Semiotext (e).

(1994) *Bunker Archeology*, trans. (of 2nd edn) G. Collins. Princeton, NJ: Princeton Architectural Press.

(1994) *The Vision Machine*, trans. J. Rose. Bloomington and London: Indiana University Press and British Film Institute.

(1995) *The Art of the Motor*, trans. J. Rose. Minneapolis: University of Minnesota Press.

(1997) *Open Sky*, trans. J. Rose. London: Verso.

(1999) *Polar Inertia*, trans. P. Camiller. London: Sage.

(2000a) *The Information Bomb*, trans. C. Turner. London: Verso.

(2000b) *Strategy of Deception*, trans. C. Turner. London: Verso.

(2000c) A *Landscape of Events*, trans. J. Rose. Cambridge, Mass: MIT Press.

(2001) *Desert Screen: War at the Speed of Light*, trans. M. Degener. London: The Athlone Press.

5 English translations of articles by Paul Virilio

(1980) 'Popular Defense and Popular Assault', trans. J. Johnston, in S. Lotringer and J. Fleming (eds), *Italy: Autonomia*. New York: Semiotext (e). pp. 266–72.

(1981) 'Moving Girl', trans. J. Johnston, in P. Lamborn Wilson and J. Fleming (eds), *Semiotext (e) Polysexuality*. New York: Semiotext (e). pp. 242–8.

(1984) 'The Overexposed City', trans. A. Hustvedt, in M. Feher and S. Kwinter (eds), *Zone 1/2*. New York: Urzone. pp. 15–31.

(1985) 'Dromoscopy or Drunk with Magnitude', trans. N. Sanders. *Frogger*, 7.

(1986) 'Star Wars', trans. unknown, *Art and Text*, 22: 15–18.

(1986) 'The Privatisation of War', trans. M. Imrie, *New Statesman*, 112 (10 October): 19.

(1987) 'Space, Time, and the City', trans. unknown, *Lotus International*, 51: 25–9.

(1987) 'Nervous Peace', trans. M. Imrie. *New Statesman*, 113 (16 January): 36–7.

(1987) 'Negative Horizons', trans. M. Polizzotti, pp. 163–80 in J. Fleming and P.L. Wilson (eds), *Semiotext (e) USA*. New York: Semiotext (e).

(1989) 'Trans-Appearance', trans. D. Stoll, *Artforum*, 27 (10): 128–30.

(1989) 'The Last Vehicle', trans. D. Antal, in D. Kamper and C. Wulf (eds), *Looking Back on the End of the World*. New York: Semiotext (e). pp. 106–19.

(1989) 'The Museum of Accidents', trans. Y. Lawrence, in *The Lunatic of One Idea*, Special Issue of *Public*, 2: 81–5.

(1990) 'Cataract Surgery: Cinema in the Year 2000', trans. A. Fatet and A. Kuhn, in A. Kuhn (ed.), *Alien Zone: Cultural Theory and Contemporary Science Fiction Cinema*. London and New York: Verso. pp. 169–74.

(1990) 'The Third Interval', trans. unknown, *Art and Design*, 7 (1/2): 78.

(1990) 'The Image to Come', trans. S. Sartarelli, *Art and Text*, 36: 90–4.

(1991) 'Head High?', trans. T. Hausman, *Newsline*, 3 (7): 3.

(1992) 'Gray Ecology', trans. unknown, in C.C. Davidson (ed.), *Anywhere*. New York: Rizzoli. pp. 186–9.

(1992) 'Aliens', trans. B. Massumi, in J. Crary and S. Kwinter (eds), *Zone 6: Incorporations*. New York: Urzone. pp. 446–9.

(1992) 'Big Optics', trans. J. Von Stein, in Peter Weibel (ed.), *On Justifying the Hypothetical Nature of Art and the Non-Identicality within the Object World*. Koln: Galerie Tanja Grunert. pp. 82–93.

(1992) 'The Law of Proximity', trans. W. Nijenhuis, in V2 Organization (eds), *Book for the Unstable Media*. Amsterdam: den Bosch. pp. 121–7.

(1993) 'The Third Interval: A Critical Transition', trans. T. Conley, in V.A. Conley (ed.), *Rethinking Technologies*. Minneapolis: University of Minnesota Press. pp. 3–12.

(1993) 'Speed and Vision: The Incomparable Eye', trans. unknown. *Diadalos: Berlin Architectural Journal*, 47: 96–107.

(1993) 'The Interface', trans. unknown, *Lotus International*, 75: 126.

(1993) 'From Superman to Superexcited Man', trans. unknown. *Domus*, 755: 17–24.

(1993) 'The Law of Proximity', trans. L.E. Nesbitt, *Columbia Documents of Architecture and Theory*, 2: 123–37.

(1993) 'The Primal Accident', trans. B. Massumi, in B. Massumi (ed.), *The Politics of Everyday Fear*. Minneapolis: University of Minnesota Press. pp. 211–18.

(1994) 'The Vision Machine', trans. J. Rose, *Transition*, 43: 20–35.

(1995) 'Red Alert in Cyberspace', trans. M. Imrie, *Radical Philiosphy*, 74: 2–4.

(1995) 'Speed and Information: Cyberspace Alarm!', trans. P. Riemens, *CTheory* (Ctheory www.com) (Electronic journal), 27 September.

(1995) 'Critical Reflections', trans. unknown, *Artforum*, 34 (3): 82–3.

(1995) 'Comforting Light', trans. unknown, *Forum*, 38: 17–19.

(1995) 'Politics of Relief', trans. unknown, *Forum*, 38: 77.

(1995) 'Memory of Air: A Policy of Relief', trans. I. Taylor, in U. Pfammater (ed.), *Cuno Brullmann*. Basel: Birkhäuser. pp. 8–9.

(1996) 'The Horizon of the Line', trans. S. Pleasance and F. Woods, in M. Jacques and A. Lavalou (eds), *Christian de Portzamparc*. Basel: Birkhäuser. pp. 74–7.

(1997) 'The Overexposed City', trans. A. Hustredt, in N. Leach (ed.), *Rethinking Architecture: A Reader in Cultural Theory*. London and New York: Routledge. pp. 381–90.

(1997) 'Cybernetics and Society', trans. C.T. Wolfe, in *Any* (editor unknown.) New York: Architecture. pp. 1–13, 19–20.

(1997) 'The Museum of the Sun', trans. L. Reijnen, in V2 Organization (eds), *Technomorphica*. Rotterdam: V2 Organization. pp. 331–62.

(1998) 'Foreword', trans. unknown, in J. Rajchman, *Constructions*. Cambridge, MA: MIT Press.

(1998) 'We May Be Entering An Electronic Gothic Era', transcribed and edited by O. Fillion, *Architectural Design*, 68 (11/12) (November–December): 61.

(1998) 'A Topographical Amnesia', trans. J. Rose, in N. Mirzoeff (ed.), *The Visual Culture Reader*. London: Routledge. pp. 108–24. (Chapter one of *The Vision Machine*.)

(1998) 'Dromoscopy, or The Ecstasy of Enormites', trans. E.R. O'Neill, in *Wide Angle*, 20 (3): 10–22.

(1998) 'Photo Finish', in L. Sabau (ed.), *The Promise of Photography*. London: Prestel. pp. 19–24.

(1999) 'Indirect Light', extracted from *Polar Inertia*, trans. P. Camiller, in J. Armitage (ed.) in *Theory, Culture and Society*, Special Issue on Paul Virilio, 16 (5–6): 57–70.

6 Interviews with Paul Virilio published in English

(1983) *Pure War*, trans. M. Polizzotti. New York: Semiotext (e). (Book-length interview with S. Lotringer.)

(1985) 'The Spirit of Defence: An Interview with Paul Virilio', trans. M. Polizzotti, *Impulse* (Death Issue), 11 (4): 35–7. (Interview with C. Mellon.)

(1986) 'Speed-Space', trans. D. Miller, *Impulse*, 12 (4): 35–9. (Interview with C. Dercon.)

(1988) 'Paul Virilio', trans. unknown, *Block*, 14: 4–7. (Interviewer unknown.)

(1988) 'Interview with Paul Virilio', trans. H. Martin, *Flash Art*, International Edition, 138: 57–61. (Interview with J. Sans.)

(1988) 'The Third Window: An Interview with Paul Virilio', trans. Y. Shafir, with a preface by J. Crary, in C. Schneider and B. Wallis (eds), *Global Television*. Cambridge, MA and London: MIT Press and Wedge Press. pp. 185–97. (Interview with the editors of *Cahiers du Cinéma*. A translation of Virilio's 1981 interview in French with *Cahiers du Cinéma*.)

(1991) 'Paul Virilio', trans. H. Martin, in *Art and Philosophy*. Milan: Giancarlo Politi Editure. pp. 139–50. (Reprint of the interview with Jerôme Sans in *Flash Art*.)

(1991) 'For a Geography of Trajectories', trans. unknown, *Flux*, 5: 48–54. (Interview with J.-M. Offner and A. Sander.)

(1992) 'Interview with Paul Virilio', trans. unknown, in *100 affiches françaises à Saint-Pétersbourg*. Paris: Demi-Cercle. pp. 74–86. (Interview with D. Joubert and C. Carlut.)

(1993) 'Marginal Groups', trans. unknown, *Diadalos: Berlin Architectural Journal*, 50 (December): 72–81. (Interview with M. Brausch.)

(1994) 'Cyberwar, God and Television: Interview with Paul Virilio', trans. Gildas Illien, *CTheory*. (Electronic journal), 17 (3): 1–7. (Interview with L.K. Wilson for *CTheory*.)

(1994) 'Gravitational Space', trans. unknown, in L. Louppe (ed.), *Traces of Dance: Drawings and Notations of Choreographers*. Paris: Editions Dis Voir. pp. 35–60. (Interview with L. Louppe and D. Dobbels.)

(1995) 'Paul Virilio', trans. G. Aylesworth, in F. Rötzer (ed.), *Conversations with French Philosophers*. New Jersey: Humanities Press. pp. 97–104. (Interview with F. Rötzer.)

(1995) 'Cyberrevolution', trans. unknown, *Telecom Observer* 16 October. (Interview with M. Alberganti.)

(1995) 'Critical Mass', trans. unknown, *World Art*, 1: 78–82. (Interview with V. Madsen.)

(1995) 'The Publicity Machine and Critical Theory', trans. N. Zurbrugg, *Eyeline*, 27 (Autumn–Winter): 8–14. (Interview with N. Zurbrugg.)

(1995) 'Century of Violence', trans. N. Zurbrugg, *Versus*, 4: 42–7. (Interview with N. Zurbrugg. Reprint of 'The Publicity Machine' interview in *Eyeline*, 27.)

(1995) 'The Silence of the Lambs: Paul Virilio in Conversation', trans. P. Riemens, *CTheory* (Electronic journal), 1 (7): 1–3. (Interview with C. Oliveira.)

(1996) 'Speed Pollution', trans. M. Degener, J. Der Derian and L. Osepchuk, *Wired*, 4.05: 120–1. (Interview with J. Der Derian.)

(1996) 'The Game of Love and Chance', trans. C. Volke, *Grand Street*, 52: 12–17. (Interview with J. Sans.)

(1996) 'The Game of Love and Chance', trans. C. Volke, *Architectural Design*, 121: 24–6. (Reprint of the J. Sans interview in *Grand Street*, 52.)

(1996) 'Paul Virilio and the Oblique', trans. unknown, in S. Allen and K. Park (eds), *Sites and Stations: Provisional Utopias: Architecture and Utopia in the Contemporary City*. New York: Lusitania Press. pp. 174–84. (Interview with E. Limon.)

(1996) '"A Century of Hyper-violence": Paul Virilio: An Interview', trans. N. Zurbrugg, *Economy and Society*, 25 (1) (February): 111–26. (Interview with N. Zurbrugg. Reprint of N. Zurbrugg interviews in *Eyeline*, 27 and *Versus*, 4.)

(1996) 'The Dark Spot of Art', trans. B. Holmes, in Herausgeber documenta Gmbtt. (ed.), *documenta documents 1*. Kassel: Cantz Verlag. pp. 47–55. (Interview with C. David.)

(1996) 'The Dark Spot of Art's Presence', trans. B. Holmes, *Metronome*, 0: 7–10. (Reprint, in edited form, of the interview with C. David in *documenta documents 1*.)

(1997) 'Interview with Paul Virilio', trans. J. Der Derian, M. Degener and L. Osepchuk, *Speed* (Electronic journal), 1 (4): 1–8. (Interview with J. Der Derian. Reprinted in J. Der Derian (ed.), *The Virilio Reader*, 1998.)

(1997) 'Virilio's Apocalypse', trans. unknown, in A. Crawford and R. Edgar (eds), *Transit Lounge*. North Ryde: Craftsman House. pp. 70–3. (Interview with V. Madsen.)

(1997) *Pure War: Revised Edition*, trans. M. Polizzotti. Postscript translated by B. O'Keeffe. (Contains a new Postscript: '1997: Infowar'.) New York: Semiotext (e). (Book-length interview with S. Lotringer.)

(1998) 'Surfing the Accident', trans. P. Riemens, in V2 Organization (eds), *The Art of the Accident*. Rotterdam: NAI. pp. 30–44. (Interview with A. Ruby.)

(1998) 'Architecture in the Age of its Virtual Disappearance', trans. unknown, in J. Beckmann (ed.), *The Virtual Dimension: Architecture, Representation, and Crash Culture*. New York: Princeton Architectural Press. pp. 179–87. (Interview with A. Ruby.)

(1999) 'The Information Bomb: A Conversation', edited and introduced by J. Armitage, trans. P. Riemens, in J. Armitage (ed.), *Machinic Modulations: New Cultural Theory and Technopolitics*, Special Issue of *Angelaki*, 4 (2): 81–90. (First broadcast on the Franco-German television channel ARTE, in November 1995.) (Interview with F. Kittler.)

(1999) *Politics of the Very Worst*, New York: Semiotext (e). (Book-length interview with P. Petit.)

(1999) 'From Modernism to Hypermodernism and Beyond', trans. P. Riemens, in J. Armitage (ed.), *Theory, Culture and Society*, Special Issue on Paul Virilio, 16 (5–6): 25–56. (Interview with J. Armitage.)

(2000) 'The Kosovo War Took Place in Orbital Space: Paul Virilio in Conversation with John Armitage', trans. P. Riemens, in *CTheory* (Electronic journal), October 18 (Interview with J. Armitage.)

Notes

1. This select bibliography of the works of Paul Virilio is a fully updated version of John Armitage's 'Paul Virilio: A Select Bibliography'. The latter bibliography first appeared in *Theory, Culture and Society*, 16 (5–6) (October–December 1999): 229–40.

2. In this regard, and apart from a large thank you to Virilio himself, I must thank James Der Derian, Patrick Crogan, Wim Nijenhuis, Mark Little, Andreas Broeckmann, Kevin Robins, Nicholas Zurbrugg, Gerard Greenway, Patrice Riemens and Andreas Ruby. Lastly, I would like to thank Joanne Parkes, Assistant Divisional Administrator in the Division of Government and Politics, University of Northumbria, UK. Suffice it to say that Joanne's magical skills with a Word for Windows character map are a wonder to behold.

NAME INDEX

SUBJECT INDEX